Mothering Through
the Darkness

∾

Mothering Through *the* Darkness

Women Open Up About the Postpartum Experience

Edited by

Jessica Smock

and

Stephanie Sprenger

[swp]

SHE WRITES PRESS

Published 2015
Printed in the United States of America
ISBN: 978-1-63152-804-0
Library of Congress Control Number: [LOCCN]

Design by Stacey Aaronson

For information, address:
She Writes Press
1563 Solano Ave #546
Berkeley, CA 94707

She Writes Press is a division of SparkPoint Studio, LLC.

For Eliza Margaret, my newest baby —JAS

For Jess. You will be in our hearts forever. —SCS

TABLE OF CONTENTS

FOREWORD

Imagine having a baby and becoming paralyzed by illness. Imagine the stigma attached to becoming a new mother and wishing your baby away. Imagine the shame of not sliding into this role with the grace and enthusiasm that everyone expected from you. Recently, professionals and laypeople alike have begun paying attention to the impact of depression and anxiety after the birth of a baby. After decades of silent suffering, we are beginning to see greater advocacy and new legislation in support of women struggling with perinatal distress. Despite this increase in public awareness and a new national conversation, mothers continue to feel marginalized and hushed by a culture that refuses to listen. Expectations of unconditional maternal bliss continue to run rampant. The prevailing notion that mothers should endlessly radiate joy, paradoxically keeps them feeling sick, longer.

Motherhood is a magnificently challenging role, asking that women continuously adapt and adjust their identities, routines, priorities, and expectations. Emotions are out of control, life becomes unpredictable, and self-care becomes something of the past. Regardless of how many books have been read in preparation or how much support loving friends and family members provide, a large number of women are surprised at the extent to which they feel overwhelmed, overloaded, exhausted, unsupported, and completely, utterly, misunderstood.

It's hard enough to be a mother when everything turns out the way you hope it will. Mommy and baby are healthy. Dad is fabulous and supportive. Extended family is available and accommodating. Even when it's idyllic, it can be a challenging journey. A woman with a postpartum mood or anxiety disorder experiences an additional and exceptionally complicated challenge. She unexpectedly finds herself face-to-face with one of life's most cruel juxtapositions: trying to reconcile becoming a mother while wrestling soul-crushing emotions unlike any she has ever even remotely experienced.

The paradoxes inherent in motherhood within the context of emotional illness are often immobilizing: The elation and the despair. The ambivalence and the affection. The fury and the indifference. The irritability and the guilt. And then, there are the maddening thoughts. Like the thought that her baby would be better off without her. Or the worry that her husband will never love her again because she is unlovable. Or the belief that she made an irreparable mistake of unprecedented proportions and she should never have had this baby. Or, perhaps most unfathomable of all, if someone knew her innermost thoughts, would they take her baby away?

To the postpartum woman in distress, these secret thoughts are unimaginable, unspeakable, and unprintable.

Until now.

The indescribable distress experienced by depressed mothers is palpable. Courageous women have assembled in *Mothering Through the Darkness: Women Open Up About the Postpartum Experience*, to share their experiences in this collection of extraordinarily personal and private stories. The distinguished group of women identify strongly with their accomplishments as mothers transformed by both their babies and their illnesses, and also by their impressive achievements as educators, editors, lecturers, students, published writers, and award-winning poets. This poignant anthology embraces the deep joy and excruciating distress of real women who believe in the healing power of self-disclosure through writing—healing themselves and healing the women who read their words. Recovery from postpartum depression and anxiety is a journey distinguished by tremendous triumphs and equally remarkable pain. It is precisely this contradiction which makes a postpartum woman's experience so unique. Still, somewhat surprisingly, there exists little understanding of these intimate experiences. Denial persists. Misinformation is widespread. My hope is that these brave women who chose to defy the stigma will enlighten others with the honest portrayal of their fragile yet victorious tales.

Sarah Rudell Beach does a wonderful job capturing one of the overriding themes of the book when she declares: *We can be shattered, and we can become whole again.*

The words and sentiments throughout this book are heartbreaking and heartwarming. They are touching and provocative. For readers who dare to believe that good mothers feel a myriad of amazing and shocking emotions, the book will truly be inspirational.

—Karen Kleiman, MSW, LCSW
Founder & Director, The Postpartum Stress Center
Author, *Therapy and the Postpartum Woman:
Notes on Healing Postpartum Depression for Clinicians and the
Women Who Seek Their Help*

INTRODUCTION

I rock back and forth in the glider, clutching my five-month-old daughter and squeezing my eyes shut. Every muscle in my body is clenched, and angry tears pour down my face. My baby wails, and I fight the urge to scream. My throat is raw with the unexpressed scream; it wants to come out. *Why won't she sleep? Why can't I get her to sleep in her crib? What is wrong with me?*

I berate myself, asking these questions over and over. I am a failure, an imposter. I have done everything wrong up to this point, leaving me with a baby who won't nap, an afternoon with no quiet, and a scream that wants so badly to come out. I am not sad. I am filled with rage. I battle against the urge to slap myself in the face. My hand twitches with the impulse to make contact with my cheek. I can feel the sting; it burns and yet soothes. But I can't do it. Women who rock crying babies shouldn't slap themselves in the face. But I want to.

—*Stephanie*

F or the first several months of my son's life he was a crier. For the first time in my life, so was I. My son cried in the morning, he cried in the afternoon, and he cried in the evenings. I cried during those times too, but it was the intensity of my own crying that shocked me. It was the cry of a woman with a broken soul, no energy, no spirit. And that's what it felt like to me at the time: the crying and the colic had crushed my spirit.

I believed that somehow, in some way, my unhappy baby was my fault. Maybe I passed on the anxiety that I experienced during pregnancy, maybe I didn't have a sufficiently positive attitude, maybe it was the glasses of wine that I drank during the last trimester, maybe—and this was the most horrible thing to say to myself—I wasn't cut out to be a mother. Now I would never finish my dissertation and never have a successful career. This was all just too hard. Maybe I just wasn't built for it.

These are the thoughts that cycled through my mind, again and again, as I tried to find refuge from the crying. When the crying became too much, I would put him down in his crib and flee—to a third-floor closet, to the back pantry, anywhere where the sound was muffled. I would crouch on the floor and sob. But I could still hear the screams, even sometimes when the baby had stopped crying.

—Jessica

When we were first-time mothers, both of us held misconceptions about postpartum depression: *Only people with a history of mental health problems get it. Mothers who have postpartum depression are sad all the time. They don't want to get out of bed. New mothers can kick the "baby blues" if they just cheer up and get out of the house more. It will go away on its own. It only happens during the first few months after childbirth. These mothers want to hurt their babies.*

None of these descriptions applied to either of us. As educated, middle-class women with support systems, we knew about which baby products to purchase and from where, the best way to swaddle an infant, how to introduce solid food.

Yet the psychological terrain of parenting remained a mystery. Nobody was talking. Nobody talked about the identity crisis that might ensue, or the fact that sleep deprivation could feel like slow torture, or the anxiety that could fill the hours of the day. Nobody was talking about the thoughts that weren't supposed to be there.

The authors of the essays in this book have broken that silence. They are talking—about all of it. Their words dispel the many myths that still prevail, bringing to light the reality of postpartum depression and perinatal mood disorders.

If there's one thing we've learned throughout the process of compiling these essays, it's that there is no universal experience of antepartum and postpartum mood disorders. Symptoms manifest in different ways: sadness, intrusive thoughts, panic, anger, obsessive-compulsive behavior, anxiety, isolation, and grief can characterize the postpartum experience in individualized forms. We also know that postpartum depression does not discriminate. According to the American Psychological Association, 9 to 16 percent of women—from all cultures, religious and educational backgrounds, socio-economic classes, and family histories—will have postpartum depression in their lifetime.

The circumstances are often unique: sometimes pregnancy or infant loss is a factor; twin births, NICU stays, birth trauma, and colic can play a role; adoption may be the trigger; marital distress can be tied to perinatal depression and anxiety as either a cause or a casualty.

As we read story after story, common themes emerged. So many of the authors experienced a shame that paralyzed them into inaction. They felt guilty about their depression—after all, wasn't this baby, this life, what they had wanted? Guilt and shame are powerful forces during the postpartum period; they often result in mothers denying themselves care as punishment for their inability to fully embrace their new roles.

The insidious myth of perfection also plays a part; women believe that if motherhood does not feel natural to them, they must be defective somehow. Kate Kearns puts it beautifully in her essay "I Love You; Leave Me Alone": "When a mother has these thoughts, how can she feel anything but shame and fear? Even though we are told the causes and warning signs well ahead of time, who can bring herself to admit to not feeling overjoyed by her new baby, no matter what the supportive scientific pamphlets say?"

The brave and honest authors of this book have shown us that postpartum depression does not make you defective or broken. It is possible to find your way through the darkness and emerge stronger.

Here Comes the Sun

Maggie Smith

I can't find the notebook.

My husband threw it away, or I threw it away, or it threw itself away.

With my son I wrote everything down: every feeding, what time he started, what time he finished, when he burped, when he spit up, what the spit up looked like, when he peed, when he pooped, what the poop looked like, when he cried, what his cry sounded like, when he slept, what position he slept in, when he woke.

If I wrote everything down, I would see The Pattern. The Pattern That Would Make Him Happy. The Pattern That Would Make Him Sleep.

The Pattern That Would Fix Him.

The Pattern That Would Fix Me.

The books all say to sleep when the baby sleeps. But he didn't sleep. And if he did, in tiny spurts, I spent those few minutes scribbling down everything that had happened since my last entry. And then he'd wake, screaming, and I'd set down the notebook.

∽

We all come into the world less than done, unfinished, our skulls still stitching themselves together. We have soft spots. *Fontanelle* means "little fountain," because of the pulsing you can see.

∽

Our daughter, born four years earlier, had been colicky, too. She hadn't slept. She'd cried insistently, refusing comfort. Desperate for lullabies, I sang her "Graceland" and "Lucy in the Sky with Diamonds," because I knew the words. I played the white noise CD on a loop. I bounced, jiggled, walked, drove. I cried in the shower, when I could steal away to take one.

I'd said to my husband, "Why did we do this?" We'd had a good life. We'd ruined our good life.

Where was my bundle of joy?

The baby doesn't look in your eyes. The baby cries like a creature, more animal than human. The baby doesn't give. The baby takes. No one tells you, for those first weeks, your life is in service to a stranger.

I'd said to my husband, "She doesn't love me—she only wants me for food!"

I'd sung her "You Are My Sunshine," as if singing it could make it so.

Our life had been interrupted. No, we had interrupted our life. We'd done this to ourselves.

With my daughter I'd cut my maternity leave short by two weeks to return to my office—mostly to escape, to row away from the lonely island we lived on together, but also to get back to the adult world, to a place where I could put in earbuds, type, and be functionally alone.

I remember dropping her off at daycare. I remember her sitting in a baby swing in a ladybug outfit, clutching a little burp cloth like a security blanket, her eyes focusing on something across the room. I left her there. I cried, but I was free.

And my dread, which I'd never treated, which I'd never even called by its proper name, began to dissolve. I could almost taste it—a hard lozenge melting in the heat of my mouth.

It took us years to decide to have another child. I was terrified of regretting it, regretting him or her. Terrified of the "What have we done?" feeling. Terrified of those bathrobe days, bathrobe weeks, the faraway look I'd seen in photographs of myself. Terrified of that hollow, scraped-out feeling.

Life was good: mother, father, daughter. We were healthy. We were happy. We slept.

What I didn't expect was that the road would be so difficult once we finally decided to travel it. I miscarried twice in 2011. I felt broken. I *was* broken.

Twice there was almost a child, as if *almost* were a variety of child, like an apple—Suncrisp, Red Delicious, Rome, Almost. And I was some variety of widow, some variety of orphan, some terrible hybrid: there is no name for a mother of an almost child.

There is no name for a mother of erasure.

There is no name for half a mother, only half of her children living in this world, only half.

∽

The year of the miscarriages was also the year of obsession. I insisted on test after test. I charted. I listed. If this, then that. If this test comes back negative, then I'll feel safe. If my levels are X, then we can try Y again. I was in the dark alone, feeling my way along the wall, feeling for a light switch or a doorknob.

We decided to try again one last time in 2012. On Valentine's Day, the day after my thirty-fifth birthday, I told my husband I was pregnant. "Here we go again," he said. We both expected the worst.

But weeks later, there it was on the fuzzy gray screen: the heart a small button clicking itself on, on, on. And this time it stayed on. Still, the bargaining, the obsessive worry, the guardedness did not resolve. For nine months, I expected blood.

∽

He looked like an Elvis impersonator when he was born. Our son, almost ten pounds, had a full head of thick dark hair. He had sideburns.

Our son was the child who almost wasn't. The last child we would ever have. If we'd believed in miracles, he would have been one. He was the sun, the light at the end of a long darkness.

At first he was so calm and quiet, I thought the curse was broken. He slept and slept, only waking to nurse. But after a couple of weeks, he emerged from the fog of birth. He screamed.

He refused to close his eyes, let alone sleep. Hour after hour, I carried him around tightly swaddled, swaying him as he blinked up at me. He slept maybe six hours out of any twenty-four-hour period, but in brutal twenty-minute increments. I found myself at the edge again, but this time with a four-year-old to care for.

This time, I felt, it was me and the baby on an island, my daughter and her father on another. We could wave to each other across the choppy water. Nursing, I had the baby attached to me almost constantly, an appendage. When he wasn't there, I could still feel him, like a phantom limb.

༄

An erasure is a kind of poem as much about the words not there.

༄

Our son was born in October. By December I was miserable. At eight weeks, my daughter had started sleeping—*consolidating sleep*, they call it—but this time eight weeks came and went without change. I couldn't put him down. I couldn't let him cry. I'd fought so hard to get him here. How could I put him down?

My mind's engine ran and ran until it smoked. I wrote everything down. I couldn't sleep. I was wired. I worried about what the next day would bring. I worried about being left alone with him. I dreaded morning.

I resented my husband for having an office to go off to each day. And when I snapped at him, when I stomped around the kitchen, slamming the cabinet doors, he said: "You chose this. This is what you wanted."

What he meant was: *You knew I'd be at work and you'd be at home. You knew it would be hard.*

What I heard was: *I told you so.*

◡◠◡

There is no name for a mother, half a mother, only half of her children living in this world, only half.

◡◠◡

I sang my son "Here Comes the Sun" and "Close Your Eyes." I gave him his own songs.

I sang him "Fire and Rain," because I knew the words, because it was sad and beautiful and so were we. Then I worried that the melody would depress him, that the notes would somehow change his wiring. Or was he already wired to be like me: too raw for the world, nerves too close to the skin?

I sang him "Here Comes the Sun," as if singing it could make it so.

◡◠◡

We all come into the world less than done, unfinished, little fountains. They call the first three months of a baby's life "the fourth trimester." Horses can practically run out of the womb. Even a deer can stand, sticky, and walk. But human infants are helpless, blind, bawling, not ready to be in the world—and you are not ready, either. You are not ready for this.

◡◠◡

This time I had no office to escape to. I'd left my job in publishing to begin a freelance career the previous year, so that I would have more time and flexibility as a parent.

This was not maternity leave. This was my life. I chose this. This is what I wanted.

If I couldn't change my life, I would order it. I created a schedule and quickly became a slave to it: set feedings, set ounces, set "naptimes" (swaddled, carried around, propped precariously in a bouncer or swing, only to wake seconds later). I couldn't leave the house. I had to stay home, keep him on track, offer him naps in his own crib. I had to swaddle, shush, sway.

I had to find The Pattern. The Pattern That Would Fix Us.

❧

It was bitter cold that winter. I was a recluse with a reflux baby who fussed and cried and rarely slept. My friends left fresh-ground coffee from the local coffee shop on the stoop or stayed and kept me company as I paced the carpet, bouncing and shushing my swaddled, blinking baby in my arms.

When my husband told me to call my doctor, when he told me that my frantic listing wasn't normal, that my anger wasn't normal, I vented to them. There is no parenting-a-newborn medication, I insisted. My life is hard, and there is no pill to make a hard life easy.

❧

One January morning, angry that my husband invited friends over for brunch, friends I couldn't face, I started cleaning in a rage. I picked up toys from the living room carpet and threw them into the playroom. The air sizzled. He texted our friends to cancel. As he whisked our daughter away for an errand, I heard her say, on the way out the door, "Let's go. I don't want to be around Mom. She's mad all the time."

I was. I was furious. All the time. Where was my bundle of joy? How could this happen twice? How could I let it? After all I'd been through to have this child, why couldn't I just be grateful?

ᴄᴡᴐ

I drove around for maybe an hour that night, between feedings, because the car was the only place where I could be alone and sob, where I couldn't hear a baby, where I could turn the music up loud.

They call it *extinction*: letting a baby cry it out, letting a baby cry until he can't cry anymore, until he gives up and finally sleeps.

I let myself cry it out.

I was extinct?

ᴄᴡᴐ

I was a mother, an erasure, a poem about what was not there.

ᴄᴡᴐ

The next day I made the appointment with my ob-gyn's office. Because I didn't want to be that mother. Because I already felt guilty, as if I had cheated on my daughter by having another child. I couldn't betray her again by changing, by having her lose the mother she'd had for four years, the mother she loved and counted on.

The nurse asked if I had thought of harming the baby or myself. Was I eating, was I sleeping, was I exercising, was I going out with friends?

No, I said. No, no, no, no.

I wasn't sad; I was mad. I couldn't turn myself off. I couldn't fix my son.

She looked at my chart. I'd been pregnant three times in two years. It makes sense, but I hadn't known it until then: miscarriage is a predictor for postpartum anxiety and depression. Of course you feel out of control: Your hormones have been all over the place. You've been heartbroken, wrung out, exhausted, and scared. You can't make your body do what it should, and now you can't make your child do what he should.

☞✦☜

Little fountains, we all come into the world unfinished, still stitching ourselves together.

☞✦☜

The nurse prescribed a low dose of Lexapro and asked to see me again in sixty days. It would take a few weeks for me to feel results, and it would be thirty days before the medication reached therapeutic level in my system.

The treatment itself was something to endure: the flat feeling, like monotone. I'd always felt high highs, low lows. I'd always been black or white. But Lexapro was gray, gray, gray. I listened to sad songs, alarmed that they didn't make me feel sad. They didn't make me feel anything. The flat gray, the deadening, was worth it—for my kids, for my marriage, for me—and eventually it gave way to shades of gray. There were almost whites, almost blacks.

When our son started sleeping more, when I felt like the worst was behind us, I weaned myself off the pills. I cried again. I was black. I was white. I was dragged into sad songs. I snapped occasionally. I was my old self, but it was manageable. I no longer felt out of control.

∽

I can't find the notebook.

My husband threw it away, or I threw it away, or it threw itself away.

I know what I would not find there: Why my son wouldn't sleep. Why I wasn't producing enough breast milk. Why he couldn't tolerate formula. Why my gratitude for him wasn't enough to keep me happy. Why I willingly marooned myself on an island with a newborn a second time. Why I thought it would be different. Why it wasn't different.

There are no answers.

∽

We are all little fountains—soft, pulsing, unfinished.

I am learning to forgive my body its brokenness, to forgive my mind its blacks and whites. I sing "Here Comes the Sun."

Today I keep two notebooks, one for each of my children. Now and then I write down the sweet and funny things they say. My last entry is this:

Looking out the back door in the morning as the sun rises.

Rhett: Snowy!

Me: And sunny!

Rhett: No sunshine.

Me: What is shining on Mommy's face?

Rhett: Rhett.

It Got Better, but It Took a Long Time to Get Good

Jen Simon

I pick at my body, obsessively, compulsively. Any scab, any scar, any loose skin or hangnail I can coax, I rip open, digging into the exposed flesh. I add myself to the mess of the apartment—bloody Kleenexes and dried, yellowed, hardened pieces of feet litter the floors.

It's 6:32 a.m., June of 2010. I have been up since four, again, and am again counting the minutes until I can go back to sleep. Sleep: I need it, I yearn for it, I obsess about it. Every moment of my day revolves around its elusiveness and how to acquire as much of it as possible. This is my life. Every day. For the last eight months. It feels like an eternity.

Snuggling into the pillow, I breathe deeply, trying to relax my body and my mind at the time when many mothers are just waking up.

Noah was born in November. He is a beautiful blond baby with big blue eyes. He is quick to smile. He latched when I put him to me. He is happy to experiment with new foods. He is meeting all of his milestones. But there is something wrong with him. He doesn't know how to sleep. His screams pierce our sought-after slumber every forty-five minutes during the night. Every night. Until he fully wakes up between four and four thirty in the morning. Every morning. This is my life. For the last eight months.

It will get better, the pediatrician says, as I cry in her office. *It will get better*, the friends in my moms' group assure me as I cry during our walks around our Brooklyn neighborhood. *It will get better*, my mom says, consoling me as I cry on the phone with her. They're all wrong. I know it. I feel it. It will never get better. How can it ever get better if nothing changes?

Nothing changes. Every night is filled with the same terrible, jolting cries. And every morning, as if on cue, Noah stands in his crib and wails until my husband, Matt, or I retrieve him. The only thing that allows me to maintain some semblance of functionality is the fact that Matt and I take turns getting up with him. But even then, I am still awake.

Perhaps worse than the crying and the aborted sleep are the fights I have with Matt. Although, no, who am I kidding—no fights or regrets or screams or full-body sobbing jags are worse than the grueling nights and zombie-like days.

But our fighting is awful, bitter and constant. Every day I plead for Matt to listen to my reasons for sleep training Noah and every day Matt is sure there's another way, an undiscovered miracle cure just waiting to be found.

Fighting is new to us; we don't know how to fight. I cry. Matt yells, stomping around the room. We both fume.

Matt doesn't harm himself, but he too has a physical reaction to Noah's cries. His whole body changes. His hands tense, becoming fists. His arms stiffen by his sides. His body is charged up and he paces, unable to contain himself or his emotion. My husband, one of the most easygoing people I have ever met, has too become obsessive. As a lawyer, he bills his time to his clients in intervals of six minutes. Every day, he tracks hours at work—what he worked on, at what time, for how long. So, wouldn't it make sense for me to do the same thing? For us to learn the baby's habits? I dutifully fill in the thirty-minute segments on the Excel sheet by color: green for sleep, yellow for awake, and red for eating. Matt pores over them, sure they contain the key to our son and his patterns, the key to our salvation.

But even though each horrible day is the same, nothing on the sheets lines up to tell us why. Why is this happening? What are we missing? What are we doing wrong?

What am I doing wrong? Because I feel like I'm doing everything wrong.

I'm not sure what to do with him, so I do all the things I think I'm supposed to do. I dress him as a miniature version of my friends, in jeans and hoodies and socks that look like Vans. We go to playgrounds where I push him on swings. We go to baby music classes and sing silly songs. We go to baby gym classes where I grab him, kiss him all over until his laugh, his unmistakable all-consuming belly laugh, fills the room and the other moms and nannies give us approving smiles. *Do you see me? Am I doing this right?* I tell myself I'll just fake it until it feels right, but it never does.

I recently stopped nursing, my broken body no longer

producing milk, so I buy organic formula and feed it to my son in BPA- and phthalate-free bottles. All of his food and my cleaning supplies boast that they are "organic" or "natural" or "green." Maybe if I can do all the "right" things for him, I can start feeling the right way about him. But the truth is I don't know how I'm supposed to feel about him because I'm too tired and numb to have feelings for anything. And no belly laughs or Plum Organics pouch or tambourine sing-along can fix that.

Every day, I kiss his smiling face while actively regretting having him. It is horrifying. I am simultaneously empty and brimming over with hate and anger. Every day is filled with these disparities.

Sometimes I feel insatiable—an empty, consuming hole that can never be filled. I am hungry, so hungry. I eat all day long—nothing substantial, but I graze—because I want something in my mouth to make me feel better, but nothing ever does. I never feel better. I never feel full.

Other times I feel like I could never eat again. There is no point in thinking about food. There is nothing, absolutely nothing that sounds like it would taste good. There is nothing that is worth either cooking or ordering or even just opening a package. The physical act of eating is so exhausting. I can't expend the energy even to open a bag and bring food or even a food-like item to my mouth. I can't be bothered to chew.

Sometimes I feel like I can't breathe. My body is a black hole of feelings and longing and lacks even oxygen—there is never enough and I'm choking and drowning at the same time. I can't stand up straight because I'm afraid my lungs will collapse in on themselves as my stomach folds over.

I am anxious. Anxious all the time about nothing and everything. I've dealt with mental anxiety before but this is different. I'm physically anxious—my arms and shoulders are always tense—and I can feel my nerves contracting, spiderwebbing across my back. I am electric.

When my mom or Matt insists I give myself a break and hire a babysitter, I spend my "free" time just as anxious as when I'm with Noah. Walking around without him feels both liberating and wrong. It's like having a giant weight lifted, but finding out that the weight was in fact a limb and you feel empty and lost without it.

I am tethered to Noah. I am untethered without Noah. He is an anchor, dragging me under, and I don't know what to do except tread water.

At 2:41 p.m. I put Noah down for his third nap. I watch him sleep. He looks like a doll, an angel. He sleeps on his belly, his bottom in the air, head turned to the side, blond ringlets framing his face. He is so peaceful. He is so beautiful. He is so vulnerable. I step away from the crib.

Lately, the terrible thoughts—the thoughts I can't admit to anyone, even myself, have started creeping into my days. I know it's normal enough to think awful things at two in the morning when I'm half-asleep, but now the awful things don't stay in the middle of the night. They haunt me at eleven in the morning, at two in the afternoon; they permeate my day.

Things will get better. People lie. But I know things will not get better if they don't change and they're not changing. So I think about how to change them.

I think about giving Noah away. I think about running away. Either with him so I can sleep train how I want, God-dammit, or without him so I can just be alone with the quiet and emptiness of nothing. All I want is a room with a bed and a door. All I want is a chance to sleep, uninterrupted.

I think about killing him. All it would take is a little extra pressure in the middle of the night while I was rocking him. Who would know? Accidents happen. He's so small. Most nights my body already feels like it's not my own. So what if I acted? It would just end. It would just be over.

I think about killing myself. Or about killing both Matt and myself so Noah won't have either of us to screw him up. I think about killing all of us, so no one would have to worry about any of us anymore and our self-contained unit of sleepless misery would be gone. Forever.

These things start to make sense.

∽

It is December 2010. Noah is thirteen months old. Things are finally better, but they're nowhere near good. No one tells you that even if things get better, they don't get good.

Mercifully, after Matt finally agreed to the cry-it-out method, Noah is now sleeping through the night. But nothing we tried broke him of his early wake time. So his morning and ours still begins at four or four thirty.

I am taking antidepressants, so I no longer feel like hurting myself or my husband or my son. But now I feel detached. And anxious. Still anxious, anxious, anxious. Better, but not good.

My former best friend—who, like all my pre-mom friends, I rarely see—is throwing her annual Christmas party. I don't want to go. I mean, I want to go and see her and my former friends and have a drink and get dressed up for the first time in forever and flirt and laugh and remember there are holidays and songs and silliness and joy for no reason other than to have fun. But I really don't want to put the effort into going. I don't want to shower. To apply makeup. To shimmy into tights and a dress when my pajama pants are so comfortable.

When I complain about my conflicting feelings, Matt says, *If you want two different things at the same time, you just have to choose one and get on with it.*

Wanting two different things at the same time: that sums up my whole life now. I don't want to be a mother, but my son has taken over my life, my identity. What would I do without him? Who would I be without him? I want to run away, get divorced, start over on my own somewhere, anywhere with quiet and sleep. But that seems like it would take a lot of energy I just don't have the energy. I want to have a second child because I've always assumed I would have two children. I want Noah to be an older brother. But there's no way I want to be pregnant or even bother to have sex. And I can't imagine replicating the hell of the last year.

Matt and I no longer have nightly, marathon fights, but there is a rift in our relationship so large that it seems irreparable. It's as if a bomb has gone off in our marriage and even if we eventually find all the pieces, putting it back together will never make things the same. We're now each on our own island, bound together by Noah, but no longer to each other. I don't know that we'll ever find our way back to one another, and if we do, if we'll be able to mend the wounds or just cover the scars.

I don't like who I am now. Before I had a child, I was so cognizant of the type of mother I didn't want to be: one defined by her child. The fact that I've become that very mother is demoralizing and heartbreaking. I don't like being with my child. But I can't be without him. I'm a failure at the one thing no one in the world is supposed to be a failure at. Sure, I've felt like a failure for most of life—for not living up to my potential, not publishing the bestsellers in my head, not making much money at my attempt at a career. But this is failure of a whole different magnitude.

Isn't raising a child the most basic, essential, "natural" thing a woman can do? And if that's the case, then why am I so bad at it? I'm an educated woman in my thirties who planned, with her educated husband, to have a baby. I'm not some dumb teenager who got knocked up by accident. So why is every day such a struggle?

Every day is such a struggle.

But no one seems to notice. I don't know if that's a good thing or not. At the grocery store, at the baby classes, at the playground—I look just like every other Brooklyn mom in skinny jeans, a fitted T-shirt, flats, and an initial necklace. We all have our children's initials around our necks. We are all branded by our children. Since we all look the same, no one can tell I'm not the same underneath. But I'm not. I'm an impostor, an actor in a charming-looking life who is just going through the motions.

I have decided to go to the party. Greeting people, I get a drink and revel in the familiar warmth as it spreads from my belly outward. I've always been a fun drunk, a happy, flirty, chatty drunk. And as I loosen up, I start talking. But now that my entire life and identity have been swallowed by a child, I have nothing to talk about except that child.

At first, I start with a cute anecdote about Noah. He is, after all, adorable. But after some more sips, my chatting gets less fun and more honest. I can't pretend like things are okay. I can't stop myself from spilling out words that I know no one wants to hear.

I've been the girl at the party who made out with a random girl. I've been the girl at the party who was too drunk and got locked in the bathroom. But tonight, I'm the girl at the party telling everyone not to have children.

∽

It is July 2014.

Noah is four and three-quarters, as he likes to say, and Ryan is one.

After trials of Prozac, Lexapro, and Ativan, I settled into a decent place, medicine-wise, when Noah was around two. And then I knew I had to do it again.

Why would you want to do that to us? Matt asked, when I broached the subject of a second baby. I didn't have a good answer. It was in part because my mother, an only child, impressed upon me throughout my youth how lucky I was to have a sister and how lonely she was growing up. It was in part because I felt we both doted on Noah too much and I didn't want to create a little prince; our devotion, I felt, was bordering on obsessive. But mostly because I felt we needed to reset. Maybe if I got pregnant again I could reconnect some of the things that went haywire in my mind the first time around. Maybe it could help us gel into a family instead of just parents with a kid. Maybe it could help me feel like a real mother instead of a fraud.

So for a year, we tried. The monthly negative tests taunted me. Both relieved and frustrated, I wondered if I was doing the right thing. Did I truly want a second child? Would it upset the delicate balance we had finally achieved in our home? Would we ever sleep again? And more importantly, would I regret a second baby like I had regretted my first for so long?

I'm happy to say that while we've had hard hours and days, things are nothing like that long, dark period in our lives. Ryan is a happy, uncomplicated baby. He's easy to love. I don't mean to imply that Noah wasn't; he was, but I just couldn't feel the way I was supposed to. I'm a different kind of mother this time around. A more forgiving, go-with-the-flow, happier mother. Contributing in no small part to that is the fact that Ryan doesn't have sleep issues and I started taking my medicine again after nursing for six months.

I feel like I've been given a gift with Ryan. All the clichés about parenting that I thought were bullshit the first time around? They all finally make sense. The time does go by fast. His laughter is glorious. Getting him up from a nap fills me with joy and wonder about who this child is and how lucky I am that I get to be with him.

I finally get to experience mothering a baby instead of just trying to survive it.

And Noah, he is smart and silly, a funny, engaging avid learner. An early riser still, he usually sleeps through the night and he usually stays in his room until 6:00 a.m. Usually. The days he doesn't are hard, but I know we will get through them, move past them, get to something better. Because for the first time in a long time, things aren't just better, they're actually good.

LIFE WITH NO ROOM

Celeste Noelani McLean

I am afraid of the baby waking. I am afraid of the baby not waking.

I am with her alone, day after day, too soon after my cesarean to be of any real use. I am so swollen from water retention that the tops of my feet jiggle when I pace the living room with my brand-new bundle. Only this isn't really pacing. It is more of a shuffle, a groaning limp as nerve pain radiates from my slowly healing incision. It is everything, everywhere, agony.

I want to call my mother, to have her take the baby from my arms and shoo me into the bedroom so I can finally sleep. She is supposed to be here. She wanted so very much to be. I think of my wedding just eight months ago. Mom rushed up to me immediately after the ceremony and I scooped her tiny frame into my arms, lifting her up off the ground.

"Hey, don't hurt yourself," she scolded. "I want you to have another baby."

"Don't worry, Mom," I laughed. "Picking up your bag of bones ain't gonna hurt anything."

We wiped tears from our eyes, a well-earned truce finally between us. Photographs of the moment show us soaked in sunshine. Radiant.

Three days later, I learned I was pregnant. Three months after that, I learned my mother was dying.

Maybe today, at home alone with the baby, wouldn't feel quite as dark and arduous if it wasn't for the nerve pain. Or leg muscles weakened by fourteen weeks of bed rest. Or the progesterone shots or the cerclage or the threat of preterm labor blanketing the entirety of my daughter's thirty-eight-week gestation.

Maybe the high-risk pregnancy would have felt more manageable, more reasonable, if I'd had my mother's hand to hold during my weekly perinatologist appointments. But instead of having her there to hold me during the hopeful dash toward my daughter's new life, I was there to hold my mother's hand as she spoke to oncologists about death.

And maybe, just maybe, the cruel timing of my pregnancy and my mother's lung cancer diagnosis wouldn't seem quite as vicious if the peace my mother and I had finally forged hadn't been sparked by my second son's stillbirth. Or if the war that necessitated our peace hadn't begun during my father's terminal illness.

Or if, or if, or if. So many ways this could have been better, but I can only deal in today's painful, hideous truths.

Today I put the baby into her swing, desperate to finally eat the strawberries and yogurt my husband put on the coffee table two hours ago. I tuck a blanket around my daughter's little body and she begins to fuss. I swear under my breath. All I want is to eat my yogurt without trying to balance the bowl on top of a baby. This is apparently too much to ask.

I should love her. I know that. And I do, but also I do not. I am angry with her and her newborn-ness. I am angry at my dying mother and my living daughter and the no room in my life for sleeping, hot coffee, or cold yogurt.

No room in my life for me.

I wanted this, I remind myself angrily. I did this to me. I worked so hard to keep this pregnancy, to manage my newly diagnosed incompetent cervix and to bring this, my last baby, into the world at full term. I have no right to the fury that bubbles like tar, black and toxic and spoiling everything with its overbearing stench. I try to quell the anger, the hate I have for the baby I know that I somewhere, somehow, do actually love.

She fusses some more and I am nearly ready to scream with full-throttle rage. The rage cycles quickly through its targets: the baby for stirring, my mother for smoking, my husband for not finding a way to take more than a week off from work. But finally the rage settles where it should have stayed all along and I dig my fingernails into the tender skin of my wrist. I look at the baby sadly, sorrowfully. If I hurt myself, hurt her, they will take her away. They will know what a vile, unfit, horrifying mother I am and they will protect her from me the way she should be protected.

Maybe that is what she needs. Maybe that would actually be a gift.

Her eyelids stay closed and I look at the clock, whisper a prayer of gratitude. She will be down for an hour and a half, and then up for an hour. This is our routine. This is the day stretching out like a battle: desperately checking and rechecking the time, merely surviving until the moment my husband finally steps through the door.

I eat my warm yogurt. Sip my cold coffee. I try to watch a television show but am distracted by the whirring motor of my daughter's swing. I take a video of her sleeping so I can show her father when he gets home. He misses so much. She changes so quickly, not just day by day but hour by hour. She smiled at me yesterday and I nearly drowned, my heart was so overflowing.

She is beautiful, really. A treasure who looks so unmistakably like family that I cannot stand to see her in anyone else's arms. I spend all day cursing the slow march of time until my husband can come lift this tiny, burdensome bundle out of my arms, yet am so jealous of the moments she spends looking intently into his face.

I want and do not want this baby. I want and do not want this entire life.

Mom calls again. I haven't been good about calling her like she needs, and she reminds me of this. She asks when I can make the drive up to see her, since she can't drive anymore. A cancer cell is compressing her fourth cranial nerve, they think. She can't move her eye anymore. She sees double everything.

"I'm not cleared for driving yet," I tell her, which is the truth. But the larger truth is that I am afraid of driving with the baby. She screams in the car the whole time and I am filled with an anxious sort of rage whenever she screams. I picture myself driving into telephone poles, just to find some quiet.

Mom sighs, a long lamentation. She tells me how lonely she

is. She doesn't cry, but only just. I don't blame her. I absolutely do blame her.

We finally drive up to my mother's apartment on Mother's Day. The baby screams in the backseat the whole way there and the whole way back. My heart races and my stomach knots. Fists clench in my lap. I am not driving so I cannot steer the car into telephone poles. Instead, I dream of opening the car door and launching myself out as my husband speeds along the highway. I pull the handle but the door is locked. It stays closed and I stay safely buckled into the passenger seat.

Two weeks later my mother has a grand mal seizure. The cancer has moved full-blown into her brain. There are seven tumors.

I change the baby in my mother's hospital room, joking with her about horrible food and even more horrible nurses. She doesn't ask me how I am doing. It is not her job anymore.

My mother's cancer ravages the last of her body. She dies when my daughter is just eight months old. My daughter starts crawling in earnest and a test to detect levels of lead in her blood comes back a little higher than normal. I begin cleaning the floors.

I clean the floors over and over again every single day. As my daughter crawls beneath the kitchen table I am beside her, wiping the floors in warm water and vinegar. I am usually the kind of person who goes whole months without mopping the floors, but now I can't go three hours without giving in to my frantic compulsion.

Months after a second blood test confirms that my daughter's lead levels are absolutely fine, I am still on my hands and knees, pushing a wet rag along the fir floors. I weep in the shower, knowing that I cannot do enough. Not by half.

I go to therapy, taking the baby with me because there is no one else to watch her while I sit and talk about how awful everything is. Only, I don't talk about how awful everything is. I am upbeat in my therapist's office. Tired, but upbeat. I report challenges, but insist on voicing the silver lining in all of them.

She asks me about being tired and I shrug, noncommittal. I talk about my routine, going over the step-by-step of my everyday battle. How I can't quite make it up the stairs to tuck in my oldest son. How angry I am at my mother for dying. My husband for not doing everything in ways that I consider right. How no matter what else is going on, there is this baby whose needs are immediate. Oppressive.

"The baby doesn't care," I tell her offhandedly, "how depressed I am. Or tired. Or that my mother is dead. Or that I can't do this. I have to keep going, no matter what. The baby doesn't care."

There is a silence between us for a moment and my mind goes on to the next topic. I open my mouth to launch into another rambling vent session when she stops me.

"Tell me," she says, "about being depressed."

I look at her. I want to cuss, but not under my breath. I have been found out and I am horrified. Ashamed.

The room is quiet except for the sound of my daughter cooing. She begins to fuss and I put her to my breast. I busy myself with the activity of nursing, attempting to stretch this unspeakable silence for the rest of our session. And maybe it works, but only sort of. When I come back for my next session, she asks again.

She asks, and asks, and asks, and little by little I answer.

I nurse the baby in front of my therapist and we talk about

my second son, the one who died. About how much my new baby looks like him, and how much I want him back. I want both of my babies. But I also want none of my babies. I am tired of babies. Bone tired. I want to be dead.

I want to be dead, and I admit to this in a way, and it is so embarrassing to admit this. But also, it is a relief. I have spoken these words and I have not died. I do not want to die any more than I wanted to die in that moment before I said it. And, miraculously, nobody came to take away my children. I want to be dead, but I also do not want to be dead. I want all of my babies and I want none of them.

I am afraid of the baby waking. I am afraid of the baby not waking.

I tell my therapist about never sleeping, not really. About staying up all night just to hear the sound of my daughter's breathing. And then being so angry with her, with myself, when she wakes up and needs me because I am worn down and exhausted and incapable of being the mother I thought I would be before I had this baby. I don't know who I am right now. I am not the person I told myself I was going to be.

She asks me about that, and I tell her I don't exactly know who I wanted to be, but I for sure know that this is not it. I was going to sleep when the baby slept. Be awake when the baby woke. Take walks and sing songs and be stronger, better, more than I am capable of being right now. I am capable of so little, yet am being asked to do so much. She says yes, this is the truth. I am not making any of this up.

This is the truth. I loved my daughter from the moment I knew that she was inside me. But I also did not love her when she was born. I was tired, ragged, overtaken when she was born.

There was no room in my life for me. Knowing this is the truth, that I was not making any of it up, doesn't fix it. Doesn't make me love my daughter any more. But it does make me hate myself a little less. And that, after a while, is what lets me begin healing. What helps me begin making room.

In the spring, my daughter starts walking. She is not a baby anymore. She holds my hand and toddles beside me as we go to the park. When we come home, it's time for lunch. She drops her spoon onto the floor, splattering spaghetti sauce beneath the table. I pick up the spoon and slip it back into my daughter's chubby hand. She laughs and throws the spoon back onto the floor, a merry game. I sigh, then laugh, scooping the spoon from the floor. Down the spoon goes again with a clatter. Up goes my daughter's voice, her belly shaking with laughter.

The floor is riddled with giant spots of spaghetti sauce. This morning's banana is down there as well. So is yesterday's rice. I'll clean it all up later. I know that to other people, a dirty floor might be a sign of a life too overwhelming. Evidence of a spiraling breakdown. But for me, it is the opposite. So when I see the grit, the grime, land on my floor, I am overtaken by a need to kiss my daughter, instead of the fiery compulsion to scrub the whole house anew. And all of a sudden, I know: I am getting through this. I am surviving, and not just in the tired, traumatic ways I was surviving in the early days of my daughter's life. Maybe I have already survived. And now that I have, I can finally start living.

I kiss my daughter. I leave the mess for later. I nurse her down for an afternoon nap and I sleep beside her, for real this time. We wake up and have a snack and read books and welcome home her oldest brother from school. We wait for her father to come home from work. I make dinner while he cleans up the mess under the table, and a few hours later we get everybody tucked into bed. The next day we do it all over again, only it's not like a battle anymore. It's not awful. It's work, and it's difficult, but it's no longer impossible.

I keep going to therapy. My therapist asks, and asks, and asks. I get better and better at not avoiding her questions. I answer. And little by little, I really do learn how to live.

AFTERBIRTH

Dana Schwartz

When my beautiful daughter came roaring out of my body on a rain-soaked April morning, I had no idea what I was in for, no idea about the darkness ahead, how her colic would consume me. All I could see were her little bow lips and the whirl of dark hair matted with my blood. I was a new mother, riding high on adrenaline and a near-perfect birth. My mother's recent death, and the cloak of grief that shadowed my pregnancy, had been momentarily eclipsed.

I was so enraptured that I barely noticed how the mood in the room had shifted. My midwife popped up with a frown and explained the situation. My uterus wasn't cooperating. Blood was pouring out. They gave me a shot of Pitocin to stimulate contractions. Some women need help starting, but I needed help stopping.

Afterward we joked about how I had filled my midwife's shoe with blood. I felt a strange sense of pride recounting the story, as if bleeding signified strength, as if almost dying but not was something to be proud of.

∽

Fast-forward one month, two months, more months. My baby wouldn't stop crying. Okay, this was not entirely true. My baby didn't cry while nursing or sleeping. The caveat was that she only slept in an upright position, preferably on me. Never on her back like the doctors recommended (or threatened) and never, ever in a crib.

My husband and I spent our days stumbling around stunned and exhausted. We took turns walking our daughter in the park for naps. He had morning shift, and she screamed bloody murder until passing out, alarming passersby. They either offered him unsolicited parenting advice or looked appalled. I took the midday nap with fewer dirty looks (mom's privilege) and at dusk we went together.

On those walks, we were often silent since our baby's screams still rang in our ears, but every now and then we'd speak, our voices low and hushed.

"Look at that baby," I'd say, pointing across the street at another couple pushing a stroller. "Sleeping on its *back*."

Or we'd hear a baby start to fuss and the parents would frown with concern. My husband would shake his head. "That's not crying," he'd say. "Not even close."

I felt a sense of camaraderie with him on those walks. He understood what we were up against whereas most people didn't. Maybe they thought we were typical new parents, overwhelmed and under slept. We were. But our baby was not typical. She was extreme.

That's what I called her after my dad tactfully suggested I stop calling her crazy. It fit. She was extreme, in every way. An extremely bad sleeper, an extremely incessant eater, and an extremely excellent screamer.

It was colic, or whatever you call it when your baby's cries are like sirens that don't turn off for months. Colic, when nothing you do, *nothing*, will soothe your baby. When your baby writhes in pain for no reason at all, or no reason your doctor can give you, while you watch with horror and helplessness.

The days unwound long and tedious, but nothing compared to the nights. As the sun went down, my baby bristled like a roused nocturnal animal. Oh, the nights.

During the day I had help. Wonderful life-altering help in the form of my husband and my dad, who came several times a week and was one of the only people who could hold our wailing baby with complete and total ease.

But understandably, he would leave at night. Understandably, my husband would go to sleep. Someone has to, we'd joke. But then the door would close and I would be alone. But of course I wasn't alone. I was never, ever alone. I could barely take a shower without hearing my baby screaming for me somewhere in the house, my heart slamming against my chest as I tried to will the shampoo out of my hair.

The nights were long and I felt so lonely, despite my companion. My baby didn't cry during the night, but she nursed on the hour and slept fitfully. When she'd finally doze off I'd stare at her, in awe and relief, but my body remained on high alert, unable to settle down. I listened to music, sobbing along to the Beatles' "All You Need Is Love" and "Blackbird," counting the minutes until dawn.

She was thriving, according to the doctor, but I wasn't. I felt a little like I was dying. But I didn't ask for help. I didn't think I needed any. Every new mother feels like that, right? We all feel like we've given up something vital, or something vital has been taken from us. None of us really know what we've signed up for until it's too late.

Right? *Right??*

My nighttime despair bled into my days. I tried to get out there. I'm a joiner. I signed up for a new mom group before I even had my baby. I went to a few meet-ups before I stopped. It was too depressing to be the only mom whose baby cried fiercely, who couldn't be put down, who always, always needed to nurse. I found better luck with some moms from my childbirth class who were patient and kind in the face of my extreme situation.

But even in their company, I felt alone on the island of new motherhood. The one person I longed for most was dead. I missed my mother so acutely my body ached.

I wanted my mom, but what I needed was help. I joined every single group except the one that would have mattered most. I vaguely remember a friend mentioning postpartum support, but it met at night. At night, what a joke! That was when I was indispensable. I could *never* leave my baby at night. How could I possibly? What a crazy idea. And that was that.

I'm sure I could've found another group that met during the day, or figured out how to leave for one night a week, or less, but I didn't. I turned away from that door. I never even bothered trying the knob.

I had little mantras I'd tick off. *I'll be okay when...*

Colic ends.

My baby sleeps.

I sleep.

When she's in school.

What I didn't understand was that I didn't have to wait. I didn't have to suffer in isolation. There is no prize awarded to the most stoic and miserable mother.

A couple years went by in a haze. Most of my mantras came to pass, and just as I ticked off the last one I got pregnant again. An event that should have brought joy almost sank me.

That's when I remembered. After years of lying dormant, a memory rose and unfolded its damp wings like an awakening chrysalis. Years before, my mother had revealed to me that she had undiagnosed postpartum depression with my younger brother. The memory of her words, spoken with unnerving nonchalance, chilled me in retrospect: "Luckily, he was an easy baby, otherwise I might have killed myself."

I wondered what might have changed if she had been alive to witness my struggle. Would she have recognized it and urged me to accept the help she was never offered? Would I have listened to her?

I'll never know. But luckily, like my brother, my son was an easier baby. Let's put it this way—he didn't have colic. I don't know what would've happened if he did. I don't know if my marriage would have made it; as it was, we had drifted miles apart and had only recently begun to repair the rift.

I don't think I was ever inches from the edge like some women, but I came close. There were many nights when I wept into the darkness, with bleak and utter hopelessness, calling out to my mother, *Please, please help me.*

If only I said those words to someone who might have heard me.

But I was too stubborn and didn't have my mother to guide me. All I had were stories. I thought about them during my pregnancy and then afterward: about my mom's natural childbirth, and then later, the birth of my brother, how she had such little help, her mother miles away, how she bore so much alone.

I gripped them tightly. They were all I had.

But perhaps that grip warped my perception. Endurance is not strength; hardships are not badges to be earned. Blood loss is just blood loss, and too much will kill you.

And I was still bleeding, as if my afterbirth had never stopped. I dragged myself through the days, the months, all the while leaking blood and growing weaker, never admitting that maybe I needed to stop pretending that my misery was normal.

The morning my daughter was born I nearly fainted on the walk back from the bathroom. All that blood loss made me dizzy. Black spots formed along the edges of my eyes. When the nurse approached, I tried to wave her away. *I'm fine*, I said, but I wasn't. She knew it, and maybe deep down, I knew it, too, because I let her take my hand and lead me back to bed.

SCAR TISSUE

Maureen Fura

*H*e doesn't know it, but I do. He is the one. His eyes are deep blue with flecks of gold that shoot out like stars in the night sky.

"Sawyer, I love you."

We are eating dinner, tater tots and ketchup. He likes to call it "ka-patch." His head tilts toward his plate, one tot in hand, mid-dip in a pool of red.

"I don't love you. I love Daddy."

I lay my hands on either side of my plate. My fingers are outstretched, the wooden table keeping me up. He is not smiling. He is not kidding.

I want to run up the stairs, slam the door, and cry in the middle of my bed.

I tell myself, "Kids go through phases." I read about it when my son was two, when he first started choosing my husband over me.

"Don't take your child's parental preference personally," the books said.

But I do. I'm his mother. He is *supposed* to love me the most. But he doesn't, and I know why.

An hour before I found out I was pregnant with my son I had my first suicidal thought. I remember it was cold and damp. I was outside, wrapped in my blue bathrobe. When I looked up at the oak tree above my porch, I saw myself hanging from its branches.

He shouldn't remember, but I know he does.

He remembers everything. Like the carpenter tool belt he got for his third birthday a year ago. The one he never played with so I tucked it in a plastic bin months ago and shoved it to the back of the garage. The tool belt he begged to play with the other day. He had only seen it once.

He doesn't forget.

Within days of finding out I was pregnant, I was barraged with impulses to take my life. The impulses soon escalated into images of harming those I love. It was an unrelenting chorus of "what-ifs." What if I fall asleep, sleepwalk, and slice my husband into tiny pieces? What if I pour bleach into his food? What if someone walks in front of my car and I don't brake? What if I drive off a cliff with my baby tucked inside me?

I wondered if it was possible to be allergic to pregnancy.

I searched the web for a diagnosis, but everything said "postpartum." There was nothing about being pregnant and losing your mind.

Therapists told me to "white knuckle it." Obstetricians said, "Be happy. You're having a baby."

Before this, I was fearless. I had traveled to India alone. I had lived in Ecuador. I'd driven across the United States by myself, twice. Now, I couldn't even leave the house.

I wonder now if my depression during pregnancy is why my son is slow to warm up when he meets new people. Is that why he's so quiet, so cautious on diving boards? Why he's scared to put his head underwater in the pool? Is this his scar tissue?

When I was five months pregnant, I went to a prenatal yoga class. The teacher was young and toned, sitting on top of a wooden platform like she was special. A furry white bear rug peeked out from under her folded legs. Dressed all in white, her head was wrapped like an Indian Sikh.

She told the room of big-bellied women to be careful of our thoughts. What we think now will shape who our babies become.

I wanted to kick her into the wall.

Friends told me it was my reaction to losing myself. But this felt bigger. Years later, I learned that the day I saw myself hanging in a tree, the same day I discovered I was pregnant, I was officially five weeks pregnant, the point in pregnancy when a woman's reproductive hormones shift into high gear.

As my progesterone spiked to create tiny organs and vertebrae, my system short-circuited. My brain went haywire.

At six months pregnant I sat on my therapist's couch. She explained that my thoughts were "ego dystonic." It meant I was aware that the thoughts were bad and therefore I was not as psychotic as I felt. She told me depression during pregnancy is the number one complication of having a baby. It affects one in seven women.

She said, "You are purposefully avoiding everything that scares you so you can make sure you never go through with your thoughts."

She was right. Every horrible thought I had, I avoided. I feared running over people; I stopped driving. I feared knives and ovens; I stooped cooking. I feared bleach; I stopped washing. I feared killing my husband when I slept; I stopped sleeping. I feared being an unsafe and dangerous mom; I was going to kill myself once my son was born.

I was put on a high-dose antidepressant that balanced my hormones. I could move through the world without fear. I found joy in the simple things again, like birds singing and sun shining on my face.

Today, I am better.

Except in the moments when my son says, "I love my daddy, not you."

In those moments, my chest squeezes tight and my thoughts race.

A voice inside says, "He knows he should be scared of you."

This is *my* scar tissue.

I LOVE YOU; LEAVE ME ALONE

Kate Kearns

I wanted to cling to her; I wanted to flee.

Let's rewind a bit.

Five months into my pregnancy, I realized I would never be alone again. To say that this initiated a progression of reactions would imply ordered, linear thought. Rather, a mosaic of feelings and questions locked into place all at the same time: panic, dread, and a hint of warmth, but mostly an alternating pattern of more guilt and more panic. It formed a brittle enclosure that was so uncomfortably close my own breath glanced off of it and came back, hot and clammy, into my face.

Panic. Is a good mother supposed to feel this way? What if I resent my child? I am happily married, and my husband waited patiently for me to be ready for this, which I was. Was? Am?

Let's rewind a bit more.

Four months into my pregnancy, my dad died. My sister and I were moving along in our lives with promise and positivity. On a Monday in early August, I spoke to my dad on the phone, and he told me he wanted the baby to call him "Grand-daddy" because my sister and I had always called him "Daddy," even into our adulthood. The next day, he was gone. He was alone. It was an accident. We didn't know for several days. Our relationship with our dad was affectionate and close but not without its flaws and frustrations. We could have used that golden time—the time people get when they know someone they love is dying that allows them to be their best selves for each other before it's too late. Our close friends, coworkers, and family circled the wagons, surrounding us with support and food. While I appreciated their help, I just wanted to grieve alone in my own home.

You see, I've never been a "joiner," and never had large groups of friends. I spend a lot of time alone, and always need to hide someplace quiet partway through a party, even when I'm the hostess. My husband and I specifically chose our house because it allows us each some personal space. I am perfectly content sitting in silence, listening to my own internal mono-logue. I never knew the true meaning of the word "introvert," or that I fit the description to the letter. Introverts are over-whelmed by crowds and need solitude to recover and charge. We like to spend abundant time alone but do not consider ourselves "lonely." When my dad died, I didn't want to heal with friends holding me together until the glue dried. I wanted to retreat, to play emotional Tetris internally, silently.

In my case, being an introvert melds with being a writer, which adds some extra nuances to the formula. I am a private person, but on top of that I find it impossible to understand and express my feelings if I'm not scratching them down on paper. Ask my mother. To my chagrin, she still has all the letters I wrote her when I was worked up about something in my youth. I'm not cold and affectionless, but I do need a lot of physical space to be a sane, functional member of society. How was I going to raise a child with clingy, loving fingers and hold on to my sense of self?

When the mosaic of panic surrounded me with its fragile, multifaceted fragments, I said nothing. Being a poet gives me an appreciation for the complexities of dark thoughts, but I couldn't trust my loved ones to get it. Was I underestimating my friends, my family, my husband? Yes. Was I still looking forward to the baby? Yes, but from that moment forward, I proceeded joyfully on the outside with a concealed electric current of anxiety and dismay snapping and sparking invisibly. I glowed, but not for all the right reasons. If ever I allowed my darker thoughts to show, people were welcome to assume I was thinking of my dad.

To return to where I began: as you expected, my daughter was born. She was awesome in the way the word "awesome" was originally intended. This hungry, gorgeous thing needed to be close to me to survive and relied on me for nourishment both physically and emotionally. The sound of my pulse soothed her and anchored her the way no one else's on earth ever could. I looked into her dark blue eyes; my panic mosaic shattered and I was trapped in place, surrounded by sharp, threatening shards around my feet.

Where was that soul-smothering, all-consuming plummet into the rosy Motherworld? Motherhood didn't make me a new person; it added a person to the me that already existed. But the "me" that already existed wanted to be by herself much more than this adorable little sausage would allow or understand.

When she fell asleep after eating, her warm little belly soft against my right side, her legs curled up under my arm, I should have been filled with something resembling completeness. I wanted to free myself from her clutches and sleep, sleep, sleep, alone.

The first night she came home, and many nights after, I cried and cried—loud, uninhibited, wide-mouthed crying. I grieved the loss of my solitude as hard as I was still grieving my dad. I wept knowing he would never meet my daughter; I wept because I resented this little creature that took up all my breathable air and the guilt was expanding in my chest as fast as my love. I wept because some unknowable imperative needed me to.

I don't look back on her infancy with nostalgia. My friends-with-children expected me to be charmed by the magic of it all, and I gave the appropriate responses. I cared for my baby. I held her close and she slept on my chest. I did not look forward to seeing her in the morning, and planned the days alone with her in anticipation of her naps and bedtime. I looked down at her conscious that I shouldn't feel able to live without her, but also knowing that, in fact, I could. It's a shadow that still drags at my heels. I couldn't speak it. Who could hear me say such a thing without thinking me a horrible person?

And that's the crux of the problem. As I write this, I keep catching myself needing to make you understand that I really do love my daughter. The truth is, it has nothing at all to do with love or lack thereof. All of the buzzwords associated with postpartum don't do justice to its biological, psychological, and unnamed complexities.

Because of this need to insist upon love, the statistics about postpartum depression are, I'm sure, tainted. When a mother has these thoughts, how can she feel anything but shame and fear? Even though we are told the causes and warning signs well ahead of time, who can bring herself to admit to not feeling overjoyed by her new baby, no matter what the supportive scientific pamphlets say? I was already an internal person before, so imagine how deep down I pressed this in order to make it through the day.

Yes, I love my daughter. Of course I do, but as she grows out of one "babyish" thing after another, I don't miss them. She is almost three now, less dependent on me for the practical things, and the pressure is easing but never gone. With age comes awareness, and her emotions are maturing as quickly as her stature. We talk, we hug and touch, kiss each other, and have fun together. She learns almost as quickly as I can speak. Her joy is infectious, her intellect astounding. She, my husband, and I are a tripod, and still, at some point every day I have to mentally restrain myself from stepping away and telling her to leave me alone. I still resent her demands on my mental energy and solitude. I still feel the breath of guilt for resenting her and for not feeling the urge to give her a sibling, which would add yet another person to my personal space.

I never had a diagnosis; I never sought one. Speaking up is not in my nature. I am *great* at being "okay," and my introspective brain keeps tabs on my well-being. Is that the right approach? Probably not. What helped? I started writing again, and it pulls me into balance, most of the time.

Right now, my husband and daughter are outside planting hyacinth bulbs. Listening to them talk to each other makes me happy, yet I have no impulse to go out there and join them. This writing is the first time I've taken the shards of the mosaic and examined them, noted their colors and contours. The reckoning has filed down the sharpest edges. Now, maybe, if I step on one from time to time, which I do often and will continue to do as long as I am a mother, they might not draw blood.

I found my own way to heal and move forward on an even keel. Soon my girl will be in school, I'll start regaining my alone hours, and I'll miss her.

A DIFFERENT SHADE
OF THE BABY BLUES

Jill Robbins

I caught a glimpse of myself in the bathroom mirror: my hair was (almost) perfect, my lipstick was actually confined to my lips, and my earrings matched. Sure, I had bags under my eyes from lack of sleep, but for a new mom, I was doing better than average in the pulled-together appearance department. If not for the sagging shoulders and the wild, panicked look in my eyes, the casual observer might think I was doing all right. But I wasn't all right.

I'd ducked into the bathroom to hide the anxiety bubbling up inside of me and threatening to take over. I wanted to scream, cry, and throw stuff. I wanted to hyperventilate and hold my breath at the same time. Hundreds of different emotions washed over me and rather than completely lose my crap in front of my family, I mumbled something about needing to pee and bolted into the john.

The woman staring back at me in the mirror was a hip,

lipsticked "still got it goin' on" forty-something-year-old mom. She had my red hair that I've always loved. She had my hooked nose I've always hated and she was wearing my favorite purple sweater. But she didn't *look* like me.

"She has no joy," was the thought that rolled through my foggy mind as I studied my reflection.

It was my birthday. I was dressed to go out, which explains the whole combed hair and matching earring thing. I'd spent the last few weeks wearing the same two pairs of sweatpants and sticking close to home. A trip to the grocery store was a major outing. You know—typical new mom stuff.

I was about to spend a few hours alone with my husband in a place where I could enjoy wine that didn't come from a box and eat food not called casserole. We would have intelligent conversation that didn't revolve around poop or snot. Instead of relishing the fact that I was about to have a grownup evening out, I was becoming unhinged over a broken vacuum cleaner.

Yes, a vacuum cleaner. It wasn't even one of those fancy-schmancy robotic gizmos that whizzes around promising a dust-free house 24/7. It was a standard cheapo upright that I'd bust out every time the cracker crumbs and cat hair threatened to take over. Hoping to clean up a little before the sitter arrived, I got out the dirt-sucking machine and flipped the switch. There was a pop and a little puff of smoke and suddenly, I was the one doing the flipping. My vacuum had chosen this moment to die, and there it was—my tipping point.

You're probably nodding your head and thinking "post-baby hormone-induced unreasonableness." You might also be thinking I'm a little old to have a newborn or that I need to get a grip about my vacuum. But everything about this story so far screams postpartum depression in all caps. Right? Not exactly. My husband and I had adopted a three-year-old boy from China six weeks before. Does that change your perspective? Would you nod your head in empathy or roll your eyes and blame it all on menopause?

Post-adoption depression, PAD for short, isn't often discussed openly, partly because there's a general lack of support and understanding. I guess that makes sense—the most common way to get babies is to have sex and wait nine months or so. Well understood or not, PAD is out there. Women like me experience stress, frustration, guilt, anxiety, and fear after adoption, and most of the time, we don't speak up because we're afraid people won't get it. Because sometimes *we* don't get it.

I'm not sure if PAD is a label that applies to me because I was never diagnosed by a professional. I was too embarrassed by my post-adoption emotional reactions to seek help. I wish I had seen things differently back then. I'm pretty sure that if I had taken the steps to get professional help, PAD would have been diagnosed as the culprit.

Our adoption was rocky. Things didn't go as planned. My life was completely turned upside down over a small human I wasn't even sure I *liked*, let alone felt anything maternal toward. The guilt over that was crushing, so I forced it in to the recesses of my consciousness and plodded forward, feeling just a little more deflated every day.

Maybe adoption looks like an easy path to parenthood from the outside, but it's not. It might look easier on the surface: no morning sickness, stretch marks, hemorrhoids, or other gross stuff that happens to our bodies when babies incubate inside us. However you look at it, the road to motherhood is hardly ever sunshine and unicorn farts. One thing adoption *is*, though, is deliberate. You might hear about "oops" pregnancies, but accidental adoptions? No. Adoption is the most "on purpose" thing I've ever done. And the hardest.

I met my son Kyle in a hotel room in China. My anticipation about meeting him rivaled that of any expectant mom waiting to see her baby's face for the first time. I'd been looking at Kyle's pictures for eight months while we waited on the truckload of adoption paperwork to be approved. I'd been dreaming of the moment I'd take him in my arms and be his mommy in real life and not just in my mind. I had a clear picture of how things would play out.

About that. Things didn't exactly go as planned.

Kyle and I were both scared that day. I was a seasoned mom. Kyle wasn't our first adopted child and this wasn't my first rodeo, but I think I could literally hear my heart thump as the people from the orphanage walked Kyle in the door to meet us. I tried to dismiss my fears and put myself in his place: yanked from everything safe and familiar and hustled toward a strange lady who spoke funny words. The fact that I was holding a cup of Cheerios and he was pretty near starving helped make our first meeting go a little more smoothly, but it was still a frightening time for both of us.

Kyle was happy to interact with me and accept my offers of food and affection. *This is going great*, I thought. But when he was left alone with us, he withdrew. He shut down, wouldn't make eye contact, and crouched in the corner of the room for the rest of the afternoon. This is a completely normal reaction for a small child who'd just been uprooted and probably understood very little about what was happening. I could relate. I felt a little like crouching in a corner, too.

By the end of my second day with Kyle, I knew something was very wrong. I knew lots of somethings were very wrong. He was sick and malnourished, which I hadn't expected, but which was not that shocking, either. After being with Kyle for a couple of days, we began to realize he had medical needs beyond the scope of what we'd been prepared to parent.

The short version is that he has congenital bowel issues that had been ignored for most of his life and explained away to us as "practically nothing." The nannies at his orphanage had managed it by limiting his food intake.

"Don't feed him too much," they advised. *"That make poop."*

I've been a mother for over twenty-two years. I have a lot of memories of being a mom, but none I remember with such clarity as sitting on the bathroom floor of a hotel in a remote corner of China thinking: "I can't do this. I can't take care of this child."

I didn't feel anything close to love for this pathetic, skinny little boy. He was sick. He smelled. He was shut down and didn't seem to want to be in my company any more than I wanted to be in his. You might think a little poop is no big deal, but as the realization that we were dealing with complex, lifelong medical needs sunk in, our family dynamic changed. We fought. We retreated to our corners with our respective thoughts and demons. This adoption knocked us on our asses.

As much as it shames me to write this, I considered disrupting the adoption and returning Kyle to the orphanage before we left China. I had a whispered conversation with my husband about this very thing, a conversation that stopped almost as soon as it began because the idea of leaving him was more unfathomable than adjusting to life with him. Although we didn't seriously explore disruption, the guilt of daring to say it out loud is something that hung over me in the early days at home with Kyle. Truth be told, the guilt pricks me to this day.

We brought Kyle home and spent the next few weeks trying to navigate our new normal. I'm not sure if it was my reaction to the sea of poop and appointments with specialists or just the fact that what I'd envisioned for our family life was so far from the reality, but I began to withdraw. I tried to talk to a few people about what I was feeling and experiencing and I got responses like:

"You should have known what you were getting into."

"You wanted this. Be happy he's got a family to take care of him now."

People weren't understanding when I tried to articulate my feelings and frustrations. Although I saw myself as a new mom, it became pretty clear that most of the rest of the world didn't see me that way. There wasn't a lot of empathy for the stress I was feeling so I learned pretty quickly to keep my mouth shut, paste a smile on my face, and assure everyone who asked that we were just hunky-dory—because no one really expected or wanted to hear anything else.

We muddled through the early days home as a new family. It was a blur and a sea of doctor appointments. It was draining and overwhelming, but we got from *"I can't handle that"* to *"okay, we can make this work."* Kyle began to settle in. He started to trust us. I watched him blossom from that scared, frail little boy I'd met in that hotel room to a fearless, outgoing, fiercely tough little boy. He's the bravest, most resilient person I know and I don't think he'll ever stop amazing me.

My feelings of hopelessness turned to resolve and the "fake it till you make it" mantra that was at the core of my daily self-talk began to sink in and become reality. "Fake it till you make it" might seem an odd way to cope with the difficulty of attaching to a child, but it worked for us. When we made the commitment to bring Kyle into our family, we put a ton of effort into facilitating his sense of belonging. I wanted him to feel safe and secure, in spite of the fear and doubt that plagued me. I fervently hoped and prayed my feelings of love and attachment would follow suit.

I am one of the lucky ones. Although I feared bonding with Kyle would never happen, it did, when I least expected it. One day when he'd been in our family about seven months, he beckoned to me from his spot on the couch, where he was curled up watching television.

"Sit, Mah-meee." Kyle patted the seat beside him. "Watch Wiggles."

Watching four Australian dudes hop around singing about mashed potatoes was not high on my list of fun stuff, but I sat. Kyle hopped onto my lap and tugged my arms around his little body, forcing me to hug him. To return the hug was surprisingly natural, and I rested my cheek on the top of his little head and realized there was nothing fake about this simple gesture of mother-child affection. I felt a surge of love and breathed a sigh of relief.

We are there, I thought.

Things didn't get magically easy in a puff of glitter and

fairy dust, but the fog cleared for me that day on the couch, with the Wiggles singing about cold spaghetti in the background. Once I got past my fear of not feeling what I thought I should feel and gave myself permission to love at my own pace, some of the guilt and panic abated. I wish I had had a better feel for the signs of PAD while I was living in it. I wish someone had reached out to me and validated the way I was feeling. I wish I'd had the guts to reach out and not give up until I found someone who would try to understand.

A good analogy for my adjustment to being Kyle's mom is stumbling while running up the side of a hill. I tripped. I struggled. I slid back when I tried to move forward, but eventually, I pulled myself to the top. I was so focused on the climb that I didn't stop in the moment to raise the SOS flag; I just trudged through.

We all think of adoption as a happy event, but some of the issues that can affect families as they're learning to become families just aren't well understood. A new mom is a new mom, and a new mom parenting a child from a hard place or experiencing fear and guilt over bonding with her child needs people to look out for her, too. If someone in your life has recently adopted, look for signs of stress or withdrawal. That person may be where I was, and it's not a very nice place to be—especially not alone.

My story has a happy ending. My birthday ended up not being a total bust. I got over the broken vacuum cleaner and my husband bought me a better one that totally didn't count as my birthday present. The wine flowed freely and I was allowed some time outside the house to relax and unplug from motherhood for a couple of hours, which all new moms need.

With patience and good medical care, Kyle's needs are managed in such a way that he enjoys an entirely ordinary life. I think I love him all the more because we both had to struggle so much in the beginning. I wish I had known it was okay to struggle and that what I was feeling was completely normal, instead of just suffering in silence and hoping things would turn around.

Not a week goes by without a friend or some well-meaning stranger telling me how lucky Kyle is to be in our family. I smile and nod, because although I don't really see it that way, I know people's intentions are kind. I know that I am by far the luckier one. I've come through some dark times as a mother and although I'm stronger for it, I don't wish what I went through on anyone.

I know that the road ahead isn't going to always be easy but I have the inner strength to get through it. I'm not planning on adopting again, but you never know what the universe is going to throw your way. Whatever lands in my lap, I think I've learned my lesson about suffering in silence. And that vacuum cleaners really just aren't that damn important.

The Comeback

Kara Overton

*S*ilence is deafening when there's no one around to break it, like a constant high-pitched scream with no volume or duration control. Mute. Where's the mute button? I need something—somebody—to shut it up immediately because I'm afraid of what might happen if it keeps going.

Or is it the incessant, compulsive thought that I'm losing my mind and no one can help me that's shouting so loud?

I can no longer tell the difference.

The two-month-old is sleeping eight-hour stretches, but I was up all night again last night, terrified that I wouldn't sleep and would have to miss another day of work. My brain taunts me, tells me that I can't be a capable mother, wife, or teacher without rest and then dangles the bait just beyond my reach; she's the cruel, heartless owner, and I'm the sick, starving dog. So I lie awake and I miss work and the unbreakable self-fulfilling prophecy continues.

Damn, the silence is loud.

I need the dominoes that started this mess here to distract me, but it's Tuesday and I'm terribly exhausted so they're at daycare. Two years ago the birth of the oldest child set off the first fall and since then the subsequent pillars have toppled accordingly. Concerns morphed into panic attacks, which morphed into paralyzing fear about her health and mine. Would I survive the monster that was sucking me dry of what used to be an ample supply of confidence and logic? How would my children, whom I really didn't deserve, go on without me?

On a daily basis I resolve to kill the beast but it seems that the harder I fight, the bigger and more powerful it becomes.

Geoff's gone too. At work, where I should be. We teach at the same high school, so when he comes home and tells me that the students are asking about me again, he may as well be handing the monster a freshly sharpened knife. I can't bear to think about how this is affecting the people around me; guilt only pushes me further down the rabbit hole.

I'm lying next to the dryer on the bathroom floor because the silence won't shut up. It's empty but running and if I could wrap my arms around the droning metal box, if I could physically embrace its constant and steady hum, I would. But of course it's too heavy, too big for one person to hold alone. So I lie on the floor and do the only thing I've been able to do since the second baby came along eight weeks ago. I cry deep, heavy sobs into the suffocating quiet.

What's wrong with me?

Postpartum anxiety. It's what the doctors said after the first was born but this—this debilitating fear that infiltrates every aspect of my life—cannot possibly be something definable. It's far too awful. No person can relate and no drug can help. I'm in this alone.

And I'm terrified.

When I finally stand up and face the mirror, a disheveled mess looks back at me. Large, hazel eyes that used to sparkle with ambition wear a bloodshot blanket of defeat. On the night we got engaged, Geoff said the energy in them was what made him fall in love with me and every day I wish I could bring it back for him but I can't. I don't know how.

I'm wearing the same oversized Sublime T-shirt that I wore when I was pregnant the first time. A happy memory of two pink lines, of nervous laughs and giddy phone calls, is tucked away somewhere in my heart. Someday I hope to revisit it without hating myself for being so naïve. The shirt's dirtier now than it was then, caked in spit-up and mashed sweet potatoes. This is not what I expected it to be.

The blonde hair that I wore in a curly bun the year I made homecoming court is tangled and unwashed. I remember when my college roommate crimped it the morning of the big football game, spraying it with black and gold hairspray that quickly clouded up the dorm room. We laughed between coughs and joked about getting high on the fumes.

I consider brushing it—the comb is well within reach—but I can't find the energy to care about an appearance that I no longer recognize.

There's nothing worse than expecting a friend and finding an enemy.

Tears—many tears—and the taste of salt. This seems to be the stranger's permanent state. I reach out and touch her reflection; she looks so heartbreakingly sad.

"Come back."

I'm not asking her. I'm begging.

"Please, Kara. Please come back."

The knot in my chest tightens as I realize that I've lost myself, that this moment of desperation is my rock bottom.

Medication, they told me. It will help.

But, Doctor, the baby's still breastfeeding. I would never forgive myself if . . . and of course I can't quit nursing because, well, because haven't you heard? Formula-fed babies are sicker and dumber and if I stop I won't be a perfect mom . . . it's true, everyone says so . . . I can't let my family down like that, especially the helpless baby who is so good and mellow and nothing like her older sister was at two months old.

"Jesus, Kara, why won't you come back?"

I remember how she used to go out with friends and say goofy things and laugh during funny movies and I miss her more than my racing heart can handle. But the silence is too loud, the thoughts too demanding, and the exhaustion too heavy to look for her. Besides, even if I do find her I won't know what to say. I'm sorry I lost you? Where have you been? Are you going to leave again?

My feet shuffle across un-vacuumed carpet and carry me to the two-year-old's bedroom, where Mr. Giraffe and Lola Monkey lie comfortably atop Hungry Caterpillar sheets, permanent smiles sewn into their faces. Daddy forgot to open the blinds this morning but I leave them down, crawl into the tiny toddler bed, and pull a faded Precious Moments blanket up to my chin. It smells like lavender bath soap and sunscreen.

Forty-eight hours since I've slept.

Her room, the same room in which I felt that first sliver of fear—*please, God, make her stop crying!*—brings me peace. I drink it in like the neglected, malnourished puppy I've become and close my eyes. Surrounded by the sights and smells of my children, sobs turn to rhythmic breathing and I finally drift off to sleep.

It's no surprise that what got me here is the same thing that gets me out.

This. This is postpartum anxiety.

Not medical books or waiting room pamphlets or WebMD descriptions, but profound sadness and deep hopelessness and a smothering fear that nothing will ever be the same. It's voices in your head telling you you're not enough and that you're ruining everything, turning you into your own worst enemy. It's being alone. Always. Even when you're not.

Three hours later I will wake up, wash my face with cold water, and type "postpartum anxiety" into the computer. For the first time since the initial domino toppled, I will encounter message boards full of people who describe symptoms identical to mine, websites overflowing with stories of despair that, with professional help and self-care, transformed into stories of victory.

This time I will cry tears of liberation because I will learn that I am not, in fact, alone after all. My hollow rabbit hole is actually full of other mothers also trying to find their way out. They're reaching for me like I'm reaching for them and when my hand touches their cold, weathered fingers I squeeze tightly.

It will be okay. We will be okay.

One month later I will call the doctor, see the psychiatrist, and take the medication. I will choose to switch the baby to formula and I will beat myself up when, for five straight days, she refuses to take the bottle. The guilt will consume me until a few weeks later when she flashes me one of her sweet, gummy grins and I'm finally able to smile back.

She doesn't need breast milk. She needs her mom.

This. This is postpartum anxiety.

Not weakness or self-loathing, but bravery and empowerment. It's discovering your strength so you can push forward, connecting with yourself so you can connect with others, trusting your experiences so you can learn from them. It's being resilient. Always. Even when you think you're not.

In *Toy Story 3*, Mr. Potato Head uses a tortilla for his body to help Woody and Jessie escape from daycare. Three months later I will watch this scene with my daughters and laugh—a deep, authentic belly laugh—as he unsuccessfully attempts to cross a window ledge and shoo away a hungry pigeon at the same time.

"I'm here," a soft voice will whisper. "I never left."

And I will smile, relieved, because it's my own.

EVEN SHAMANS GET THE BLUES

Alana Joblin Ain

I can drive up and do an exorcism," my mother offered. My baby girl, Autumn, was two months old and my depression wasn't being cured by a cocktail of lemon balm, Chinese herbs, and fish oil.

"I'm comfortable communing with the spirits," she assured me. "And I'm not afraid of my gifts."

I was afraid of her gifts.

I was afraid of everything in those months following Autumn's birth. Sleep became a separation akin to death. Dreams were like a "best of" horror reel of scenes from *Pet Sematary* and countless Holocaust books I'd read in Hebrew School. Most prominent was the house where my mother's father had taken his life, seventeen years prior—half my life ago. It didn't take long for sleep-time to give way to full-blown panic attacks.

At a new mothers' group, I sat in a circle with other women. The conversation turned to sleep deprivation: moms revealed concerns about separating from their newborns, coordinating shifts with their husbands, clogged milk ducts. An "A" student and rabbi's wife, I considered myself a cheerful member of new social groups. I didn't mention the Auschwitz nightmares or the suicide in my grandfather's basement.

"Mom, I don't think there's a demon inside me. I have postpartum depression. It's a real syndrome."

A speech therapist turned shaman, my mother tried to fix and arrange everything through magic. Even my pragmatic pharmacist father, her husband of forty years, was not immune to her spells. She made me a collection of powerful amulets. I had a "transition" necklace, to mark leaving an office job for a more creative path, and an "intention" amulet, which she believed brought me my husband, Dan, whom I was set up with shortly after she bestowed it. And I had a "birthing" pendant, meant to bring an easy labor. It was with that last gift that I realized the limitations of magical thinking.

"We don't have depression on my side of the family," my mother said, "but I guess it's possible you got it from Daddy's side."

"Mom, your father killed himself."

I was too wrecked to be polite.

"Well, there's that," she conceded, "but the women don't have it."

My mother wasn't the only person remiss in identifying my postpartum depression. At my eight-week OB checkup, I told my doctor that I was suffering moments of extreme anxiety and grief, beyond the realm of anything I had experienced in my thirty-three years of life. I suspected it was a clinical postpartum disorder, but my doctor told me, "No, that's where you don't want to take care of your baby; you don't have that."

I wanted to take care of Autumn—more than anything—

yet as the days and weeks turned into months, I wondered if I would be consumed by this darkness my mother thought to be the devil. Something erupted and tore me raw—not just physically—after the birth. I thought the love I felt toward this small girl could kill me, that maybe I just did not have the mettle to be a mother.

"In a few weeks you'll forget you ever felt this way," well-meaning friends suggested. It was just the "baby blues," the "normal" adjusting of the hormones that takes place following the birth. Deciphering the poetic from the clinical was always a challenge for me. But this time there was physical pain in my chest, a shift in body temperature, sweating, pacing, insomnia, inability to eat. I was unable to cry, which felt much worse than familiar weepiness. I did not believe this awfulness would ever pass.

My mother, who was the runner-up in her Pennsylvania town's local Farrah Fawcett look-alike contest shortly before I was born, had never experienced any such thing.

"Maybe because I was so much younger than you when I gave birth," she suggested. She wasn't wrong. It must have been easier to give birth at twenty-five surrounded by dozens of extended family members while living in a house with a back-yard and a dog—not in a cramped city apartment.

Even though I suspected I was getting worse, with panic attacks that left me unhinged for days at a time, I held out hope that it would just go away.

My idealized vision of creative people didn't help. I just assumed they didn't need medication, and instead, when times got tough, they lived out the "dark night of the soul" over and over, weaving their suffering into their craft.

That's what my mom seemed to be doing: shaping mosaics,

sewing fiber-art-shields, stringing colorful glass beads, keeping her anxious animal fingers in constant movement.

Eventually, Dan, who was not alarmed by expressions of anxiety and depression (*Our people have endured worse challenges*), suggested that I see another doctor.

The psychiatrist, a slight woman in her sixties, a veteran in her field, diagnosed me within our first five minutes of conversation:

"You have postpartum depression. You have a family history. You need help. This is not going to just go away," she told me.

I began crying. I was scared to take medication. I didn't want to lose the ability to feel things, I told her.

"The goal of medication is to make the pain feel *tolerable*, not to make it go away. It's okay that you'll still be in some pain," she told me.

"You know about that writer David Foster Wallace who killed himself after he went on antidepressants," my mom mentioned, as I headed into the city to meet up with Dan at a Shabbat dinner he was leading, one week into my 50 milligrams of Zoloft.

I anxiously stuffed challah in my mouth, trying to suppress the fear that I was on an inevitable path to suicide, until I finally took aside one of the other guests and confided in her.

"Fifty milligrams—that's candy," she told me. "I'm on 150. And your mom got it wrong: David Foster Wallace killed himself after he stopped taking his meds."

I was not alone. Thank God, I discovered, at this Sabbath of the afflicted. It became clear that my mother's commitment to magical healing and my own idealistic expectations were making me worse.

When I admitted to the unsavory feelings, I found that I was in good company in other social realms, too. People I'd known for years, even decades, had struggled with depression and had been helped by medicine at various times. It had just never come up. This was my new minyan.

With the help of Linda, a therapist, I accepted that the trauma of the childbirth had created chemical unrest, but also a collision of past and present, where I finally confronted the roots of my anxiety.

Early on, Linda asked if I had any rituals. I answered that I said the same prayer every day, blessing all of my family members.

"Do you say their names in a specific order?" she asked.

"Yes," I answered.

"And what happens if you say their names out of this order?" she asked.

"I start over."

There were a lot of things like that—private ways to make order out of chaos. Things no one else would ever notice. I saw Linda a couple times a week. I listened to her meditation CD. I took my meds. I spoke honestly and openly with other women.

A few months in, I knew that I was starting to improve. When I said the prayers out of order one day, I just kept going.

Then, one morning, I noticed a collection of splattered paintings tacked upon Linda's wall. It looked like the sort of thing my mother might enjoy.

"Are other patients doing art projects?" I asked, wondering if there was some alternative to all the talking.

"Yes," she answered. "Would you like to try?"

"Yes," I said.

"You seem to be doing really well," my mom told me during a spring visit when Autumn was nine months old. I tickled my baby girl's legs and belly, both of us laughing, and I leaned over her growing body, kissing her chubby cheeks.

"And you look like you're enjoying motherhood," she added.

"I really am, Mom," I said. I saw her looking at me, seeing me.

"I think," she paused, and added gently, "You might even be a better mom than me."

His Baby Watermelon Head

Kristi Rieger Campbell

A blend of intentions, life mishaps, and other priorities meant that I didn't have my first and only baby until I was forty years old. At the time, I'd been raising my teenage stepdaughter for more than a year. I didn't tell anybody but my husband that I was pregnant. Even he waited for my news for twenty-four hours, four pregnancy tests, and too many self-affirmations for me to count. I had to work up the nerve to say it out loud. That I was pregnant. That I hoped.

For one, I didn't believe that the pregnancy would stick. For another, I didn't believe I deserved it to stick. My pregnancy announcement at almost six months along was met with heartfelt congratulations and jealousy that I was so lucky to have a fifteen-year-old at home.

A built-in babysitter.

Usually, I nodded and smiled and agreed that I was lucky. I didn't tell anybody that my teenage stepdaughter would never watch my son. That nobody would watch him for years.

I didn't tell people a lot of things. I certainly never spoke about how I felt. I didn't talk about my incompetent cervix, sure that I'd jinx my son's arrival if anybody knew how undeserving of him I was. To this day, my heart beats faster when I remember calling my husband from the parking lot of the doctor's office after finding out that my life had just drastically changed: simply walking my dog or cooking dinner meant that my son's umbilical cord might actually fall out of me, and that he would die if that happened.

My new reality meant bed rest and twice-a-week monitoring for the rest of my pregnancy. Nobody witnessed the humiliation and fear I felt when I had to call the boss that I hated to tell him that I wouldn't be at work for a long time. Only my car and my coat held my embarrassment and my tears.

I didn't mention I was convinced that I'd lose my baby to miscarriage the way I had before. That the beginning of the end of my first marriage was because I needed something from my then-husband on the day I miscarried. Something that he never gave.

I didn't speak of how I already worried that The Universe would never allow me the honor of becoming a mother. I didn't share with anybody how I had to take back all of my unanswered prayers from years before, when I asked God to give me a terminal illness that would take a mother away from her children.

I was convinced that I'd remain childless forever. Certain that I deserved to lose my babies. All of them.

I deserved every bad thing. Every loss coming my way.

I figured that I deserved all of the bad things that may happen during my AMA (advanced maternal age) pregnancy.

I knew that I didn't deserve to be a mother.

I hoped though. At least a little bit. God, really, I hoped a lot. Somewhere between the "thens" and "befores," I found a way to believe that I might actually have a child. I did hope.

That pregnancy test that I kept to myself for twenty-four hours from my husband and six months from the rest of the world one day became viable. Sure, there was bed rest and there were scary moments. I had doubts and worries and cravings and sleepless nights. But I also had hope.

Finally, after a minute or months, one day, I became a mom. It was then that I realized that life is more forgiving of me than I am.

My worries shifted. From me to my baby.

Somehow, I realized that thinking I didn't deserve to be a mother wasn't the point. Falling completely in love with my teeny tiny human knocked me on the head with an understanding that my self-indulgent bullshit was just that—bullshit. I found a new love for myself, a tenderness toward the value of my life. I became important because my newborn needed me above everybody else.

One night when my son was about eight weeks old, for whatever reason, he had fallen asleep easily and allowed me to place him in his crib and walk away, which wasn't the norm during those early days. That particular night, I armed my husband with the monitor, made him swear to keep the volume down on the TV in order to hear every single noise from our son, and I went for a walk in the dark. Fall was approaching—it was still warm in DC—and it was one of those almost perfect nights in which the humidity wasn't as oppressive as usual. I walked, and then I stopped. I don't remember the exact details of my thoughts, but I remember feeling simultaneously content and desperate. I felt connected, present, alive, and thankful. I also felt terrified.

I sat down in the middle of the sidewalk and looked at the stars. Inhaled. Exhaled. Wished. Prayed. I calculated the timing of my wishes and prayers just so—to be "off" and have to re-request would surely render the magic moment pointless. I figured out what, exactly, to wish for, found a bright star, anchored my hands on the cooling concrete, and said, out loud, "Please. Please let me live to be at least eighty-five years old. Let my baby live to be the same, and grant me closeness to him for all of his years."

It was that simple. That was all I wanted, and really, it still is.

For the first time in years, I knew that my living mattered. That I was here, on purpose. The living, crying, suckling life of this boy, this boy who was of me and yet completely himself, was why. He was why.

Because of him, I went from skydiving and unworthiness to safety gates and bravery.

I knew that parenting might be rough. I'd been warned about sleepless nights, baby spit-up in my hair and on my prized new sofa, and about the wonder and horror associated with breast milk coming in.

I expected to love the unexpected. The things the books didn't tell me about. I looked forward to it.

And honestly, mostly, at least with hindsight, I know that I held on for the rides. Waking myself with snores at 3:00 a.m., sitting in his nursing chair with my neck and my boobs dangling down while he slept on my lap, was cool with me. I hadn't read about it, but I figured we won. We slept, anyway.

Still though, there was unexpected ugliness. The type that brought me to my knees, over and over.

I didn't expect that sometimes, on some days, my brain would turn against my heart, and scream to me about how horrible I was. How the hateful whispers of *"you do not deserve"* would make me want to cover my thoughts the way that children cover their ears. I knew that anybody who'd lived the life that I had, full of past binges, a divorce, smoking, and all the other things, just didn't deserve.

Nobody told me that I'd picture my perfect little newborn's head going "splat!", bright red and broken, like a dropped watermelon on my hardwood floors. That I'd picture his broken head, every single time I carried him.

One afternoon, my husband tripped on our stairs while carrying laundry. He stumbled down the final three and landed, hard, with his shoulder against our wall and put a three-foot hole in our drywall. He felt awful and silly and stupid and kept apologizing to me for it. All I could think was "Thank God you were carrying laundry and not the baby." I think that to this day.

None of the online baby forums or books I'd read mentioned anything that prepared me for the reality that, while simply walking across the street with my son's head tucked safely in my hands and his body strapped uncomfortably to my core, I would vividly imagine every disgusting detail of what a car crashing into us would look and feel like. How I'd hoped my un-lost baby fat would protect my baby's watermelon head.

None of the books said anything like that.

I rode in the backseat of the car next to my boy until he was five years old while my husband navigated alone in the front seat. Once, I glanced over at the car next to us and saw a young woman in her twenties staring at us. I was both embarrassed and nostalgic, remembering how I, too, may have once seen now-me. Back when I was childless and knew everything, I'm sure it would have seemed like overkill and helicopter parenting to see a passenger-less front seat, mother and child in the back.

For mama-me though, riding in the back next to my son seemed practical. Handing him a bottle or a snack or simply putting my hand on his head to help him to sleep seemed like something every mom might do. And maybe it is. My prayers and rituals seem a little embarrassing now. As if my hands and whispered mantras held the power to protect my little boy from a runaway truck.

Too afraid to share my fear, I lived all of my horrible, sure-that-one-of-us-would-die thoughts alone. I assumed they were normal.

Now, five years later, I am almost certain that those thoughts weren't normal. That I should have shared what was in my head with somebody besides my husband, who didn't know how to comfort me and also didn't know what to do other than to assure me that my thoughts were crazy, unfounded, and that mostly, babies are okay. That mostly, babies live.

It's not that anybody in my past had told me that having depression or anxiety was a weakness. We never talked about it when I was growing up. Our family was more likely to say "Snap out of it!" than to ask whether somebody needed outside help. We weren't strangers to therapy, however. My brothers and I saw a family therapist for years after my mother had a nervous breakdown, attempted suicide, and left us with our father at the ages of thirteen, eleven, and eight.

While neighbors gossiped and tsk-tsked our sad situation, nobody ever used the word "depression" or "anxiety." We heard words like "selfish" and "wacky" and "fucking crazy," instead.

I assumed that coming home from a walk, closing the door behind me while feeling thankful for being safe and alive, and then bursting into tears was due to hormones and a body that didn't feel like my own. I figured that sleeping pretty much every single time my son slept was due to exhaustion more than it was an escape.

My son is now five and he has developmental delays. I'm still working on believing that these things are not my fault. That we are safe and that satellites don't fall from the sky very often and that millions and millions of people grow old each year. I continue to be terrified that a car will break us both open. Or worse, only him.

I can say that I no longer picture his not-so-tiny head splattering on my floor. That somewhere along the way, I found hope when it comes to climbing and jumping and all of the boy things.

I continue to pray to an unfamiliar God, make wishes on stars, and beg myself and the universe for forgiveness. I thank this life for the moments of magic. Of wonder. For brief glimpses into knowing that this—right here and right now—is momentarily perfect, and that it is enough. That I am enough. That we're okay. Safe.

I live. And I struggle. Maybe, we all do.

Did I experience postpartum depression? Anxiety? I don't know. But I wish that I'd asked. That I'd reached out. That I'd gotten help. I wish I'd found a way to not wake up breathless with worry about the splat of a tiny watermelon head.

OPEN SESAME

Elizabeth Bastos

I sat in the pediatrician's waiting room staring at the ficus. At my feet was the car carrier that contained my week-old son. He was bawling. All tiny fists. Tiny feet kicked off the socks some well-meaning great-aunt had knitted out of baby blue yarn. From the beginning they were impossible to put on.

I stared at the ficus, the potted tropical plant, ignoring my infant, ignoring the socks, and wondered what life must be like for that plant. Its ancestors were in the Amazon, but here it was an immigrant in this sunless space of a medical office waiting room. I thought about how my great-grandmother must have felt leaving the old country to come to America.

I waited for my name to be called, and when it was, I picked up the car carrier. I abandoned the socks. I had a high fever from a breast infection and had just started antibiotics, but I knew that was not the only reason I was out of my mind.

"How is the nursing?" the pediatrician asked. I answered by

pointing to my enflamed chest, and behind it, to my heart, which felt like a stone.

I was no pastel Mary Cassat painting, all pink and bliss. I couldn't sit without a specialty donut because I had cracked my tailbone in labor and delivery. I wore an undergarment because I peed myself regularly; I didn't have the muscles to stop the flow. My hair was a mess. My breasts were infected. I felt jittery. Wired.

I said, "He's not latching on. Can you show me 'the latch' again?" I used this vocabulary because I had learned it. I was parroting, but it meant nothing—who the hell knew what a "latch" was really? We were a failed "nursing couple."

"Keep practicing," the pediatrician said.

"How are *you?*" she asked. She was going through a check-list. This was the postpartum depression screening. "How are you sleeping?" "Are you eating?" "Do you have any thoughts of harming yourself or the baby?"

There were obviously right answers. They were: *Good. Fine. Yes. No, of course not! I adore my baby.*

How could I say to anyone that when I saw him for the first time, and he was placed on my chest, I had the sense I had plunged headfirst into a pool in a quarry? And that the feeling would last for years?

I felt no balloon of affection expand in my chest. I didn't even *like* my son. I watched like a cold-blooded reptile while my husband, swoony with love, went with the delivery nurse to give our boy his first bath as I got the tears in my perineum stitched up.

My son was born with fluid in his lungs and I felt no compulsion to go to him and try to fix it, to hold him upright, to pat his chest. His sounds were an irritating snuffle. I hated them. He was born with a birthmark on his forehead, which the nurse said would fade by the time he was five, and I hated that too. The nurse was right. By the time he was five, there was just a whisper of redness there, but I had convinced myself that the birthmark was evidence that I—Snake Woman—had marked my son.

He seemed to loathe me right back. He wouldn't take my milk, though I dangled my breasts every which way, even trying to nurse on all fours like a cow with him beneath me propped on pillows as the midwife nursing specialist recommended.

His gaze seemed vacant. He wouldn't scan my face the way I had learned in birthing class, the way all newborns are supposed to thirst for connection with their mothers. There was no mystic gazing.

When I looked at him all I saw was, *birthmark*. So I stopped looking at him.

I would leave him in the crib to walk to the bathroom and then not make it and urine would trickle down my leg and I would clean it up with a rag while he screamed. The house seemed possessed by us.

I willed him telepathically to *just shut up* and my mother, who was there to help, to fly home to Maryland. I didn't want any more casseroles. I didn't want another bunny blanket. The stuff—carriages, bouncers, walkers, cars, boosters, bath toys, baby books—smothered me; it felt like so many bricks in a wall of the castle of Motherhood that was being built around me in which I stood alone, The Queen, trapped, as on an island.

I took no pleasure in his small slipper-shoes with trucks on them, or the rattle that had been mine. I seemed to have no maternal ON switch. I watched hours of *Nature* documentaries about mammals and how they care so sweetly, so *humanly* for their young, swinging them up to cling to their backs, and determined that I was an insect.

It was as if my feeling of "unlove" was a thing. A pestilence. I felt plagued and ashamed.

I passed the screening for postpartum depression by lying, saying things like, "I feel okay," "Just tired."

To this day I am surprised I got away with it, that I was left to my own devices. I was acting placid, but churning like hell under the surface to keep from drowning. I washed and rewashed and then zapped the baby bottles in the microwave to disinfect them.

Medicine, thank goodness, has gotten better since then. I should have immediately been put on medication, but I wasn't. It took years.

As my son grew and met milestones (first laugh! first roll-over! first steps!), I wanted the whole thing to be over. Even as he pushed his Cozy Coupe around the neighborhood looking adorable, I wanted out. I wanted to blink my eyes and my son would be forty, gainfully employed and living far away, with an infant that would be my grandchild, but of whom I would know little.

Being a hands-off grandmother—having the work and the bottle washing and the defeat behind me—sounded like bliss. I wanted to live in Florida, to play canasta with my lady friends, and to sit in the sun on Miami park benches. I wanted to never visit during winter.

And then my son learned to ride his bike. He was about

four-and-a-half—he'd been using this push-bike without pedals with the skill and determination of a gifted future X-gamer— and we took him to a bike shop to get fitted for his first bike. My son scrambled up onto the saddle like ascending a cliffside (the bike was so big-seeming and he was so small) and suddenly he was *riding* in the parking lot. Like Alexander the Great on his great war horse Bucephalus. I felt my heart pound in my chest.

As he confidently rode past me, he looked at me directly in the face and said, "Watch me, Mom! Mom, are you watching? Mommy! Look what I can do!" He wanted me to look! Me! I made contact with his wide blue eyes and out flew a "Wheeee!"

Until then, I had not clapped my hands for him without assuring myself that it was the correct behavior, a play from the Loving Mother playbook that everyone else seemed to have in their back pocket. I was always working to manufacture the gestures that looked like caretaking, the glances that were filled with the devotion I didn't actually feel. I had never spontaneously, authentically given him my love, as if I had a bottomless well of it. I dipped it out in spoonfuls, ever certain I would return to the well and it would be dry.

I am not the mother I thought I would be. I'm brave enough to honestly say that I am a grasslands mother, a savannah mother, a nature show mother. In the emotional landscape of myself there are droughts. But there are holes that contain sweet water, too. I've learned that. When I find them, I say, "Come, drink. Let me nourish you in the ways that I can, knowing that it will never be enough, and the next drought will surely come and for that I am so sorry." I *wish* I were the Amazon. Surely I've shed as many tears.

I wish I could have those years back. I wish I could say that there are no longer days when I feel fenced in, queen of a parched country, or a zoo animal pacing the cage.

It's on those days that I will myself to pour the milk, and to review fractions. I temple my fingers and put them to my forehead: a headache is coming on again, but I continue to listen to my son haltingly read *The Hobbit*. When he elbows me, trying to get into the bed to snuggle, I bear it stoically, like a lioness does her cub biting her tail. I stroke his hair when he is sleeping. I whisper things I know he finds funny like, "You're the cat's pajamas." But I physically yearn to have that moment back when I could have held my son to my chest for the first time when he was first born, now that he's nine and I've already spent over half of his at-home life with him.

But time is an arrow as they say, and I can only continue from here, today, to take this moment, to inhale the bread-crusty, young-boy smell of his wrestling clothes before I toss them into the laundry.

Fragments of a Fractured Mind

Eve Kagan

I guess I should have known. The story of my mother's struggle with postpartum depression had become somewhat of a family anecdote, the gravity replaced with a wink: *your uncle had to come over and drag your mother out of the house in her bathrobe to take her to his shrink.* And yet as I embarked on the journey of motherhood I held fast to the daughter's sacrosanct mantra: I am NOT my mother.

Then the moment arrived when I hooked my thumbs under my own daughter's slippery armpits and pulled her out of me, flushed and new, nuzzling into my breast for the first time. She was here. It was surreal. I rode the oxytocin wave for weeks on end; days and nights were merely distinguished by the light in the room. It was soft and warm skin-to-skin hazy bliss.

And then we moved. First across the country and then across the Atlantic. My husband had secured a postdoctoral fellowship in Munich for the year, and just as the baby girl inched into her third month of life, we left everything we knew behind, save for some clothes, books, and our slobbery sweet English Setter.

In truth, the ecstatic high had already begun to dissipate, leaving behind a dull, sleepless emptiness like the once-vibrant color drained from an ancient photograph.

Just before leaving for Germany, I wrote a pseudo poem hinting at the cracks beginning to fracture my mind:

The sharp edges of exhaustion brush up against my molten heart
Like Eskimo kisses between razor blades and goose feather down
Like nails on a chalkboard and warm cherry pie
Never felt such unsteady bliss before
Screams squirms smirks smiles and a dimple to die for
Wrapped in the Moby we tromp down the road her left cheek hot
pink against my chest leaving the echo of her ear sketched into my
skin, her right cheek cool in the crisp fall morning air

Five months in I stood crying as my homemade minestrone soup boiled on the stove, filling the windowless kitchen of our Munich flat with steam and hysteria. My husband was holding the baby who had refused to nap again. She was fine. I was not. Sleep had been an issue since the beginning. She was awake every few hours to breastfeed in the night and she only napped for thirty minutes at a time. I was always on call, and had been since the day she was born, alone. It was a prison of my own making: it seemed ridiculous to me for my husband to get up and warm a bottle in the middle of the night when my breasts were full and tingling with milk at her mere whimper. So we never introduced a bottle—we didn't even own one.

Her refusal to sleep was wound tightly around my own deprivation and every moment she spent too long awake made me want to run to the bathroom and slash my wrists so I could dream forever. Somehow these thoughts didn't strike me as strange or suicidal. I didn't long to die; I just longed to sleep soundly without stirring at the slightest creak in the bedsprings. When she cried, I felt like a raw nerve electrocuted. The image of myself silent in the crimson burning water, unable to hear her scream, seemed like a logical solution. I was shattered. Everything soft and warm in me, the giant beaming heart my husband so often references when reminiscing about our courtship, had become brittle.

I knew I was not myself. But I had no idea who I was anymore. When people asked me what I did I couldn't fathom how to answer, since every definition I had previously used was now past tense: I *was* an actress. I *was* an educator. I *was* a writer. What I had become was a woman obsessed with the unpredictability of motherhood. I didn't feel qualified for the job. I searched the Internet desperately for answers to inane questions that often resolved themselves before I could land on a decent solution. I pushed the stroller a little too roughly through the Englischer Garten, praying to a god I didn't believe in that the baby would nap. It was not just my identity, not simply the label that did not fit; I was unrecognizable. My mind was a whirlpool of doubt: *What have I done? I should have never been a mother. I am not meant for this. I am a horrible mother. I don't love my baby enough. I don't know what I am doing. I am failing. I am a failure. I am damaging this little being. What have I done?*

I never thought it was postpartum depression. Perhaps it

was because we were in Germany. While I had spent a large portion of my twenties traveling the globe, from Kampala to Kathmandu, visiting and working in developing countries, this was the first time a place felt truly foreign. The austerity of the language and demeanor of the Bayern was a stark contrast to sunny, sweet Santa Barbara where the baby was born. My village was nine hours behind and six thousand miles away and Skype only provided my family with brief interludes that focused on baby face time. Perhaps it was because I was still functional for all intents and purposes. I put on mascara every morning, washed my hair when it was dirty, sautéed garlic a perfect golden brown, sang original lullabies, had orgasmic, sometimes angry sex with my husband, wore the baby in the Björn on the 16 Tram to the BioVolet to buy organic Süßkartoffel (sweet potato) to mash up for her first taste of food. I did not need my uncle to come over and drag me out of the house in my bathrobe to see his shrink.

And, yet, I felt utterly alone all the time. I never wanted to hurt my baby; I only wanted to hurt myself. I suddenly understood how people could cut themselves—the need to see all of the pain within come to the surface in the form of a wound. I never picked up a knife or a razor blade. I did, however, hit my head against the wall.

I tried to connect. I took the baby to classes where she chewed on communal toys, giggled at bubbles, and practiced crawling on purple foam exercise mats. I joined an expat moms' group. We met for lunch each week at a local café—run by a flirty, freckled Irishman and a shy, doe-eyed Turk—that boasted candy-colored chandeliers, a play area with a miniature white picket fence, and giant pieces of sinfully moist zucchini cake.

While my interactions with these lovely women were genuine, they never dipped below the surface.

Pleasantries were exchanged, along with translation mishaps and where to find the German equivalent of favorite American products, while breasts were suckled shamelessly at the table. I never assumed any of these women were suffering as I was—they all seemed at ease with their babies but perhaps I projected the same. I had this picture of what I thought it would be—no doubt drawn from the glossy photos in the magazines I once read while waiting for my ultrasound in which mommies with perfect smiles delighted in baby toes—which I could not reconcile with my reality. *What is wrong with me? Why can't I be grateful? Why is this so fucking hard?* I wanted to scream, but I kept quiet. I didn't want to risk losing my place at the table. I felt like a shell and a shadow, hollow and insubstantial.

How had this happened to me? My pregnancy was amazing. I was so confident and calm, and even somewhat audacious in my work: managing a yoga studio; teaching a theatre workshop to teens; completing certification as a prenatal yoga instructor; directing, producing, and performing in a small production. I practiced yoga and meditation regularly. I embraced the transformation of my body as a metaphor for life itself: constant flux. I felt empowered knowing that everything I did was in direct relationship to her. I ate well, slept well, loved well, all in the name of creating a safe and sacred space inside me for this little being. When we found out I had a two-vessel cord and needed additional monitoring to be sure she was growing properly, I stayed relaxed. I trusted in my body's ability to be pregnant, to nurture and shelter our daughter. I trusted that everything was going exactly as it should. It felt right. I felt like a mother.

I labored naturally for over twenty-four hours, through excruciating back spasms, and double-peaked contractions that lasted over two minutes, but only when my midwife said my uterus could not continue and I would have to acquiesce to an epidural did I cry. Perhaps that was the beginning of the end, the moment I lost control. As much as I had convinced myself that I was going with the flow, there was without a doubt a sense of perceived control while she was in my womb. I was the only one who knew how to take care of her and I trusted my ability to do so completely. Somehow she was more alien to me once she emerged as an independent, brilliant little being.

We returned to the United States just after her first birthday and I suppose I naively hoped being back would quiet the demons rioting in my mind. There was comfort in the familiar: street signs, menus, and assembly instructions written in English; vegan chocolate chip cookies from Whole Foods; calling my best friend on the phone without counting back the hours on my fingers. Yet I continued to struggle, waffling about every minute decision, worrying that the choices I made would be wrong. I took intermittent solace in her incredible evolution: *she is thriving so I must be doing something right.* But I wondered at times whether she was so incredible because of me or in spite of me. When her sleep schedule was solid I could briefly find the light, but when it was erratic and unpredictable I slipped back into the darkness of old patterns.

While I can write with lucidity when these moments over-whelm me, and they still do sixteen months in, I feel possessed by the anger and anxiety. I cannot see beyond the cycle of thoughts fraught with contradiction. *If I put her in a footie, will her feet be too warm? If I put her in a romper, will her toes get icy? Should I use the wool sleep sack or the cotton one? Should I turn up the heat or turn it down? Should I put her down earlier since her nap was shorter? Should I put her down later in hopes that she sleeps in? Should I drop a nap? If I go back to more naps, won't I just have to start this process all over again? But is she too sleepy at the end of the day without more nap time?* And on and on and on. Once I emerge it is as if an exorcism has taken place and my mind returns at least somewhat to a state of brief equanimity.

I know I will regret all of the time wasted on these thoughts. I already do. They take me away from the present moment with my sweet baby girl when all I want is to be with her fully, to bear witness to her as she delights in the world.

The reality of my postpartum disorder is now undeniable. While the anxiety and depression are no longer pervasive, they are easily triggered. I still wake in the middle of the night drenched in sweat, sure that the baby is awake even though she sleeps soundly. I don't think it is possible to return to who I was before, but there is an opportunity to once again embrace change as I did during my pregnancy, to transform into something new.

Every time we read *The Very Hungry Caterpillar*, which we do with fervor on an almost daily basis, I am reminded of the potential to become a butterfly. So instead of praying to a god I don't believe in for things to resolve, I make this commitment to myself (in print, no longer silent or ignored): to work with my mind to recognize that thoughts are ephemeral, to confront the anxiety and depression directly so that they will no longer imprison me, to breathe when I feel overwhelmed, to soften my heart, to let go of the picture of what I thought would be and rest with what is.

SOMETIMES THERE AREN'T
ENOUGH BAGS OF CHIPS

Katie Sluiter

'm lying on my side, scrunched into a twin-size bed next to my five-year-old son, Eddie. We read a couple of books together, chatted for ten minutes about everything from the igloo he and his friends are building on the playground to why God lets babies die. Now, his breathing has slowed. He has turned toward me so his nose touches the sleeve of my bathrobe. One of his hands rests on my arm. He tells me he feels warm and safe when I lie next to him at bedtime.

I remember the first day we were alone together. Eddie was about ten days old and my husband's paternity leave was over. Eddie started to cry early in the morning, so I took him to our bed to try to lull him back to sleep with a bottle. He was not having it. He would take a little, then scream.

And scream.

And scream.

I started to cry, panicked. A first-time mom, I had no idea

how to soothe my baby. He had a clean diaper, had slept a normal amount for a ten-day-old infant, and didn't seem to want to eat. Something had to be wrong. Was the bottle not working? Did the formula hurt him? Why wouldn't he stop screaming?

I called my husband, Cortney, and begged him to come home. He couldn't.

I called the nurse, and she gave me a few things to try. Things that didn't work. So I called my husband again, pleading this time. I was failing.

He said he just couldn't come, that maybe I needed to rock Eddie. I had tried that. I had tried it all. I called the nurse again and again. They couldn't help me. They said it was normal.

Nothing felt normal.

We cried together all day.

In fact, we both cried for the first three months of his life because he had colic and I had postpartum depression, and neither of us knew what was going on with ourselves, both new to this life.

There were days when Eddie would cry so hard and so loudly that I would wonder if a baby could cry himself to death. If the act of screaming to the point of no sound could harm my little boy. Yet there was nothing I could do to soothe him.

We switched him to soy. We put corn syrup in his bottle. We gave him gripe water. We bounced on the exercise ball. We wore him. We put him in the swing. We rocked him. We put him in his crib. We held him. We tried everything. Everything. The crying just kept going.

This incessant wailing would take a toll on anyone, but for me it was different. It was unbearable. I wasn't just physically worn out from it—I was mentally exhausted. I started to notice that my mind would wander to really ugly, scary places. I would shock myself with the narratives that played out in my brain, narratives that made me put my sobbing baby in his crib, go to the bathroom, turn on the water, and cry. I wanted to escape.

One time when I was bathing a small, wailing Eddie, I started to picture his face completely submerged under water and how quiet it would be. I immediately felt nauseous and wanted to shut the story off, but for some reason, my mind kept playing out all the gory details of what would happen next.

It was like when I saw *Jaws* for the first time in fifth grade. I wanted to stop the VCR, but it was at someone else's house, so I covered my eyes. But the movie was still going. When these thoughts would start, I would mentally cover my eyes and wish I could turn it off. But I couldn't stop the thoughts once they started. It had to play out to the end—the disgusting, scary, awful end.

I felt like if anyone knew, they would take Eddie away. If Cortney found out, he would leave me.

Part of me knew this couldn't be normal, but I was so tired. Maybe it was just exhaustion and lack of a "normal" schedule?

I thought things would get better when I went back to my teaching job and I wasn't with Eddie all the time, but they didn't. Around the time I went back to work, Cortney got laid off from his job. The stress just kept piling on and I wasn't coping with it well. In fact, the intrusive thoughts escalated.

On my drive home from work, for example, I would start to panic and envision myself driving off the expressway going eighty miles per hour and straight into a tree. The idea of sleeping forever was glorious, and I would think of all the ways I could make it happen. The only thing that kept me from actually doing it was the pain I knew I would cause my husband and family. But the bubbling feeling was starting to get unbearable. I knew I couldn't keep it contained for much longer.

I honestly thought at the time that all of this was stress from work and having an unemployed husband. I thought it was "normal" for someone in my position and if I just worked harder, it would get better. I never associated these feelings with anything that was mentally "wrong" with me. I was teaching an honors class for the first time and had a lot of pressure on me to do well. I had a baby I couldn't soothe. I had a husband who was laid off during a terrible recession. Feeling like I wanted to go away forever seemed justified, something that would get better with time.

If anything, though, it was getting worse. I started thinking that I wasn't cut out to be a good mom or teacher or wife. At least not all three at the same time, and that made me feel sad, afraid, and inadequate. I wanted to "do it all." People would say to me, "If anyone can handle it, Katie, it's you! You're so organized!"

But I wasn't handling it at all. Inside, I knew I was failing, but I just kept plastering a smile on my face and acting like everything was fine—that we would get through it.

At some point the feelings of inadequacy and failure turned into a blinding rage mostly directed at my husband and my mother. There were times when I actually felt like I hated them. I was like two different people. In front of all of the world I was a hardworking first-time mom who was working so hard, she was even picking up an evening class at the local community college. It was as if I wore a sign that read, "Look! Everything is fine! Great, even!"

On the inside, though, the rage was about to boil over. I let it pour over in front of Cortney and my mom. I had to let some of the steam out, or I knew I would explode, so I focused it at the people who loved me the most because in my mind, they were the ones making me feel like the biggest failure.

My mom could get Eddie to sleep when I couldn't. She was so calm and patient. Due to his unemployment, Cortney stayed home with Eddie and knew him better than anyone. Why were they so good at this and I sucked? How did my mom keep such a clean house, work, and go to school when we were kids and manage to put a full meal on the table every night, when I couldn't even get my baby to sleep?

I did not consciously think, "Man, I hate these people who love me so much," but I did pick fights. All the time. It was my way of letting out the steam so I didn't boil over in front of anyone else.

I've blocked out a lot of my breakdowns, but one of the worst fights is still vivid in my mind. It was the first time Cortney and I realized something wasn't right.

I was attempting to make dinner, and I was trying to get something out of our always-too-full-and-messy pantry while Cortney was in the kitchen feeding Eddie. It had been a long day and we were arguing about something stupid. In fact, I can't even remember what it was. But I was yelling.

"Kate, you don't need to yell. You're getting all worked up."

"Fuck that. I can yell whenever I want to!"

"Really? Swearing in front of Eddie?"

"He doesn't even fucking understand anything yet. And why the fuck can't I ever find what I want in this damn house? Why does everything suck???"

"Kate . . ."

"FUCK THIS HOUSE AND YOU AND THIS FAMILY!"

Then I threw an entire bag of chips at my husband, and broke down.

I am not one to swear like that. Not at all. I was yelling and saying shocking things because I could not keep the bubbling rage in me anymore. I blocked out most of the times I screamed and belittled my husband, because who does that? Who curses out and calls the guy who is doing everything in his power to make the family work, "useless"?

It wasn't long after the chip-throwing incident that I broke down again after Eddie was finally in bed for the night. I sat on the ottoman in the living room and admitted that I needed out. I couldn't do it anymore. Just days before I had read the blog of a good friend in which she admitted that she was seeking help for postpartum depression. None of her symptoms were what I thought of when I thought of PPD, but they sure did sound a lot like my life.

I didn't say I needed help. I said I wanted out.

I'm sure Cortney was scared and concerned for a very long time, but to hear me say that out loud rattled him.

"Do you think you should talk to your doctor?" he gently asked, knowing I could explode on him at any moment.

"I guess so," I said, more defeated than anything.

I had no fight left in me. I thought that for the past nine months I was "getting by" and fighting a fight that only I could win. That conversation with my husband was me admitting that I was a failure. At least it felt like that at the time.

I stayed home from work the next day to get a same-day appointment with my doctor. As I sat with my hands between my knees, retelling all of my frustrations and feelings, she smiled and nodded.

"You have a postpartum mood disorder. Definitely."

"You're that sure?"

"Oh, yes. There are medications I can prescribe, but I would also very much recommend you get into therapy. Pine Rest is right across the hall and I have referred lots of moms there."

Knowing full well that none of my doctors are big drug pushers, I realized this was serious business.

"Will I be on medication for this forever?"

"Maybe. Maybe not. You have to see how it goes. But you do need help. You are right."

That appointment was five years ago. I have been officially diagnosed since then as having postpartum depression and anxiety. When I got pregnant with my second child, Charlie, I struggled with antenatal depression, and then after with PPD, PPA, and OCD. My psychiatrist at the time also diagnosed me with PTSD from my miscarriages before Eddie, and from my traumatic birth experience with Eddie (I had an emergency C-section that went well, but was very much an emergency).

As I write this, I am pregnant with my third child, a girl. I still take my antidepressants because depression, anxiety, and OCD are here to stay.

A lot of my time in therapy was spent on the guilt I held on to about those months of rage. I knew Cortney and I were good. We had talked about it and he (and my mom) were happy with my progress. But what about Eddie? Had I messed up our relationship permanently? Could I ever repair the lack of bonding from his first year of life?

From time to time I think of this worry, then bedtime comes around. Eddie and I read together, discuss books and life. We talk about big things and little things. He snuggles in, whispers, "I love you, Mommy," and I know. We are good.

LEAVING THE ISLAND

Randon Billings Noble

*H*alfway through *Robinson Crusoe*, the protagonist finds a human footprint in the sand. He is terrified. After fifteen years alone on his desert island, the thought of another person drives him nearly mad with fear.

I did not see a footprint. I saw a sonogram. But it was not just a single image. I was carrying twins.

My husband and I have no history of twins in our families. We had no help conceiving them. That particular month my ovaries, perhaps feeling the pinch of time, decided to fire off both barrels, sending out two eggs instead of one, two eggs to be fertilized, two eggs to implant, two eggs to hatch into two new human beings, twice as much genetic material to fling against eternity.

I pretended to be shocked into silence when the sonogram reader said, "It's twins!" and my husband smiled through his happy tears and pressed my hand. I pretended to be merely stunned when the nurse took my blood ("I'm a twin!" she told me brightly). I pretended to be simply overwhelmed as I filled out forms and made our next appointment and kept my eyes slightly wide and my mouth pulled into what I hoped looked like a bemused smile. But I, like Crusoe, was "terrified to the last degree."

When I stepped into the elevator, I entered what would become my nine-month Island of Despair. I put on my sunglasses and cried. I cried in the elevator, in the lobby, on the walk to the car, in the car, on the drive home, and then flung across my bed. I cried through the afternoon and evening and sporadically through the night. When I woke up—eyes swollen, nose blocked, heart dark and dry—I felt nothing but despair at the wreck I thought my life had become.

In the morning after his wreck, Crusoe is comforted by the sight of his ship driven nearly to shore, and he spends the first day salvaging what he can from it. But I could not see a way forward with twins. I was convinced that I would be completely consumed by them, that I would be unable to have any kind of independent life, that I would have to somehow hold myself in suspended animation until they turned eighteen, when maybe, just maybe, I might be able to recover some of the things that made me me. While everyone else was thrilled by the news, I felt myself sinking further and further into hermetic misery.

Robinson Crusoe is a novel that explores what it is to be an individual in isolation. Crusoe is cast off from human company and stranded for nearly three decades on his South Pacific island, which the locals call Masafuera: Farther Away. During the first few years he goes through cycles of grief and resignation, faith and despair, hope and fear. But all this time he is making practical improvements to his island—a fortress, a

garden, flocks, furniture. And that is part of what makes this
book so compelling. We can't help but ask ourselves what we
would do in his place. What home would we build for ourselves? What books would we wish we had? What fantasies and
philosophies would we spin out into the barren days and silent
nights?

But depression is a different kind of island. It is also isolated, but its resources are inaccessible. Depression is a place no
one can really fathom until or unless he is there. It is a place
where logic fails. It is a place where the laws of gravity are more
powerful than any other force. It is a place almost impossible to
revisit or describe once you've left.

That fall my island was my living room, my fortress an Ikea
Poäng chair. I did not make practical improvements to my
environment other than the most basic preparations for the
twins: two rocking cradles, a changing table, diapers, blankets,
onesies (a word I didn't even know how to pronounce pre-
pregnancy—oh-ness-ies?). I tried to work on an essay, or at least
write some journal entries, but I couldn't seem to make sentences form. I tried to read some of my favorite books—*Anna
Karenina, The Hobbit*—but after staring, unseeing, at their pages
for many minutes, I burned through all the Sookie Stackhouse
novels on my Kindle, ordering the next only minutes after
finishing the last. When reading became too difficult, I tried to
watch movies like *The Life Aquatic with Steve Zissou* and
television shows like the new Sherlock Holmes on PBS, but
then I realized I couldn't follow a simple plot let alone an intellectual mystery, so I streamed series like *Firefly* and *The Hills*,
clicking "watch next" over and over and over again. I could

barely believe how stupid I felt, but I would do anything to distract myself from my fears of being cannibalized and colonized from the inside out. It turns out there was some truth to these fears.

Later I read that a woman's brain can shrink by eight percent over the course of her pregnancy. The fetus siphons off all her juicy omega-3 fatty acids and other brain-plumping nutrients and her brain downsizes to compensate. I have become convinced that, carrying twins, my brain shrank 16 percent.

And then I read that cells from a fetus can migrate through the placenta and take up residence in the mother's body. A mother's brain might contain her child's cells. A child's cells could indeed colonize his or her mother's brain.

This condition is called chimerism, named after the mythological Chimera that Homer describes in the *Iliad* as "a thing of immortal make, not human, lion-fronted and snake behind, a goat in the middle, and snorting out the breath of the terrible flame of bright fire." In Greek myth a sighting of the Chimera might portend storms and shipwrecks, but Crusoe never saw one. He has little warning of the violent hurricane that drives his ship off course and into his small island.

The footprint, however, warns of a different kind of danger. Lying awake night after night, he is at first convinced that the footprint is the Devil's, and then tries to convince himself that it is actually his own footprint. But he finally concludes that the print belongs to one of "the savages of the mainland," a cannibal. Crusoe spends the next few years camouflaging his living quarters, securing his livestock, and making his presence on the island as invisible as possible.

But there is no hiding a twin pregnancy. Around my fifth

month people started asking me when I was due. "Mamma's gonna pop!" a man yelled at me on the street. But by my third trimester I wasn't going out much anymore. My waist had reached Henry VIII proportions. I had outgrown my maternity clothes and took to wearing a tank top and two receiving blankets pinned together to make a loincloth. My physical self kept growing as my internal self was slowly eaten away.

After fantasizing all kinds of fears, Crusoe finally sees evidence of the "savage wretches" who use his island's beaches as a feasting ground, leaving behind "skulls, hands, feet, and other bones of human bodies." He muses, "Fear of danger is ten thousand times more terrifying than danger itself," and then spends quite some time planning ways to eradicate this "evil" by killing the cannibals through elaborate plots involving pits full of gunpowder. But then he has a dream. Crusoe rescues one of the cannibals, and civilizes him, and in gratitude the former savage shares his knowledge of the sea, allowing Crusoe to escape the island.

And that, of course, is exactly what happens. The rescued Friday becomes his "servant, and, perhaps, a companion or assistant," and the two become inseparable, leaving the island and, after many adventures, returning to England together.

I did not have a dream to show me the way forward. In fact, I was barely sleeping. My days were a fog of crushing weight, itchy skin, swollen feet, and endless thirst; my nights a darker and lonelier version of the same. I was in no shape to rescue anyone, least of all myself. I gave in to the island and waited.

At four o'clock in the morning on the day the twins were born, I heard the first birds of spring singing outside my window. My hands were shaking so badly I could barely sign the hospital admittance forms, but my mind was a smooth sheet of calm sea. When I delivered the twins, my body was not wrecked but carefully cut open and even more carefully repaired. I was not cannibalized or colonized, and when the twins left my body, my terrible despair did too. Perhaps it was the relief at being sole again. Perhaps it was the ebb of a hormonal flood. But that first night, as the twins slept in their hospital cribs, I turned to my husband and said, "Don't tell anyone, but they're pretty cool."

I was delivered too.

RECOVERING MY STRANGER-SELF

Jennifer Bullis

At age thirty-eight, I thought I could handle raising a child. Even though I'd never taken care of a human baby, I'd loved and nurtured many, many animals. I'd kept horses for twenty-seven years. Along with my husband, a small-animal veterinarian to whom I'd been married for fourteen years, I had fostered dozens of homeless cats that had found their way to, or been dumped at, our barn. I'd raised an orphaned kitten. I'd given hospice care to all our aged beloveds: three cats, seven guinea pigs, and my thirty-four-year-old horse. Even though I had never wished for a child, even though I had put off motherhood, I did think I was sufficiently tender.

And sufficiently tough. I'd endured a hostile graduate program to earn a master's degree, then a doctorate. I'd completed a dissertation and survived the hazing ritual of the oral defense. I'd prevailed in the academic job market and attained, against steep odds, a tenure-track position. I'd earned tenure through a lengthy process of proving my value. I'd chaired my department during a contentious and difficult period of change. Parenting would be a challenging new job, and I assumed intensive effort would enable me to succeed at this work, too.

∽

I told my husband, *Wait. I'll be in the horse barn.* I added to myself, *Shoveling through your patience and avoiding what's hardest: holding that baby and making him mine.* Experts say that the maternal gaze bonds mother to infant and creates the infant's attachment to her. My husband held the baby out to me. *Just look at him,* he said to the sobbing breaths I choked out on the cold front step. *He wants you. He doesn't know how to wait.*

Both of them would have to.

∽

I spent the first half of my pregnancy vomiting. The scent of food made me retch, so my husband couldn't eat his meals in the house. He couldn't even brew a cup of coffee; coffee was the worst. He scrambled eggs using a portable burner he plugged in on the far side of the barn, downwind of the house. Some days, so long as I didn't smell the cooking, I was able to eat a little. The only liquid I could drink was lemon-lime Gatorade, since water had too rough a texture. But more than a few mouthfuls of Gatorade would make me throw up, too, so I was perpetually dehydrated.

I had to cram teaching, office hours, paper grading, horse care, and whatever small meals I hoped to keep down into the four hours each afternoon that I was functional. The rest of each day I spent holed up in my bedroom, chilled and drowsy from hunger, hiding from intruding smells. I had to negotiate a reduction in my teaching load and bow out of a panel presentation at a national conference.

I couldn't find a doctor to help me. A local baby boomlet was developing, and none of the obstetricians or midwives I wanted to work with had any more room in their schedules for patients with October due dates. So at eight weeks pregnant, I began to call general practitioners who delivered babies. I went to an intake appointment with one. When he spoke, he addressed my husband. He was very concerned about the things that could go wrong as a result of my age. He markered a large, red *AMA* for "Advanced Maternal Age" on the front of my chart and wrote up orders for an amniocentesis. When I asked him what could be done about my nausea, he instructed me to relax and enjoy my pregnancy.

I didn't go back, nor did I have the will to phone any more doctors. Until eighteen weeks, when I learned of an obstetrician who was taking new patients, I sought no prenatal care. Looking back, I wish I had tried harder, since it's possible that a perceptive doctor would have flagged me as a postpartum depression risk. It's also possible that my inaction was a symptom that I was experiencing some depression already.

I had two good months—months six and seven—of my pregnancy. My husband and I made two interstate trips to visit our families, and I took a two-week writing workshop in a nearby city from a poet I greatly admired. The nausea had abated, and I was able to eat again, even sip an occasional coffee. But in the eighth month, I started to feel overwhelmed—both by increasing physical inertia, and by the baby showers, at which I was obliged to display to friends and well-wishers a cheerful anticipation that increasingly I did not feel. My husband was working hard to prepare our house for the arrival of the baby, but I became so anxious I could barely participate.

∽

That gray fatigue looked a lot like grief. Late at night, after the colic abated, I would see myself from outside myself: slumped in the rocker, gazing at the finally sleeping baby and wishing I could copy his new contentment—his curling into himself and into the warmth of his own repose—after hours of walking, bouncing, nursing, soothing. I would watch myself get up with a lurch and feel my perceptions follow me from a few inches behind. Now that I was standing, I'd forgotten what it was I had intended to do, once vertical. So I'd stand for a moment and, in a dim glimmer of awareness, find that immobility was taking me no closer to rest. Collapsing back into the rocker, I'd close my eyes and wonder, really, what I could possibly stand to lose.

∽

Losing much of my hair more than half a year after our baby was born should have been a clue that my thyroid function was changing. Instead of getting my thyroid-hormone levels tested, via simple blood draw, a psychiatric nurse practitioner put me on an antidepressant. It helped enormously—within days, I became able to sleep, relax, and feel hope—but it took me eight years to taper off it. (Even if brain chemistry is not initially to blame for one's depression, taking an antidepressant *will* alter one's brain chemistry.) The nurse practitioner was correct in telling me, "Depression is what happens when you get exhausted by anxiety." What she didn't pursue were the physiological roots of my anxiety: decreased thyroid production, accompanied (or perhaps caused) by adrenal depletion after a difficult pregnancy and breastfeeding. If I had begun taking thyroid hormone—which I did not know to ask about until after the baby turned two—I may have been able to avoid getting hooked on the antidepressant.

◠◡

Unrealistically, I had assumed that as a mother, I'd be able to do without the things that had constituted my identity—riding, hiking, teaching, writing—during my earlier adult life. On the other hand, I didn't think I'd have to give up *all* of those things, and certainly not all at once. However, consumed as we were by our baby's colic, teething, and inability to sleep, I could engage in very few of the things that had previously given me joy and purpose. My husband and I could not go outdoors for more than an hour at a time, since our baby would soon grow uncomfortable in the front pack or jogging stroller. Unsteady as I was, I no longer felt capable of riding my horse, a gorgeous mover but quick and spooky, and unridden since the beginning of my pregnancy.

At work, I used up my leave (first paid, then unpaid) and then, incapable of returning to a full-time workload, I resigned my tenured position. Subsequently, as a part-time adjunct, I could no longer stay on campus to meet individually with my students about their writing, and thus lost my chief means of satisfaction in my teaching. My own writing ceased, since I no longer recognized the interior of my own mind. Every time I did sit down to attempt to write, the baby would wake up, as though aware that I was turning my attention to something other than him. Months of this convinced me that I would never be able to write again, and the grief of this loss pierced me more than anything else.

My husband felt heartbroken. Both of us were desperate and perplexed. We thought that since our baby was so unhappy, we must be terrible parents. Nobody reassured us otherwise. We knew we must be doing everything wrong and blamed each other. We were stung by criticism from other family members who told us we were spoiling our baby by breastfeeding him and giving him so much attention. On the other hand, the parenting resources in our progressive community advocated "natural" methods so strongly that I felt deficient for not being able to tolerate co-sleeping or extended baby-wearing. Our doctor had no answer when, at the six-month checkup, my husband asked, "When do we get to start enjoying our baby?" The baby that my husband had always wanted cried perpetually, and I, his wife of fourteen years and companion of twenty, was falling apart. It took him a long time to forgive me for adapting so poorly to a role I'd thought I could handle.

∽

The hairs on your head are numbered, I remembered reading, and so I resolved not to worry about the baby's cradle cap or the tiny wisps of golden-brown peeling from his head, still nearly bald at seven months, nor about my own hair falling out in clumps so thick I'd begun browsing wigs. Dutifully shampooing the baby, I realized how far I'd let myself slide. So one morning, what a great gift to feel something as the baby fingered his hair and then mine. We began to reflect each other to each other, and I began to see that we were cherished.

໑

Parenting class was the best and worst. One week, after the facilitator left the room to take a phone call from her school-age son, another mom said to me, in front of all the other moms and babies, *Maybe he's crying because you're not making enough milk. Maybe he's crying because you you you you.* Another week, the facilitator handed out a pamphlet on postpartum depression. On the cover was a drawing of a mother holding a baby in front of a window with blue curtains. Yellow sunlight was streaming in, the baby was smiling, but the mother's eyes were huge and sad. In her face, I recognized my own. That's when I knew.

໑

Weird medicine, this, I thought while halving a twenty-milligram pill into two tens, *to hoist me from the hole in which I've failed to find my own mental bootstraps.* That morning, eight months on and clean out of *If I can just make its* (through the colic, through the teething, until weaning, till we get some nighttime sleep), I called the psychiatric nurse practitioner recommended by my obstetrician's office. She ordered me in, then scolded me for not knowing that the prolonged cases of postpartum depression are the ones most likely to result in suicide.

∽

Everything I did felt out of season. The previous fall's tree pruning, put off by the baby's arrival, scented the house with sap and wood through the windows open to the August air. Maple, apple, birch, fir—ghosts sweet and pungent floated in and away on the heat from the branch-bound yard. Inside, sitting in the wicker chair, I nursed the baby. His hand, a tiny maple leaf, brushed the skin of my belly, his touch even lighter than no touch at all.

∽

For a year after I started the antidepressant, I frequently played a game called *at-this-time-last-year* with myself. "At this time last year, I was too anxious to sleep." "At this time last year, I was too exhausted to do Christmas." "At this time last year, the baby started teething just as he was getting over the colic." "At this time last year, my hair fell out." "At this time last year, I had to resign from my job." "At this time last year, we had to take the baby on a plane trip." The point of the game was to contrast how miserable I had been with how much better—how much more relaxed, how much more capable, how much more in love with the baby—I now felt. I continued to play versions of this game off and on for the next several years to remind myself that even though it had been awful, I was much better now. In the game, I played at returning to the situation that had made me feel helpless to escape from. I went there in memory to remind myself that I would never, in reality, go there again.

Our son is nine now, and we are all doing well, both as a

family and individually. One morning, when our son was two and a half, and I'd been receiving treatment for my hypo-thyroidism for four months, I looked in the mirror and recog-nized myself. It was a flash—a sighting—and a huge relief. I perceived that finally, after a long absence, I had returned to myself.

Not to my previous identity, but to someone I recog-nized as capable of finding balance, humor, and competence as a mother.

FEAR OF FALLING

Dawn S. Davies

*A*fter the birth of my first daughter, I developed a fear of flying. More specifically, a fear of crashing. The airplane ride itself—fun. Fine. The crash, if it must happen . . . okay, I guess. Everybody goes sometime. It was the idea of falling toward earth before the crash that scared me, because I have an impressive imagination and I know, in those few minutes of free fall, I would have time to realize what I was going to leave behind. I had a baby now, a responsibility to raise this child. I had to stay alive so I could do it right.

This fear developed out of the blue when my daughter was six weeks old, on a return flight after visiting family. We were settling into our row, buckling our daughter's car seat in the middle seat, when I had a quick, startlingly detailed image of the airplane at thirty thousand feet—sun glinting off of the metal side, etched with thousands of tiny scratches—ripping in half and plunging out of the sky. My husband, because he is a tall man, was quickly decapitated by a sharp piece of debris that flew across the top of the seats, and the baby's car seat was sucked out of the hole. I had no choice but to leap out after it, pointing and rocketing down toward it, then wrapping my arms around it, watching my howling daughter's perfectly oval face while we fell at 120 miles per hour. This thought worked at the speed of a neuron, and before the flight attendants could sit down, I was up, tugging at the car seat, and headed for the closed door of the plane.

"I can't do this. I have to get off." I announced this to no one in particular. Two flight attendants shot up the aisle after me, and my husband pushed past them. He wrenched the baby out of my hands, pinched me in the crook of the elbow, and said, "Everybody's staring at us. Get back in your seat."

"This airplane's going to go down," I said. "I'm going to die before I get a chance to raise this baby." I could feel the stares while we walked back down the aisle, but I didn't care. This was before 9/11 and heightened security, and I was simply a nutty young mom, not a security threat.

"You're embarrassing me," my husband said through a fake smile.

He put the baby in the window seat, sat in the middle between us, and buckled me, then himself. He put a hand on my forearm and gripped it so tightly that I couldn't get up.

"Let me off this plane," I said. "It doesn't feel right." He gripped my arm tighter. At six weeks postpartum, hormones can be unstable, and lead women to believe things that may not be true. I did not know this at the time. In my mind, I was acting rationally.

"Stop it. We're going home. You're flying." The baby and I both started crying. He looked at the seat back in front of him and didn't speak to me again. Of course we made it home with no trouble—planes don't just crash because you think they will —but there was a distance between us after that. I had shown a side of me that neither of us had known existed, an irrational side, a weakness, yet a strange, primal urge for survival.

After the trip, I felt unsettled and sad, though my baby was healthy and beautiful. Often, I would daydream while nursing her. I would see, instead of her losing her first tooth, or carving a pumpkin, or doing the long jump, or going on her first date, images of starving children with flies in their eyes, rotten meat, acres of garbage, beatings, immolations, bloated whale carcasses washed up on the shore. I would feel a spinning in the room, which would cause me to hold tight to the baby, lest she be torn out of my hands. Because my husband had shown he was not interested in my irrational thoughts, I didn't tell him how I felt. I was ashamed and afraid of what would happen if I did share them. Gradually, things got better, but it took until well after my daughter's first birthday. I toughed it out because I didn't know any better.

When my daughter was seventeen months old, I got pregnant again. My hormones soared and I felt wonderful through the pregnancy. But within a few weeks after the birth of my second daughter, they crashed and I felt worse than I had the first time. I had solved my fear of flying by deciding never to fly again, but had developed intrusive thoughts that something I accidentally did would kill the baby and it would be my fault.

Around supper time, I would put the baby in the windup swing in the kitchen, crank it up, and let her swing while I cooked. My older daughter would play with her toys nearby. Within a few days, I had to move the swing several feet out of the kitchen because I had recurring thoughts of the butcher's knife, which I had used adroitly for years, somehow tumbling out of my grip and piercing the baby through her fontanelle. I was afraid to walk her outside because we lived at the top of a large hill and I had thoughts of losing my grip on the stroller handle and sending her plummeting down into traffic at the bottom. I was also afraid to bathe her, because I was sure that, despite my good intentions, and despite my two years of baby-bathing experience, I would lose hold of her soapy body and she would slide under the shallow water of the baby bath and drown. And if she didn't die right away, the bathwater she inhaled would set off a pneumonia that would kill her later.

Worse than this, I was afraid to tell my husband, or anyone else. I was afraid that they would take my children away from me, so I managed it by force of will, with the irrationality of it bleeding outside the lines of normalcy like a stain.

During this time, I also became obsessed with the beginning of my own end. I began to prod my breasts for lumps. Every day I found several—I was breastfeeding after all, and the ducts were impressively lumpy because they were full of milk, not tumors. These lumps would cause a spinning fear that would take over and ruin, several times per day, whatever I happened to be doing—coloring with my older daughter, watching the baby make funny faces, reading, hanging laundry, stirring a sauce. When this happened, I had a sensation of falling that made me break out in a sweat, and called for me to grab on to things.

I compulsively inspected my skin for mole changes, felt my groin and armpits and clavicles and jawline for swollen glands. I was exhausted from being up in the middle of the night with a new baby, but hormonal logic, an oxymoron if there ever was one, told me that it must be leukemia, or lymphoma, or lupus, and not simple exhaustion. Every headache that developed was a brain tumor, but not a minor league, benign one—an astrocytoma that would leave my daughters alone to one day button up their own wedding dresses.

"You're too sensitive," my husband would say when I tried to bring it up. "You have two perfectly healthy daughters and all you do is worry about ridiculous things. I don't understand you." I would try to explain how I felt, but when I did, he stopped responding to me in any way. He would turn his back on me in the kitchen, or in bed, and I was left alone with my thoughts, embarrassed and ashamed of my weakness. Besides, I did have two healthy daughters and a nice life, and I felt guilty for having these thoughts.

I would read *Goodnight Moon* to the girls before tucking them in for the night, weeping quietly in their dark bedroom because I was about to lie down for the night myself, and I might get a blood clot in my sleep, because Margaret Wise Brown, the author of *Goodnight Moon*, had died from a blood clot after flinging her leg in the air while abed. Each night, I would crawl into my bed afraid that I wouldn't wake up the next morning, and what was worse, my daughters would be raised by a man who wouldn't say nice things about me to them after I was gone. No one had told me to not trust myself right after having a baby, that the psychological and emotional effects of plummeting postpartum hormones could be serious, and that I should probably take it easy for a while, or maybe talk to someone about it.

One night, when the baby was almost twelve weeks old, I

awoke with a strange pain in my abdomen that caused me to think suspiciously about the obscene mound of baked cauliflower I had eaten the night before. Cauliflower usually ignites in me a prodigious, occasionally debilitating gas factory, but if this were gas, I had outdone myself. Although there was nothing vague about the pain—it was acute and very real—I could not pinpoint its origin. It was high enough to be the pancreas or gallbladder, yet low enough to be my appendix. In my misery, I executed my German grandmother's trick of lying on your stomach with the buttocks in the air—the gas rises and you soon have the relief you are seeking, at the expense of anyone else in the room, but in this instance, nothing helped. I switched positions, and took a deep breath. Nothing changed. I shook my husband awake.

"Something's wrong," I told him. "I have to go to the hospital right now."

"What is it?"

"I have a pain in my side. It's bad."

"You're joking."

"I'm not."

"What do you want me to do, drive you?"

"I don't think I can drive."

"Well, I'm not getting the girls up in the middle of the night, and we can't leave them alone."

"Something's really wrong."

"The keys are on my dresser." I crawled over him, and pulled pants on under my nightgown, hunched, unable to stand up straight, or even place my feet on the ground without pain shooting through me.

"I have to leave for work by eight, so try and be back by

then." He rolled over toward the window before I even left the room.

Real pain will quickly eclipse any sentimental thought of suffering and death. I was in too much pain to cry, in too much pain to worry that my husband didn't seem concerned, and in too much pain to fear dying. In fact, the pain was so severe that I quickly began to believe that death was a better option than feeling the way I did. I drove down the dark, empty, shiny Boston streets, hollering out loud in agony, the echo of my voice filling the empty car. My goal was to stay in the right lane and not crash. I followed the subway tracks to Beth Israel Hospital, pulled up to the emergency room main entrance, left the car running, and walked in through the double doors, where I managed to notice a terribly shiny measure of sea foam tiles and chrome chairs. For some reason I had time to think, "I don't want to die here. It's too reflective," before vomiting all over the waxed tile floors and passing out.

I woke up on a gurney in a room to the smell of rubbing alcohol. A thick, red-bearded man bent over me to start an IV. I thought he was Jesus. I rolled my head and vomited off the gurney.

"Am I dying?" I asked.

"No, ma'am."

"Oh, God, can you please kill me then?" I could not sit still, so I tried to crawl up the back of the gurney. I draped myself over the top and vomited again.

The nurse pushed a button and an intercom came on. "Page housekeeping, please," he said. "Hold on there, little lady, I'm going to give you some morphine as soon as we get some information from you."

The next five hours were spent giving blood and getting tests. I would sleep in a drugged stupor, then wake periodically to revisit the pain, see stone-carved faces of old men floating down from the ceiling to leer at me, retch into a pan, then fall back to sleep, only to wake feeling like I was falling backward and headfirst off the gurney. The nurse came in periodically to check on me. A CAT scan had identified a stone in my right kidney. It was my job to pee it out, they told me, and they gave several quarts of IV fluids and a strainer. I hobbled up every fifteen minutes to either throw up or whizzle blood-red urine into the toilet. Around sunrise I peed out a tiny speck of dark sand, which, when I looked at it closely, looked like a jagged, knife-edged moon rock with an evil face carved in it. I had a hard time believing this was the stone.

"That's it?" I asked the nurse. He peered into the strainer.

"Looks like it. Lucky you."

"So I'm not going to die?"

"Why? Do you want to?" He winked.

"Sometimes," I said, and he stopped what he was doing and looked at me. Maybe the morphine had loosened my tongue, but I told him about the perseverations, about the fears I had of accidentally killing the baby, about crying every day, about how I spent the previous afternoon in the rocking chair holding the baby with two hands, the house getting dark in the early spring light, my older daughter playing in the fireplace with a shovel and a bunch of ashes. I told him I was afraid that the house would burn down when I turned on the stove, and that when I sat quietly, I could feel the earth spinning on its axis, and that if I let go of the girls, they would fly off and fall into space.

"How old is your baby?" he asked.

"Three months."

"You have postpartum depression, sweetie. Women get it all the time. They say it's horrible. You'll get over it when your hormones regulate, but you need to tell your doctor. Call them as soon as you get home. Will you do that?"

I drove myself home, against the doctor's advice, in a morphine haze, just in time for my husband to meet me at the door and hand me the baby.

"Well?" he asked.

"Kidney stone," I said. "And postpartum depression, I think." I handed him back the baby and went to lie down on the couch. Aftershocks of pain shot through my flank and down my leg, and I was weak and shaking. The baby started a low cry that rolled into a full boil within fifteen seconds.

"Is it out? Well, that's good. Here, can you nurse her? She's about to blow." He handed her back. She screamed in my arms and rooted for my breast.

"I can't. They gave me morphine. I have to pump and throw all milk away for twenty-four hours."

"There's a bottle on the counter. Sorry, but I have to leave."

I cried when he left, grateful that there was a name to what I had, and oddly happy to know that I wasn't the only one. If there were others, I thought, I could find them. I could tell a doctor and they wouldn't take my children away from me. Maybe my husband would understand. I slept randomly and dangerously throughout the day. I woke once, during lunch, with my head on the kitchen table, to my two-year-old trying to see if a green bean would fit inside the nostril of her tiny sister, who was at least in the baby swing, and not out in the yard somewhere. And most importantly, I called my doctor and made an appointment.

My husband and I made it three more years before we said the word "divorce," though I think the beginning of the end was that day on the airplane when I was so afraid of falling out of the sky, of losing control. The day I showed the vulnerability that comes when you give birth, the vulnerability that comes when your body takes over by creating a baby inside of it, then turning you inside out, then righting itself again, as if it had been through a storm.

There are better ways to treat a postpartum woman than disdain and withdrawal. What my husband could have done was ask me why I was afraid. What he could have done was hug me, and tell me we weren't going to fall out of the sky. What he could have said was, "You're not going to die, hon. You're scared because this is new. You're a little kooky because your hormones need to get back to normal. We're going to have a great life. Besides, it's not the falling that kills you, silly. It's the landing. Here, hold my hand."

LIGHT IN THE MIDST OF DARKNESS

Michelle Stephens

I hear the freezing rain as it hits my bedroom window. I bounce on a yoga ball in last night's pajamas with my seven-week-old baby wrapped on my chest. I am trying to soothe the both of us. Sleep didn't happen much last night. She slept in fits and spurts and I slept even less, trying to keep her content. It is now 3:00 p.m. and I am exhausted. She has finally succumbed to sleep and my four-year-old daughter is quietly playing after what seemed like a million questions and three meltdowns. Today, there will be no pictures taken. None posted to social media for the world to judge. These are not the moments I want to share.

I bounce softly, humming "You Are My Sunshine." I tried singing it to the baby, but the words got caught in my throat. Tears come easily these days. Lack of sleep and her recent birth have brought all sorts of emotions close to the surface. Add the guilt of lacking patience for my older daughter and it doesn't take much for them to escape. The bags under my eyes are a testament to that. But the bags are ok, because today, there will be no pictures. These bags are not how I want to be recognized.

I stop bouncing for a moment to give my body a rest. I take a deep breath; I can smell her still-new head. I look over at my big girl and watch her as she draws quietly. Tears well up in my eyes. Gratitude and a deep sense of sadness are battling for control. The baby settles back in and I pull my hair back into a ponytail. How long has it been since I last washed it? Three days, maybe four? It doesn't matter; there would be no pictures today. No, today was just for me, for us. Today is too raw with too many emotions vying for my attention.

Yesterday I pulled myself together enough to go to the grocery store. I had woken with a feeling of anxiety but tried to brush it off. I dropped the four-year-old off at work with Daddy and treated myself to coffee before heading into the store. By the time I had settled the baby on me, in a carrier, I was feeling better. I was able to peruse the aisle and sip my mocha. Then, out of nowhere, I could feel my head fill with panicked thoughts. My vision dulled as my heart raced. Panic washed over me as I stood in the freezer aisle, clutching my coffee in one hand and my sleeping baby with the other.

I managed to get through it. I managed to breathe and slow my heart rate enough to think a little more clearly. I managed to fool the people around me into thinking I was just another mom, out grocery shopping for her family. I didn't take any pictures yesterday. I don't want to remember the fear I felt in the freezer aisle.

Today, I am exhausted. My hands are still shaking from the thoughts that filled my head all day yesterday. Even if I tried to take a photo, it would be nothing but a blur. Maybe that would be more representative of my mind these days, blurry and soft with beautiful lighting but no actual details. I take another deep breath and look at my sleeping baby and then at my four-year-old. We have been through so much already, the three of us. I struggled to conceive them both and had a tough pregnancy with the second. My oldest walked the halls with me as I labored with her little sister.

The baby snuggles against me while I cry tears of guilt for yelling at her sister for the hundredth time. I wonder if they know the amount of strength they give me. I wonder if they would ever understand it. My shaky hands swipe the screen of my phone, revealing photos of smiling faces, calmer days. There are none from today, though. Not yet anyway.

This is my life, unedited. It is beautiful and amazing and hard and exhausting. Some days are better than others and I try to keep it all in a delicate balance. Otherwise I will be washed up in sadness brought on by postpartum depression, anxiety, and an ever-growing feeling of isolation. No, today there would be no pictures. No visual reminders of the tough days. No sharing of the darkness. This is for me and my eyes alone.

The baby squirms and repositions herself. She takes a deep breath and releases it with a sigh and a coo. It doesn't take much digging to find moments of light even in my darkest days. I bounce a little more so she can get the rest she so desperately needs. That I so desperately need. I close my eyes and just enjoy the quiet. The shaking in my hands slowly subsides. There will be no pictures today; they can't capture the silence anyway.

She stirs again and this time she wakes up. She is sad and hungry. I am sure her diaper is wet. I slowly unwrap her and lay her on my bed. She has been fussy for the past three days. She eats, sleeps, and cries. I am guessing a growth spurt is to blame but I still feel helpless. I change her diaper and she makes a funny face midcry. I can't help myself and I burst out laughing. I need this release. This levity. She stops crying and gazes straight into my eyes and smiles a big, toothless, full-of-adoration smile. This time I am the one crying. Maybe today there will be pictures.

I grab my phone with my now steady hands and capture her smile. You can see that she had been crying; her face is red and splotchy and there is a tear in the corner of one eye. But, despite all that, she is smiling at me. With my dirty hair and messy clothes. With my too-close-to-the-surface emotions and guilt-driven self-doubt. She is smiling at me because none of this matters to her. She smiled at me in the freezer aisle yesterday and she will smile at me during my darkest times tomorrow. She loves me unconditionally and absolutely. The purity of her emotions takes my breath away. I snap a couple more pictures and put my phone down.

My four-year-old comes running in. She asks to kiss the little sister she had so desperately begged for just a year earlier. As she nuzzles the baby's tiny head, I bend down to listen to her whispers. "I love you more than the stars shine and the moon glows." I can't control the tears. How did I get so lucky? And why isn't the beauty that surrounds me enough to fight this depression? Enough to fight the constant nagging anxiety? I reach for my camera and snap a photo of my girls sharing the sweetest of moments. It is these moments that I will draw strength from when I need to fight my demons.

My four-year-old looks up and sees the tears in my eyes. She asks me if they are happy tears or sad tears. "A little of both," I answer.

"Don't be sad, Momma! I love you, too! I love you more than the stars shine and the moon glows!" she says, smiling. She looks down at her baby sister, her eyes twinkling. "And a little bit more than that," she whispers to me.

I fight off more tears, not wanting to make my sweet girl think she said anything wrong. No, she said everything right. I am the world to these girls and they are mine. I will beat this darkness. I have to. For them, for my husband, for me.

There were pictures today. Pictures to remind me that during even the darkest of days, there are tiny rays of light, rays of light that don't notice any of my flaws and couldn't care less if my eyelashes are curled. Rays of light that make the isolation of motherhood a little more bearable, rays of light that were once just dreams.

Tomorrow there may be no pictures or it could be a well-documented day, filled with beauty. It is unknown, and the unknown is a struggle for someone like me who plans for everything. I am learning to let go, to live in the moment. These struggles have taught me that I am stronger than I ever thought and can get through anything. Some days are easier to conquer. Others, I have to just let go. I have to snuggle in close and stay in my pajamas.

Today was a bit more challenging, yesterday was worse, tomorrow might be better. All I know is that, in the midst of the freezing rain and too-close-to-the-surface emotions, my little girls smiled at me and there were pictures.

The Breast of Me

Suzanne Barston

My baby was crowning, my obstetrician was knitting, and my husband was holding my left leg up in the air. This wasn't how I pictured my birth experience. None of my Lamaze classes had covered what to do when your doctor was more concerned with the sweater she was making her cousin for Christmas than the infant barreling down your birth canal. And I'd wanted my husband by my head, stroking my hair and murmuring supportive phrases into my ear. Not catching the afterbirth.

None of that was bothering me, though. I was too focused on the strange fluorescent aura that had suddenly descended on our delivery suite, sucking all the happiness out of the room. I had compiled a playlist of appropriate songs to accompany my son's entrance into the world, and now I couldn't listen to them. I begged my husband to turn the music off, and he put on a cheerful Trey Anastasio album instead.

This was no small thing, considering how much thought I'd put into this playlist. For nine months, I'd been listening to these songs, imagining the moment my offspring and I would lock eyes in a moment of perfect understanding and love. I'd wanted to time it so that Snow Patrol's *Open Your Eyes* started just as I began my final pushes. The lyrics seemed perfect: I'd pictured my future child in a war, fighting to break through and become an actual living, breathing baby. He was stuck in this dark place and I would finally get to pull him into the light. And in doing so, pull myself back into the light, too.

When it came to reproductive matters, my body had failed in nearly every way. My husband, Steve, and I had no problem getting pregnant, but I couldn't seem to hang on to a pregnancy. Two cycles in a row, I'd seen those two pink lines pop up and immediately felt an undeniable connection to the new soul making its home in my body. And then I'd lost one, then another.

Even when I did manage to keep a pregnancy, this body of mine still couldn't get its act together. My stupid womb had screwed up its only job: to keep my baby safe and growing. We'd seen a big, healthy, perfect fetus at every ultrasound exam up until my last requisite one at thirty-three weeks; in fact, at that last exam, my baby had been measuring about two weeks ahead. But five weeks later, an additional, unexpected ultrasound provoked by some troubling symptoms showed that the baby had stopped growing right at that same thirty-three week mark, which, along with a dangerously low level of amniotic fluid, put him in peril. I never found out why this happened, but according to the specialist who ultimately insisted that I deliver right then and there, something had gone very, very wrong inside of me.

My doctor finally put down her knitting needles and ambled over to my bed.

"Okay, take a deep breath and push. I can see the head already."

"Really?" I cried. This was the moment. The one I'd been waiting for. Cue the Snow Patrol.

"Yep, there it is. He has a lot of hair! Let's see if I can braid it," she murmured, finally paying attention to what was happening between my legs.

Steve and I laughed nervously. We weren't sure she was kidding.

The labor and delivery nurse was staring at my doctor incredulously. She shook it off, turned to me, and suggested that I might want to give another good push. "I think you just need one more!" she said encouragingly, with a pointed look toward Dr. Distracted.

I mustered up the energy for one big push, and held my breath.

And with little fanfare, and the completely wrong music, my son Leo was born.

∽

There he was. In my arms. Perfect. Everything I'd been dreaming of and working toward in the past year.

So why wasn't I happy? I couldn't even smile; my face kept twitching, lower lip trembling, crying that wouldn't stop. I held my brand-new baby and stared at him, baptizing him with tears, a pit of fear gnawing at my sore insides. I wanted him safe in someone else's embrace: with my husband, whose happiness was so intense that it almost pierced through my bubble of emptiness, just barely missing the mark, or with the nurses, who handled him with a confidence I doubted I'd ever possess.

Looking at him, it seemed impossible that he had come from me, been inside my belly, had any part of me in him. I would have more easily believed that he'd been delivered to my hospital room like a get-well-soon bouquet. I looked at his chest, moving steadily up and down, and told him I loved him. But all my emotions felt filtered, distant. It felt almost like sadness, but no, sadness wasn't the right word. It was—what? Empty?

The nurse suggested I feed him. I brought him to my breast; his mouth opened, closed down on me. It felt fine. Weird, but not painful.

"That's a perfect latch," the nurse proclaimed, like she was proud of us.

It only lasted a minute. Then they pulled him off of me and took him away to get cleaned up.

∾

Hours later, in the windowless room that would be our first home as a family of three, they wheeled our baby in. He was crying, making guppy-like movements with his mouth. It was time to eat. Steve carefully lifted him out of his glass-walled bassinet. He looked so natural with our baby in his arms, and I felt an odd twinge of fear. I didn't even know how to pick up a new baby, and I was supposed to be the one with the maternal instincts. Something felt off, but I quickly dismissed it as lack of sleep and food, and the newness of it all.

As my husband gently placed Leo on my belly, my fears subsided for a moment. This skin-to-skin thing was as comforting as the books had promised. I could lie here all day like this, I thought. Unfortunately, my son had other ideas, as he started whimpering and rooting around for my nipple. I shifted around, trying to get him latched on without harming his fragile little head.

"The nurse just shoved him on there," Steve said. "Want me to try?"

"No, I think he's . . . oops . . . wait a sec . . . ouch. Ouch!" I cried, wincing. "I think he's latched. It hurts though, really bad. Do you think it's supposed to hurt this much?"

Steve shrugged. "I'm sure it gets better." I tried to nod in agreement, tried not to cry. It didn't feel like a simple matter of raw nipples—it was too early for that, considering Leo had only attempted to feed once before, and for only a few seconds. This was like a lightning bolt of searing pain, shooting through my left breast.

After about five minutes, tears were streaming down my cheeks. "I can't do this," I snapped at my husband. "It kills. This is fucking ridiculous."

He ignored my anger. "Why don't you try switching to the other one?"

I shifted him as gently as I could to my right breast and attempted to guide him to my nipple. But this time, he couldn't seem to latch on. We kept trying for a good forty-five minutes, eventually switching back to the left despite the pain that still pulsed through that side of my body, but by this point, the kid was screaming and wouldn't have any of it. Defeated, my husband ran out into the hallway to summon a nurse. The one he found looked about sixteen and seemed embarrassed to even say the word "nipple," but she did manage to force Leo's tiny mouth onto my right nipple and hold him there as he squirmed around for a bit. "There," she proclaimed. "He's eating. They don't need much at this point, anyway."

This scene was repeated every two hours for the rest of our hospital stay. We told ourselves we just had to hang on until the lactation consultant arrived. It was like waiting for Santa Claus. Of course, we were Jewish: waiting for Santa had always been rather futile, and it started to become clear that our anxious anticipation of the lactation consultant would be equally unfulfilled.

She did come, eventually, but it wasn't worth the wait. She gave my breasts a cursory examination, watched Leo move his head lazily around the general vicinity of my breast, and told us he was "just lazy" and would do better once he "woke up a bit."

I don't think she looked me in the eyes once during her visit. I was nothing more than a disembodied pair of dysfunctional breasts. I told myself that was okay, that it wasn't about me but about Leo. So be it, I thought. This is life, now.

༄

An orderly wheeled us down the hallway, me in a wheelchair, Leo lying in my lap. Every person we passed smiled and congratulated me. I watched their faces with fascination, marveling at how their smiles reached their eyes. When I tried smiling back, it felt more like a grimace.

As we waited for Steve to pull the car up, Leo started wailing, and I knew I couldn't make him stop. He was hungry, but I still hadn't figured out how to feed him. I tried to hush him, telling him under my breath that we'd try again as soon as we got home. *Figure it out,* I inwardly scolded myself. *It's the most natural thing in the world.*

But even as I thought this, I wondered. What if breast-feeding were natural, but I wasn't? It would be natural to feel awe toward my newborn, not ambivalence. Natural to want to hold him, rather than scared to do so. Maybe my breasts just knew something I couldn't admit to myself. That I had no capacity to nurture, no ability to nourish. That I wasn't fit to be a mother.

༄

We arrived home to a hero's welcome. My in-laws had decorated the garage with "Welcome home Leo!" signs and an impressive collection of balloons. They waited outside like paparazzi, cameras in hand, as we pulled up, documenting Leo's journey from car seat to front door with frantic flashes and clicks. I stuck that familiar frozen smile on my face, opening my eyes wide in what I hoped resembled a look of happy surprise and good cheer.

My parents were at the door to greet us, along with our dog, Dizzy, who'd been our first baby, in the most clichéd, yuppified sense. He spun around in excitement, licking my shins and sniffing curiously at the infant carrier, where the demise of his spoiled existence lay sleeping.

As Leo's genetically connected fan club crowded around him, I huddled in the corner with Dizzy, soaking his silky fur with the tears I'd hidden from my in-laws' cameras. A constant buzz had settled in my ears, along with the mist in my field of vision, casting a gray pallor on everything around me. Dizzy was black and white, so at least looking at him wasn't too disconcerting.

I escaped upstairs to take a shower, hoping that the warm water would have its usual restorative powers on my mood. The stream from the showerhead was like a thousand tiny lashes on my stitches and engorged breasts. I figured I deserved it. I was screwing this motherhood thing up royally, and it was only day three.

As I gingerly toweled off, I heard Leo whimpering downstairs, and my husband calling up to me.

"Suz, I think he's hungry. Should I bring him up?"

I responded affirmatively, settling into the new red glider we'd purchased for Leo's retro-circus-themed nursery. Maybe all we needed was the right chair, I thought. Time to think positive! Positive thinking could do wonders! As Steve pounded up the stairs with our hungry baby, I willed my breasts to work, repeating my mantra: *It's the most natural thing in the world. Figure it out.*

I tried pulling him gently to my nipple, sticking it into his crying mouth like the hospital lactation consultant had just a few hours before, but he wouldn't latch on. Steve tried to help, adjusting and readjusting Leo's body to find the magic position that might help him feed successfully. We spent about thirty minutes contorting my breasts and our son's head before giving up out of sheer exhaustion.

"Maybe he wasn't hungry?" my husband suggested hopefully. I nodded, but it had been hours since he last ate—if you could call any of what he'd done in the hospital "eating." I attempted to reassure us both, repeating what I'd read on so many blogs, in so many books: "Yeah, their stomachs are like the size of a thimble at this point. He probably doesn't need much. We can try again later."

From downstairs, we could hear our parents talking in

what they assumed were hushed tones, wondering why we didn't just give him formula like they'd done with us. We'd turned out just fine, after all.

I looked at my husband, cradling our wailing baby. Steve had turned out fine. He never got sick, he was happy and successful, and obviously he knew how to parent. Then there was me. There was nothing "fine" about me. I couldn't handle the most basic biological functions. My body couldn't hold on to pregnancies, couldn't sustain them properly. I couldn't look at my son with anything other than despair.

I couldn't give him formula. Because all I *could* give him was breast milk. Not love, not laughter, not focused attention. My only job was to feed the baby, and if I failed at that, I'd be rendered completely irrelevant. I couldn't give up.

૮ન૭

Weeks went by, and the fluorescent film persisted. Each time I tried to feed him, Leo would scream and arch away from me. *He hates me,* I thought. This realization didn't surprise me or even upset me. It felt like old news.

Despite suspecting something was seriously wrong with me, I was hesitant to seek professional help. I had a checkered history with those in the psychiatric profession; I'd been hit on by one therapist at the age of fifteen, and told by my college-era shrink that I should just "face up to the fact that I wasn't pretty" (this from a woman who was supposed to be helping me with anorexia and body dysmorphic disorder). The only thing that had ever helped me was Zoloft. It had literally saved me, and as much as I hated the idea of being dependent on a drug—

the prospect gave me such anxiety about long-term effects that it was almost a wash between the good outcomes from the medication and the bad—I knew it would be a lifeline in this case, too. But according to every study I read, there was no conclusive proof that Leo wouldn't suffer side effects from ingesting my SSRI-tainted milk. I wouldn't stop breastfeeding just because I was stupid enough to get depressed.

Aside from whatever was going on with my serotonin levels, I felt that some undefinable bond between Leo and me had been irreparably destroyed; every time I got close to him, he would scream. This seemed so contrary to all I'd heard about breastfeeding being the easiest and best way to comfort a newborn. Instead, every feeding session started and ended with my husband comforting Leo, while I sat there symbolizing nothing but pain and frustration for my son. I imagined that the two of them were looking at me with disappointment and regret—why hadn't they chosen a better wife, a better mother? One with a body that worked the way it was supposed to and a mind that didn't crumble at the first sign of adversity.

⁓

He never could latch, despite our earnest attempts: visits with various and sundry lactation specialists, a procedure to "untie" his apparently restricted tongue, a few optimistic moments with a nipple shield. I started pumping instead. If he couldn't have an adequate mother, he'd at least have an adequate supply of mother's milk.

And so I pumped. And pumped. I spent hours upstairs in my bedroom, hooked up to a milking machine. At first, it was a welcome respite, the perfect escape. I could cry in peace, even with my in-laws downstairs, with their watchful, searching eyes, expecting—no, needing—me to be happy and "normal." Dizzy would follow me into the bedroom, looking curiously at the machine as it whirred steadily, sucking all it could out of me. I swore it was talking to me, murmuring *you suck you suck you suck* as it did exactly that. But Leo grew, and so I pumped.

Then Leo broke out in a rash so vivid that friends could hardly say the requisite "he's beautiful" when they saw him for the first time. The contents of his diapers were startling, streaked with blood and mucous. On the advice of the breast-feeding websites, I stopped eating dairy, wheat, soy, corn, and leafy green vegetables. I lived on bread and water, like a prisoner. I gladly accepted this, my penance for the unspeakable crime of being an ambivalent mother.

He kept getting sicker. He cried before eating, and after eating, and between eating. With Steve back at work, my pumping routine morphed from break to bondage. I'm sure there are worse things than being unable to comfort your wailing baby because you're too busy trying to produce his next meal, but at the time, I could imagine no greater torture.

Still, I kept pumping. Still, he kept crying. As did I.

∽

It was Leo who made the decision for me, the choice that helped me be his mom. Now, at six years old, he believes he's smarter than I am. I can't really argue with that. He's been that way as long as I've known him.

A little over a month after he was born, he was diagnosed

with a severe milk protein allergy. The pediatrician suggested we try a hypoallergenic formula, "just to see what happens." Within twenty-four hours, he changed from a miserable, sickly creature with a rash to a gorgeous, happy, alert baby.

My own metamorphosis took longer, of course. But that same day, I gave myself permission to stop. To stop pumping. To stop measuring my self-worth in ounces of milk. To leave my bedroom and the milking machine and go for a goddamn walk. To stop being the source of pain for my child, and to become his mother.

I filled my prescription for Zoloft, returned the rented, hospital-grade breast pump, and stuffed my sports bra with cabbage leaves. Everything dried up, eventually. Milk. Tears.

One morning, not long after, I sat in the red rocker feeding him. I began to sing softly, not a lullaby, exactly, but something similar. Something from that forgotten playlist from his birth, a song about leaving dark rooms, hand in hand.

As if on cue, his tiny fingers curled around my wrist, pulling the bottle closer. Our bodies relaxed into each other as he drank. There was no pain, no screaming, no anger.

I gazed into his eyes, which were a misty blue, like sea glass. I'd never noticed. I couldn't recall ever having the chance to look at him, so calm and still.

There you are, I whispered, to my child. *There you are,* I whispered, to myself.

And there it was, wild and colorful and warm. *Love.* There it was.

THE SAVAGE SONG OF MY BIRTHRIGHT BLUES

Estelle Erasmus

*N*othing about my pregnancy went according to plan. In my midforties, after treating my age-related infertility with the help of modern medicine, my husband and I were overjoyed to learn that I was expecting a baby girl.

With a bill of good health from my doctor, I was supposed to bask in nine months of bliss, while devouring bonbons and spreading bonhomie, much like the pregnant midlife celebrities we see smiling on the covers of *People* magazine.

Instead, severe, palm-sweating nausea presided over my days, making me dizzy and forcing me to feverishly suck on lemon ice pops—a panacea against fainting and throwing up. I never fainted, but I did vomit copiously before and after dinner each night like clockwork.

Oddly, by the beginning of my third trimester, I had gained seventy pounds while subsisting on a diet of pizza, watermelon, and fruit juice.

My feelings about my new body were complex. All previous vanity shrank in the face of the new normal I saw in the mirror. As my body enlarged, the old me disappeared, becoming invisible. My already buxom breasts burgeoned to porn-star proportions. My fingers swelled so much that I couldn't don my rings. My legs lost their definition and resembled tree trunks, or "Oompa Loompas," as my husband lovingly referred to them.

I couldn't have wrapped my legs around my husband if I tried. Though brimming with life, I felt unsexy, full of burps and flatulence instead of passion.

Terrified of acquiring stretch marks as an unwanted "medal of honor," I bought elixirs online and in between frenzied bouts of spewing, spent hours obsessively rubbing the slippery salves all over my belly and buttocks, as a benediction of sorts.

I was scared of more than just the stretch marks.

I hoped that the salve would protect me against the incoming onslaught of postpartum depression, a fate that I believed to be my birthright.

My mother had suffered from postpartum depression, during a time when there was no label for her mood swings and unexplained ennui. Her friends and family chalked it up to hormones and exhaustion and left her alone. My aunt told me my mother was reluctant to hold or feed me, leaving me mostly in the care of other relatives, until one day, while I was still in swaddling, she suddenly snapped out of it and willingly donned the mantle of motherhood. My mother refuses to talk about it, so I have no clear picture of what really happened. Just that something did.

I vowed to my husband that for me, genetics would not be destiny.

If it takes a village to raise a child, I told my husband, then let's build that village.

Our plan was the armor I girded myself with to fight off the specter of postpartum depression. Using military precision we devised a strategic scenario of support: a highly recommended baby nurse would meet us at our home the day we returned from the hospital, our cleaning lady would increase her monthly visits to bimonthly, we'd prepare and freeze meals in advance, I'd join several local mothers' support groups. We painstakingly set up everything in my life after I gave birth to assist with the baby, minimize stress, and allow me to smoothly flow into my new maternal role.

We added to the blueprint: My husband would avail himself of his company's paternity leave, and then take his accrued vacation, after which he'd work from home for a week or two. Once he returned to the office, his mother would travel from New Zealand to stay with us for several weeks. Our three-month meticulously designed plan would culminate with a family summer vacation to the shore.

As I lay in our bed, heavy with child, I thought we had it under control, figured we'd anticipated every possible circumstance in which postpartum depression could sneak up on me. I might have had moments of sadness, but I'd never been truly depressed before, I reassured myself, so I'd see it coming and have time to deflect. History would not repeat itself this time.

The vomiting stopped at the thirty-second week of my pregnancy. That's when the heartburn kicked in, causing sleepless nights despite the comforts of my man-sized body pillow, which by now I referred to as "my other husband."

Then, the night terrors began. I had long dreaded the physical act of childbirth, couldn't imagine a baby winding its way down and then emerging from the dark cavern of my body, but I had filed those worries away to be taken out and examined at a much later date.

They came thundering back with a vengeance, as if I were a doomed character in a horror movie, always looking over her shoulder. I awoke gasping from suffocating dreams, bathed in pools of estrogen-smelling sweat, convinced I felt the pain of a child emerging from my womb and tearing me asunder amidst the bloody rites of birth and the medical detritus of a labor and delivery room. I cried in the morning after my husband went to work so he wouldn't know how badly I was falling apart. He was worried enough about me, I told myself.

I also had been recently let go from my job with a medical communications company I had a brief stint at after a long career in publishing. I wasn't brokenhearted at the loss—which was due to a restructuring—because I had mainly taken the position for the benefits, good salary, and close proximity to where I lived. I hadn't planned to return, opting to stay home and raise my daughter, which I suspected they'd figured out.

Although I didn't care, several of my colleagues took their dismissals very hard, complaining about the way they'd been mistreated by an unrepentant management. I took to holding the phone away from my ear as they vented, too caught up in their emotions, unable to separate and create the boundaries I desperately needed in order to feel serene. One well-meaning colleague told me, "Good luck carving time out for yourself after you have the baby. It will be a challenge," exacerbating my already rampant trepidation about the lifestyle changes looming.

I had attributed my constant crying, night terrors, over-arching anxiety, feelings of sadness and impending doom, and difficulty concentrating to pregnancy hormones, heartburn, and the stress of constant prenatal monitoring. With hindsight I see that I was facing antepartum depression—or depression during pregnancy—a condition that is often a precursor to postpartum depression.

I wasn't alone. Statistics from the American Congress of Obstetricians and Gynecologists suggest that between 14 and 23 percent of women (one out of every eight) suffer from some form of depression during pregnancy. Although it can happen anytime, the majority of women find themselves depressed starting in their thirty-second week of pregnancy, like I did.

Because I believed that any drug I could possibly take for my "nerves" would go through the placenta and affect the baby, I never considered taking medication or an antidepressant. I didn't even bother to ask my ob-gyn about it. In retrospect I realize that was a mistake. She might have been able to provide other solutions.

"You need a doula," a friend told me after I cried on her shoulder for the umpteenth time.

"What's that?" I asked.

"Someone who can help you navigate through your pregnancy and then be there as you deliver," my friend said. I was sold.

Like a Midwest-born, prairie-skirt-wearing Mary Poppins, sans umbrella, the doula appeared at my door, with a huge satchel filled with patchouli-scented pillows, pregnancy-approved essential oils, and home-cooked quinoa. I told her my fears about my pregnancy and she told me that she was there to help me.

The doula never said I was depressed—although I believe she must have known—but her words and actions kick-started my healing.

She told me about the harmful effects of processed food on my growing baby's brain—so I threw out the TV dinners I'd eaten for years and bought salads, whole grains, and even quinoa, which I found I liked.

I went through a sort of feminine energy boot camp over the next month that got me over the worst of my anxiety.

I relaxed during meditation sessions. I listened to tapes of soothing whale songs and channeled my female ancestors while asking for protection for my baby and me. With each chant and affirmation, my fears began to dissipate.

With my doula's encouragement, I enrolled in a prenatal yoga class at the hospital where I'd deliver my daughter. By exercising I increased my body's mood-elevating serotonin levels while decreasing its mood-dampening cortisol levels.

My doula set up a session for my husband and I to talk about our concerns. We were in the process of selling our home, and I found it very stressful to have strangers going through it, sneezing and touching my furniture, so I asked my husband to remove the listing until after I gave birth.

Finally, my delivery date arrived. Because my baby was supposed to weigh more than nine pounds, my ob-gyn, who was pregnant herself, decided to induce labor at thirty-nine weeks. My husband tenderly fed me lemon and strawberry ices, and my doula massaged my temples and lower back, as I listened to a tape of meditative music. My water broke early on.

Once a woman's water breaks, I learned, the baby needs to be delivered within twenty-four hours, or it could be risky for both mother and baby.

It took fifteen hours of hard labor, five ices, twenty sips of water, three increasingly aggressive inquiring phone calls from my parents (that my husband fielded), and finally one epidural to find out that the baby hadn't moved, and I hadn't dilated. Finally, at 8:00 p.m., my doctor suggested that I undergo a C-section, because the anesthesiologist was available and with several other cases needing attention, he might not be later on, when I had to have the baby, or if we found ourselves in a life-threatening situation.

I asked my husband what he wanted. He said, "It's your body, do whatever you feel is best for you and the baby." His response made me fall in love with him all over again. I knew what I had to do.

I turned to my doula, "Help me, please. I'm so scared to have this baby. You've helped me so much. Is there anything I can do to get rid of my fear?"

I'll never forget her answer. "Estelle, I know you studied opera and you love to sing," she said. "So why don't you sing as they deliver your baby. The act of changing your focus should stop you from having a panic attack." I thought that was a brilliant idea and thanked her as they wheeled me into the sterile, white operating room.

"I'm so frightened," I said to my doctor, the anesthesiologist, and the rest of the operating room staff. "Do you mind if I sing while you cut me open and deliver my baby?" I nervously asked as they prepared me, let my scrub-garbed husband into the room, and moved the curtain partition over my belly so

I wouldn't see the machinations of birthing my daughter. To my relief, the staff smiled and laughed and agreed.

So there I was, in the delivery room I'd had nightmares about for months, my husband holding my hand on one side, a kindly nurse holding my other hand on the other side. Emboldened by their response, I opened my mouth, took a deep breath, and called upon my operatic training to entertain them and set me free. Soon the room was filled with a robust, slightly giddy, and definitely too loud rendition of the appropriately bluesy yet hopeful song "Summertime" (*Summertime and the livin' is easy*) as my daughter was lifted out of me at eight pounds twelve ounces and I welcomed my beautiful girl into this world.

I felt the energy around me become lighter as I stopped singing and gazed into my daughter's dark gypsy eyes. I could see the view ahead and it was beautiful. And my daughter was beautiful. I felt my love for her take me over, as the antepartum depression had tried to, and I knew that I had won.

I learned that even during the shiniest moments of your life, an unwelcome guest like depression can lurk in the background, catching even the savviest of planners, like myself, unaware, taking every resource and strength you possess to fight it off.

I'm so fortunate I found the village that helped me to do that.

My Face in the Darkness

Denise Emanuel Clemen

*W*e didn't want children.

My husband had once envisioned life as a Catholic priest or a Benedictine monk, until I'd lured him away from all that. Parenthood had never been in the cards for him. I was blunt with anyone who asked me about starting a family. "Nope," I'd say. "I don't want kids," while silently, I'd make the correction: *Any more kids.* I had relinquished a son for adoption after a secret pregnancy when I was seventeen. I didn't deserve another shot at motherhood.

But like all good plans, our idyllic vision of just the two of us went awry. On our regular Saturday morning walk, we found a toddler wandering the streets of our neighborhood. His sodden diaper probably doubled his weight; still, I didn't mind holding him. As we walked up the porch steps of the nearest house, I was already hoping he didn't belong there. And he didn't. But the woman who answered the door knew where he'd come from. "One of theirs," she said, pointing at the house across the street and clucking her tongue.

It took some time for the woman at the next house to answer the door. It was chaos inside. Kids everywhere. She barely glanced at the baby on my hip before grabbing him and slinging him across one of her own. There wasn't even a thank you before the door slammed in our faces. *You could do a better job than that,* said a little voice inside my head.

Sometime after that, our only set of friends with a baby asked us if we'd take care of him for a week so they could step out of the world of parenting and back into the kingdom of coupledom—in Hawaii. We said yes. The kid was eighteen months old, and his round brown eyes were a match for my own. Everywhere we went people said he looked just like me. The kid liked bacon, and the second morning that I cooked him some he called me Mama. At the end of the week when we went to the airport to greet his parents, the little bacon-eater clung to me and screamed. It wasn't until the five of us settled into our friends' living room that he'd even look at his parents.

You'd know better than to leave your child with friends for a week, said the voice inside my head. *Your kid won't be calling anyone else Mama.* The next thing I knew I was off the Pill and we were in Paris, where we conceived a daughter we'd name Colette.

My pregnancy brought benefits. My acne vanished. My mood stabilized. I could indulge in the occasional chocolate malt because I was eating for two instead of worrying that a casting director might think I could lose a few pounds. The labor and delivery were straightforward too. Sent home from the hospital after a breakfast of steak and eggs the next morning, I couldn't wait for some new family cocooning.

The crying started the moment we stepped out of the air-conditioned hospital and into the heat. The Santa Ana winds were like a blast furnace incinerating us as we got into our unair-conditioned car.

The wailing continued. Walking the floor replaced cocooning. Breastfeeding was more difficult than I had imagined. And the responsibility of caring for a newborn filled my head with questions. *Why wouldn't the baby stop crying? What was wrong with her? Was she sick? Why couldn't I stop crying? Why was I such an inept mother? Why couldn't I sleep when the baby slept like people said I should?* I insisted that my husband remake the bed so my head could be at the foot of the bed closer to the cradle. Now I could watch the baby all night long. The world was turning upside down.

It's like prison, I told myself when I rocked my daughter. Every day is a calendar square. In eighteen years, I'll be out. Wheelchair, I'd mistakenly say when I tried to tell anyone how much time I'd spent in the rocking chair that day.

I'm sorry, I'd whisper to my son, imagining his face as I cradled my daughter. It had been sixteen years since I'd held him, but I was certain that my daughter looked just like him. He'd cried when I put him into the arms of the social worker at the adoption agency. No wonder my babies didn't like me. I'd given one away, and this one knew I wasn't to be trusted.

I could not muster the will to leave the house with my daughter. My husband's colleagues delivered an expensive, beribboned stroller one night as I sat on the floor in the shower crying. It stayed parked in our hallway. La Leche League meetings provided support for breastfeeding mothers just a few miles away, but when I put the baby in the car and she began to cry, I turned around and went home, my heart pounding. I had only one friend with a baby, no relatives closer than a three-day drive, and my husband worked a dozen hours a day as he devoted himself to his new law firm. Trapped in a one-bedroom apartment with a crying baby, I careened down the precipitous slope into depression.

ᗡᐤ

It's almost thirty years since my daughter was born. A lot has happened in the past three decades. A few months ago my boyfriend died from lung cancer. In the aftermath of his death, more than two months passed before I spent a night alone. My younger daughter slept on my bedroom floor for the first few nights. My older daughter traveled across the country and stayed for a week. Friends came and stayed with me, cooked for me, took me on outings. When one left, another arrived, and the phone calls and e-mails and Facebook messages kept coming. As a society, we often lament our ineptitude at coping with death, but we might be worse at dealing with birth.

While death is a full frontal attack, birth is a stealthy assassin. Some magnitude of sadness and depression are expected in the bereaved. When a woman becomes a mother, her old life dies, yet she's expected to rise from her ashes and immerse herself in the jubilation of being completely responsible for a helpless human being. In the understandable urge to celebrate that new bundle of joy, friends and family often fail to thoroughly acknowledge the physical and mental toll wreaked by birth and motherhood.

I was sold my own particular bill of goods as a new mother: A baby I could keep was supposed to be the solution to my problems. In 1970 when I gave up my firstborn, I was assured that I'd move on, have other children, and that all would be well. In the sixteen years that elapsed between the birth of my son and the birth of my next child, not one day went by when I did not think of the baby I'd handed over to strangers. I stuffed my sadness deep inside, self-medicated with alcohol, and did the best I could until I unwittingly pried open my Pandora's box of grief by giving birth to another child.

Your daughter knows you're a bad mother. God is punishing you for what you did. The voices of doubt and self-loathing rang in my head night and day. I cried when the baby cried, ate cold soup out of a can, and couldn't figure out how anyone with a new baby ever prepared a decent meal, took a shower, or got dressed. Convinced that something was wrong with my daughter, I insisted on at least a half-dozen extra visits to the pediatrician in the first couple of months. She was diagnosed with colic, while I was not diagnosed at all.

After a few weeks, my siblings, though almost two thousand miles away, banded together and sent my mother out to California to stay with me. The two weeks she spent sleeping on a rollaway bed in the living room helped a lot. She held the baby while I showered, made my breakfast, sat with me, and walked at my side as I developed the confidence to push the stroller around the block. She even convinced my husband that he had to be home no later than 8:00 p.m. Every one of these contributions was a lifeline.

I had a handhold on sanity, albeit a shaky one, when my mother's visit ended. My husband began taking the baby on an early morning walk while I slept, and every afternoon at four I unplugged the phone and nursed my daughter and myself to sleep for a nap. The sleep gave me the stamina to go on walks with the baby. I also found the energy to get together with my friend and her little boy. Eventually I even made it to a La Leche League meeting. La Leche League became the cornerstone of my support with not only support group meetings, but play-dates in a nearby park as well. Still, even with these changes, the dark cloud loomed.

I'd lost my old self somehow. The self that persevered. The self that could hold everything in. The self that could ferret out solutions. There was no solution. I had a baby. A baby I was anxious about. A baby that evoked loss. A baby I couldn't comfort because no one could comfort me. Even now, all these years later, when I think back at the person I was then, I feel the grayness descend.

One summer on a vacation to visit my husband's family in Nebraska, my daughter bucked in her high chair, kicking and crying while her cousins sat nicely at the table. "Do something with her," my husband commanded. *Do something.* The voice rang inside my head as I pulled her out of the chair and stormed into the evening. I cried all the way to the highway where I had every intention of crossing to the train tracks and lying down with her. It seemed obvious we'd be better off dead. A few days later I cried all the way to the airport and on the plane ride back to Los Angeles.

When I got pregnant again, my mother and my aunt decided that they would come to California for the birth and stay for a while. The way I recall it, the announcement of the pregnancy and their plans for a visit happened in the same phone conversation, along with a family story about some aunt or cousin who had plopped her baby into a pot on the stove and would have cooked it if her husband hadn't walked in.

My mother was well qualified to care for me. Her very first full-time job was as a mother's helper. "She'll tell you that you can go home, that she doesn't need you," she was told by the woman's husband, "but don't let the baby out of your sight." One night while my mother was sleeping, the house was in engulfed in a ruckus, and she woke to find the mother being hustled off to an asylum. The baby was then put in the care of its grandparents and my mother was out of a job. While I never told my mother about the incident in Nebraska, maybe it was this experience of hers that so readily led her to come stay with me. When her two weeks of vacation were up, my aunt stayed with me for an additional month.

I grieved secretly for my son after the births of both my daughters. When I think back on those days, the memories are like ruined snapshots and even today, almost three decades later, I feel the rekindling of that dark anxiety in my body. I thought my children might be better off without me, yet simultaneously, I was terrified that I would die and leave them motherless. It seemed as if a tape ran constantly inside my head portraying the worst possible thing that could happen at any moment. Air travel was nearly unbearable. I worked unceasingly to seize these terrible visions and imagine them shattering or turning to dust.

What I believed to be the germ of my grief, the birth and relinquishment of my son, was secret, so it was difficult to seek help. And when I did, the results only compounded my misery. During the first session with a therapist, I immediately confessed that I'd gotten pregnant at sixteen and had given my baby away, but I said that I was over it and that I didn't want to talk about it. What I wanted to talk about, I said, was how stressed I felt at being a mother. The therapist stared at me and then asked if I thought I might be a danger to my daughter. The question terrified me. What if something I said caused my daughter to be taken from me? I never returned for another session.

Motherhood, it seemed to me, was a silken coat that most women slipped into effortlessly. My coat felt dirty and tattered and ill-fitting. This divide is further evidenced, I think, by our reactions to stories in the news of mothers with postpartum psychosis harming their children. The silken coat crowd asks how anyone could do such a thing, while the rest of us hang our heads, fearing bath time, the carving knife, or the drive around the lake.

When my daughters were two and five, I searched for and found my son. We were happily reunited, and I divulged my long-held secret to family and friends, but it was years before I could tell the story about my son or my postpartum misery without visibly trembling. Now, more than twenty years later, I've cast off the rags of that unhappy existence. Certainly, life has continued to deliver its blows, but most days I not only feel resilient, I also feel worthy of life's joys.

I'll never know if the loss of my son was at the heart of my postpartum depression. I'll never know if an official diagnosis from a doctor might have delivered an effective treatment. Maybe the enduring anxiety and sadness I experienced after the births of my daughters would have happened anyway. Maybe even if I had been diagnosed and treated early on, my suffering would have continued. What I do know is this: Nowadays as I care for my ninety-year-old mother, I hear her stories over and over again. When she recounts the story of her first job and the night that young mother was carted off to the asylum, I imagine a woman in a long nightgown with tangled hair, eyes wide with confusion and fear. But that face in the darkness is my own.

We Come Looking for Hope

Alexandra Rosas

*W*hen we are in survival mode, we don't recognize it as such. One day blurs into the next, and living becomes nothing more than just that: staying alive, minute by minute.

As a little girl, I dreamed of the day I would have my own baby. I never wanted to own Barbies or to play dress-up—all I wanted was a chubby baby doll that I could diaper, feed, and softly sing to sleep. A mother is everything that I wanted to be. In school when asked what we wanted to be when we grew up, I would answer that I wanted to be a teacher, but I would say it with my eyes cast down, because I was lying. I wanted to be a mother.

At the age of thirty-five, my lifelong dream finally came true. On April 17, 1995, the most beautiful dark-haired, blue-eyed boy I could imagine was born. He was my son, Alec. The moment I first saw him seemed so surreal that I could only stammer, "Is he mine? Is that him? Is he mine?" over and over. I thought my heart would burst open from the love I felt for this baby. I felt that way until five days later, when despair, coupled with anxiety, took over my life and made it impossible for me to sleep or eat.

If I tried to describe those early days of motherhood, words would pale the experience. It's times like these that I wish I were an artist, because the battle for your life needs colors and sweeps of a brush to show the swirl of panic, fear, darkness.

There was a labor and delivery nurse in the hospital, Mardi, who cared for me in the days after Alec was born. We got to know each other because Alec was born at thirty-four-and-a-half weeks and spent five days in the NICU. On the day of our hospital discharge, Mardi sensed something off about me; she would later tell me it was in my eyes. For reasons only she could sense, she called to check on me at home within the week.

On the morning she called, at the sound of her voice asking me how I was, and if everything was all right, I could only answer by choking with tears. She asked me for my address, told me to sit and wait, and promised, "I'll be there in twenty minutes." I held on to the phone, and the emotion I'd been hiding from everyone else burst through.

The depth of this sadness brought me to my knees. Clutching my chest, I sobbed. Heaving and gasping, and not understanding any of what was happening to me. There was no reason for this weight in my chest. The baby I had long awaited slept in the next room, and I adored him. None of this made any sense to me. I didn't know where to go, or what to do, or how to think. I was lost in my own life and there was no trace of who I used to be left inside of me.

Tears streamed down my cheeks as I stood at the window and watched for Mardi. I had to make it, to hold on, for the twenty minutes until she got there. My life had become just that—surviving small blocks at a time.

Finally, I saw her. She jumped out of her car and ran up our front steps. This nurse who was intuitive enough to see what no one else could see, rushed up to where I had run downstairs to meet her. She saw my face, and pressed me into her chest. I couldn't even recognize the sounds I was making—they were so broken and trapped. Over my cries, she spoke into my ear and saved me: "I promise you, you will get better."

I wanted that promise of "better" for my baby. Ever since we brought Alec home at five days old, something wasn't right. In the pitch black of the night, my heart would race. During the day, I couldn't even see through the tears that filled my eyes for no reason other than sadness. It had been like this for close to two weeks now. I prayed over the pounding in my chest that I would be normal again. But what if I would always feel this way?

Mardi was next to me, asking me to believe her and her promise. Was she promising hope? The part of me that was too terrified to believe, too scared that I wouldn't get better, shouted back, "No. Not me. I'm not going to be one of the lucky ones." I tried to explain to her that it all felt too impossible to ever find a way back.

I was afraid to believe, in case she was wrong. I had no hope. But Mardi did. She told me that all I had to do was believe her. For my baby. I told her that my days seemed endless and that the nights were a hundred times worse. I hadn't slept since we brought Alec home. I tried to describe to her how every moment felt like I was standing on a cliff, looking out over my life while the world whirred on with me lost in the cyclone of it. Thoughts roared in my head constantly, telling me to *just give up. Run away.* That everyone would be better off without me.

I imagined myself leaving my baby in the better care of my husband, and I wondered how Alec would know that I had left out of love for him. But as I spoke, Mardi's voice was louder, and she made me hear her above the storm of my thoughts. She was promising me that I would get better, and saying she had proof. I asked her how, how does someone get better from this?

She told me she worked with people like me. That she knew people like me, and that they had gotten better. She told me that having been seen and treated early, I would be one of them. I knew that I had to decide. My mind battled; I was standing in between two worlds. I could either believe her and try, or I wasn't going to make it. I knew that much. I knew that there was no way that I would survive this alone. I loved Alec so much. I took Mardi's hand, and told her that I trusted her.

Somehow through the darkness, something in my heart opened. A resolution, like a light, and my soul took on the fight for me and my baby. I decided to believe. It was more than optimism; it was far more powerful than positive thought or statistical probability. What I felt was the possibility of hope. Together with Mardi, I called my doctor and we made an appointment for that afternoon. Within a few minutes of talking to me later at the clinic, my doctor got on the phone and called a mental health specialist. I had an appointment for that same afternoon. I was started on a prescription medication that was safe while breastfeeding and had therapy sessions three times a week.

I was saved by a woman who knew just what I needed. The hope that she gave me is the only way that I survived. I've learned that hope is not on a continuum—it's not measured on a spectrum or by degrees. It is a complete giving-in to a desperate belief in something when you have nothing else. My postpartum depression and anxiety remain the blackest period of my life, and I survived, because I was seen early, because someone spoke up after having a gut feeling.

Nineteen years ago, when I became a mother for the first time, I needed to believe in something more than words can describe. Hope became that tangible thing I could hold on to when I was barely able to believe anything.

Hope was my lifesaver.

Hope told me I would be there for my child.

Hope gave me belief that I would survive, one day at a time.

One morning when Alec was ten weeks old, after I had been seeing my therapist for a few weeks, I held him, singing off-key but with my whole heart. He looked up at me, gurgling, and then his face broke into a smile. I blinked, not able to take in what I had just seen. It was Alec's first smile, and it was for me. I burst out laughing from the incredible joy of triumph. I saw how beautiful, indescribable, and faithful hope is.

In the months that followed, I continued with therapy, along with Mardi's postpartum group. Hope kept showing me its face with flashes of the gift that life is.

It is this gift of hope that has remained flesh-and-blood real to me. I now speak to new mothers' groups, where I share honestly about my slow, struggling climb out of the early days as a new mother. I don't cover up the true despair of what that time was like for me. I tell my audiences, in a voice that breaks every time from the fierceness of the memory, that I need them to believe me. That this seemingly put-together woman standing in front of them now was once so sure that she'd never feel normal again. That once, I was that frightened new mother, right there where some of them may be now.

When I look out at those women, teary-eyed, I see them listening. And there is always that one there. The face I instantly recognize. I know what she's come looking for today. Her desperation for belief in my words is so visible, so clear in her eyes, in the same way that I wanted Mardi's promise of hope for me to be real.

In the clearest voice I can, I look back at her, and just as Mardi did for me nineteen years ago, I promise her, she will get better. And I tell her to never give up hope.

No Stranger

Nina Gaby

ow do you know?" the patient might ask. I lean forward a bit in my office chair, a magic mix of silence and empathy, or so I would like to think. The woman sitting across from me may be dabbing at her eyes with her fingers. If her nails are chewed to bloody shreds, I will fold my own more tightly in my lap.

"I've been a nurse practitioner for a long time," I will say. "More women than you think go through this. It's hormonal . . . ." But her attention might wander as I began my spiel. Mary—let's call her that, a good neutral name—isn't interested in any scientific explanations for how the hopelessness and the voices in her head and the cocaine crash or the desperation to hang on to some man made her put her kids in a closet with a bottle of liquid Benadryl and leave her newborn with her dealer's nine-year-old (or something like that) instead of going to the hospital emergency room to tell someone what she was really thinking.

What she was really thinking was that the children would

have been better off without her and that meant, in the twisted logic of severe postpartum depression, not taking them with her. Wherever that might have been. She is now thinking that she protected them. The closet and the nine-year-old babysitter seem like safer choices than being with *her*, after all. "It's the best thing I could have done. Them in the closet could sleep and the baby was with somebody." She looks up at me and I do not judge. I think of Susan Smith who drove the car into a lake with her children strapped inside, and Andrea Yates who saw the devil and drowned her children in the bathtub. I do not judge them either. I think how much worse this could have been, this hormonal crapshoot.

I probably didn't meet this particular Mary until long after the closet incident. There have been so many "Marys"; 9 to 16 percent of women will experience postpartum depression according to the American Psychological Association, and women "develop medical or social consequences of addiction faster than men," say Harvard[1] researchers.

By this time, she'd already been in jail and the Termination of Parental Rights was probably already instituted and the kids were somewhere else and she was probably in my office because heroin had become much cheaper than cocaine and maybe she got busted for attempting to carjack an old lady in the Kmart parking lot and court sent her to us. "Us" being whatever agency or facility or emergency room I might be in at any given time. Mary was probably eight months pregnant again when I met her, although you can barely tell, and we were probably busy making arrangements for both her and the newest newborn to be discharged to a facility that could put the baby on methadone immediately. I would have picked at my ragged nail bed to distract my thoughts, to divert the urge to consider how those babies might have been better off.

"How long have you been depressed?" I ask her, jotting details.

"Forever," she tells me.

There was good reason for her to be depressed. She came by it naturally. Maybe her mother was institutionalized shortly after Mary was born. Or her mother was abused. Or Mary herself was the product of parental rights being terminated. The rest of the story repeats itself in my office session after session, patient after patient. Like I said, there are many more Marys than you can even imagine. Trauma. Desperation. Rehab. Incomplete trials of antidepressants. Pregnancies. Relapses. Jail. Thinking the unthinkable. Repeat the cycle.

"I can't give you an antidepressant right now," I apologize. "Too risky in the last trimester." She raises her eyes to mine—a tacit acknowledgement that we both realize how ridiculous that statement is, given all the heroin and whatever else she's been using. "But we can talk about something stronger, maybe some Risperdal."

I don't want her to suffer voices again, and an antipsychotic medication is safer in the third trimester than an antidepressant. Even though this baby will probably be whisked away immediately and the likelihood of Mary getting adequate follow-up treatment is unlikely. She will begin to self-medicate immediately. And her baby will live. These babies, these mothers, they are testimony to human resilience. They do the best they can. I remind myself every day that that's a good thing.

All I have to offer are some recommendations (stay clean and sober and use birth control and take your meds and go to counseling and journal your grief and go to Twelve-Step and move out of the drug house and exercise and diet and don't forget to hydrate) and a prescription. I will hug her. If I live long enough, I will see these babies in my office one day. Or my daughter will see them. My daughter, who is in graduate school for social work. My daughter, who reminds me every day of the good cycles in life.

So how do I know? Although I know nothing of their desperation, my compassion will ring true. Sometimes I will tell these women a bit about how crazy I got after my daughter was born, how crazy I was even before she was born. But only if my words are completely in the service of their recovery. A means of normalizing—if that's even possible—their experiences, putting them in a scientific framework. Otherwise, it would just be me telling my story, a story that under some circumstances might even seem funny, heroic to the innocent listener who has never heard the bigger stories. And I never tell those women for whom the outcome was tragic about my story. My outcome was not tragic. Obviously. My daughter is in graduate school and I'm in my office.

When they ask me, "How do you know?" I may refer to "not being a stranger to a bit of postpartum myself." In the spirit of minimal self-disclosure I have settled on the phrase "I'm not a stranger to" . . . whatever they have to say. They trust me, but have no details about how my experience pales next to theirs. Or wonder how a person as crazy as I was can help them.

I had hoped that my "pre-partum" depression would "pre-pay" my karmic bill. I had very minor depression, anxiety, and OCD traits throughout my life, had adequate trials of antidepressants, and became a psychiatric nurse practitioner and crisis therapist. I knew how lucky I was—the minor part. Early on I figured that postpartum depression was a risk for me, but expected I could balance my emotional happiness and stability against my physiological tendency toward clinical depression, if I was ever so lucky as to get pregnant. And besides, I was a professional. With training and resources.

So here's the thing with training and resources: depression robs you of the clarity to use any of those skills or supports. I describe it as "Vaseline over the camera lens—the view is distorted but the object hasn't changed." Which is still way too much abstraction for the depressed person to deal with.

The quick story is that I met a great guy and got married at thirty-seven and could finally afford a child and then didn't get pregnant. Me, the girl who got pregnant right out of college while using two forms of birth control. The very first fraying threads of my depression began, as I look back, at my fortieth birthday party a week before my actual birthday. The photographs show me distracted and sad. I recall now my preoccupation with how maybe because I'd had an abortion at twenty-three I would never be allowed by the powers of the universe to ever get pregnant again. This is not normally the way I think, and finding it crazy, I mentioned it to no one.

On my actual birthday, after a week of compulsive potato chip eating and a flulike malaise, I took a pregnancy test that came back positive and began a panic attack that lasted for well over nine months. Thrilled but terrified. My father had just died on top of everything else, and I was having a hard time navigating this barren terrain of loss, again not adequately acknowledging any of it.

I quickly established a vision of how this "elderly prima

gravida" (the diagnosis in my chart indicating that I was pretty old for a first baby) was going to handle it. So what if I was in a panic? I was going to get on the Nautilus and the StairMaster till moments before birth. I would not miss a single day of work. I was on a psychiatric crisis team back then, and sometimes, in my office with a patient, I would put a protective hand over my belly, hoping I could drown out the things my little fetus was hearing. I worried. I became more superstitious. I listened to a lot of patients talk about how and why they had lost their children. I listened hard, as if the very act of listening was a talisman against tragedy.

A colleague told us over lunch one day that when they brought their second son home from the hospital, their older boy said, "That looks like it would fit just fine in the garbage disposal." I laughed along with everyone else, but the image stuck. My brain was roiling with dysregulation, imbalances that would later be fueled by the crush of hormones and Fentanyl and Dilaudid. Chemicals that were all a part of the C-section that I most assuredly did not want to have. The C-section was necessitated by a failure to progress, after an early scare resulted in two months of bed rest. I was unable to settle down.

Bed rest took me out of work, which made me feel helpless. I gained an enormous amount of weight. I watched Geraldo Rivera and the soaps and refused to answer the phone. While some women I knew were having professionally produced videos of their home births (wearing nothing but expensive French lingerie), I was yelling at anesthesia residents to "get out of my room and get me the attending *immediately*." I stomped around in a bloody johnny and kicked my mother and friends out of the hospital. I hummed loudly throughout the C-section because

I feared if I heard a word they said during the procedure, or heard the clanking of the instruments, I would lose my mind. I had observed too many emergency C-sections in nursing school and could not bear to imagine what was happening to my belly as I lay there trembling.

"Crazy" worsened as I hallucinated from the Dilaudid, but as a psychiatric professional, I knew I better not mention that there were tiaras atop my newborn's head. That I was seeing shifts in the pattern of the hospital room's wallpaper. Or that I was becoming paranoid. Angry. Goddammit, didn't I deserve for this one time to be perfect? I wouldn't let the nurses take my baby to the nursery because there had recently been mix-ups in another hospital and babies had been stolen. If it happened once, it could happen again. Another woman, also a profes-sional, had recently died from bleeding out after her C-section. *How much good did her professional standing do her? I thought.*

I made my nurse friends come up to my room and check my sheets for blood. I wouldn't walk the hallways unless my husband was there. I yelled at the staff for putting pacifiers in my baby's mouth. "This is for *you*, not the baby!" I bitched at the nurses. "You just don't want to hear her cry." I knew too much to be a patient, but the Vaseline was covering up my ability to look at anything from a reasonable professional vantage point either.

It was a quick jump from the image of a garbage disposal to the image of a microwave. A baby could fit in a microwave just like it could fit into a garbage disposal, right? Once when I worked in a restaurant, the cook put a whole trout in the micro-wave and we watched it explode. The eyes went first. Just the idea of it made it impossible for me to go into my kitchen once we got home from the hospital. I was discharged after five days in the hospital; the pediatrician wanted us to stay longer, and I now realize that while the baby was beautiful, healthy, and fine, the mother was not. I realize that he, as well as the OB team, figured I would probably be OK; I was a colleague, for god's sake. And I *was* OK, eventually. I do not want you as the reader to become anxious wondering how the whole microwave thing played out.

I managed my terror as best I could.

I did not want to put the baby in the microwave, I had no plan to put the baby in the microwave, but because it was *possible* to put a baby in a microwave, all I had to do was not go into the kitchen. The second my husband left for work in the morning, I called my mother. At eighty-five, she could barely walk or drive, but as long as the weather held out, she would come over. I have no idea what I would have done had she not come over. I could not go into the kitchen, which meant that I could not eat or drink myself, which would mean that I would not be able to nurse, and the nursing wasn't going well anyway, so I'd not have been able to get the supplemental formula, and it would have been kind of like my equivalent of the closet and the Benadryl.

My mother never asked what was going on. She just sat in the rocking chair where I placed it near the kitchen, and waited until I told her she could go home.

As an advanced practice nurse, I diagnosed postpartum depression in others. I was the person who called child protective services about *other* people. I had decided, in my fragile and depressed state, that my daughter would be taken away if anyone knew I was afraid of the microwave in my own kitchen. While I could easily have talked to any of my colleagues or found an antidepressant that might have been safe while nursing, I chose to keep this a secret. It was too crazy to bear and I had lost my moorings.

This is what it taught me: depression is like shallow flood-water around your ankles—it looks like nothing but the undertow can drag you away.

These secrets. Even my husband, a licensed social worker, as understanding and responsible as they come, had no idea. I felt he was shouldering enough of a burden while I stayed home on maternity leave, *doing nothing*. I had *never* not worked. Two months of bed rest and then a leave—again my perception was flawed. I needed to protect him from my failure. I could not share this. It wasn't fair to him, I reasoned. If the term can even be applied here.

He came home early one day to take me for a walk. It was an icy February and I was worried about falling; I felt I wasn't healing from the C-section but he insisted I get some fresh air. My mother was there for the baby. I ventured outside, clutching his arm, vulnerability was everywhere, I was not me anymore.

"I have to tell you something very serious," I said, stopping on the sidewalk. I told him about the microwave.

He could have laughed—who wouldn't be tempted to use a defense such as humor to protect against the idea that their wife was going mad—but of course he didn't. He took my shoulders and said very calmly, "You would never hurt that baby." My terror burst like a balloon and floated up into the gray February sky.

Can any of us get our heads around the unthinkable? My craziness stopped at tiaras and shifting wallpaper patterns where some might envision the devil. My irrepressible thoughts stopped at the microwave, where another woman not as fortunate might perseverate on something else. A bathtub. Or a small lake. I had resources and I wasn't living in a drug house. I had synapses that calmed and began refiring safely, efficiently. I soon returned to work, better for all this.

We cannot ignore the effects of hormones, of neurotransmitters, of imbalance. Of the things that we do under the influence of those potent chemicals. I am older now, devoid of these risks. The "complete hormonelessness" that poet Morya Donaldson[2] describes in "When I Am Old" provides a peace. No more PMS, no more postpartum. No more horrible life decisions during perimenopause. I have entered a quiet where, as I say to my patients, I am no stranger to the ravages and yes, I do know. Tell me.

1 Harvard Health Publications, January 2010.
2 Donaldson, Morya. *Selected Poems.* © Liberties Press, 2012.

NEVER, NOW, AND ALWAYS

Karen Lewis

week one

Anything that the new year promises hides beneath surfaces of champagne and dancing and unopened cookie-fortunes.

week three

A small blue plus sign appears on the test. Your almost three-year-old son is curled up in his fort of blankets and you snuggle in with him, trying to stay warm on a January morning. Your husband is working out of state, a couple weeks gone, a few nights home. It's been like this since summer. Your baby blues nudge you from somewhere invisible, long before the baby is born.

week four

You make an appointment at the clinic to confirm what you remember, New Year's Eve, when you'd mutually decided it was time to toss birth control into the trash and dream of another child.

week five

You are thrilled that your son will have a sibling. You worry about the months your husband was deployed overseas. What he might have been exposed to. The years you lived near a nuclear power plant. You listen to morning radio news and realize the whole world is probably doomed. You double-guess your choice to bring children into a fractured world. You are almost thirty-five, so you decide to get tested, to be sure your baby is okay.

All day, every day, nausea reminds you of seasickness. You and your son pretend you're in a boat of bubbles in the bathtub. You subsist on peanut butter, carrots, and macaroni. Safe harbor is weeks away.

weeks six, seven, eight, and nine

Your son loves stacking firewood and learns to count the pieces. He pretend-cuts with a toy chainsaw that was a gift for his third birthday. You take long walks in the woods, even on rainy afternoons, and wait for your man to return from sea. You feel isolated and alone. Some mornings, you attend an exercise class that offers friendship, childcare, and a safe playground.

week ten

You drive to the city to visit the medical center for state-of-the-art prenatal testing. The day before, you visit a dear friend. You became mothers the same year; her daughter and your son are playmates. Your friend is supportive and excited about your pregnancy. She confides that she still grieves for the child she could never conceive. She tells you that they hope to adopt again. She offers to watch your son while you go to the clinic. You park four blocks from the medical center and savor the long walk up a steep hill. The teaching hospital is busy, and you wait more than an hour for your turn. The CVS probe through your cervix feels like a thousand cramps. They can't seem to get the right tissue sample.

You realize it was a mistake to do this test. You should have waited a few weeks for amniocentesis. You try to phone your husband, but can't reach him. On the hundred-mile drive home, you're exhausted and stop along the highway to barf. Your son hands you his juice box and a toy tractor to cheer you up.

week eleven

Your husband returns from a distant state and tells you that he doesn't want to be so separated. He wants to live all together, up north. You close up your cottage and drive almost a thousand miles to the small port where he keeps the boat.

week twelve

Your husband works fourteen-hour days. He is also building a second boat and the bills keep coming in and he keeps pressing forward. One evening, you suggest a family day off. You want to explore the islands, or maybe Seattle. Whenever you try to talk about slowing down, it turns into an argument. His anger scares you. Therefore, you're not entirely upset that he is gone all day, every day.

Your son loves painting. His wild colors brighten up the drab décor of the transient motel. You feel like you're living in a movie set for a grim film about sad people doing bad things. On rainy days, you prolong every excursion to the grocery store, just to avoid the dreary motel room. You lack energy to play the way you once did. Your son begs to go for a bike ride, but you can't get it together. You are anxious about strangers, about strange noises outside on the sidewalk of this strange town where everything is gray and damp and bleak.

week thirteen

The medical center calls to say, "Your fetus is chromosomally normal." You are relieved. They ask if you want to know the gender. You reply that you want to be surprised. You grew up with two sisters and have no clue about raising a boy, let alone two. In fact, you're having issues with your husband. You glance with envy at other couples, who seem to be enjoying each other's company. You slowly slip into a thin, icy crevasse of doubts.

The person you now see in the mirror wears a faded blue bathrobe and baggy yoga tights, and she can't find her hairbrush. She has an extremely rough acne outbreak on her forehead and a rash on her swollen breasts.

week fourteen

You're trying to park your husband's heavy-duty pickup in a narrow slot outside the fast food place. You're eating for two, always hungry now that the morning sickness has abated. Your son wants to play in the happy fun zone. You like the happy fun zone, too. But there's a problem. It feels wet between your legs.

You notice blood seeping onto the truck seat. "Let's just drive through," you say. You try to make your voice cheerful, but something inside is falling apart.

"You promised we could play," the small boy says.

"Not today."

You order two fun-meals. Your boy is strapped in his astronaut-style car seat and you wonder how to protect him from whatever is about to happen while you hemorrhage to death in a fast food parking lot.

You're cramping and panicked. You don't know anyone in this town. Your husband is out at the islands. He can't be reached by phone. You wonder if you have the strength to drive back to the motel where you've been quasi-living for the past month. You could try the marine operator, but aren't sure what to say.

Your son is amazing. He entertains himself with French fries while you listen to a Dylan song on the radio that tells you how a woman can *break just like a little girl*. You vaguely remember seeing a hospital sign, somewhere on the other side of the harbor, but then—you can't think clearly at all—you realize it would be too weird for your son to go into an ER with his mommy bleeding like crazy from down there.

You arrive at the motel and try to climb down without your son seeing the crime-scene-sized bloodstains. He notices, of course.

"What's that, Mommy?"

"Must have spilled some ketchup," you lie.

You let him unlock the motel door, to buy distraction time. When you burst in, water is running full volume in the bathroom. Your husband comes out and grins. He whirls your son around in the air making helicopter noises.

"Weather picked up. Got a day off!" he says.

His steel-blue eyes miss nothing, though. He turns cartoons on the TV, plops your son on the bed with an excited bounce and offer of a blankie for a tent. Then, your husband pulls you into the bathroom. Your planet is swirling off-center. You don't need to pretend to be strong anymore. You're sobbing, and he holds you with a tenderness that you have forgotten. You collapse on the grimy floor, wishing the bathroom were a cave. He wraps his thick winter jacket around you.

week fifteen

Somehow you find yourselves at a small, under-equipped, rural hospital, where they bring a portable ultrasound into the ER. The radiologist tells you it is week fifteen. Miscarriages at this stage are common. Very common, they emphasize. They offer to let you wait it out on the cold steel table, until you can be seen by the ER doctor, who is busy with a heart attack victim. Or, they could call in the ob-gyn for a quick D and C. You say you don't want plan A or plan B, or a D and C, you just want everything to be normal. They say that normal is different for everyone. They tell you that your baby is a girl.

One of the deckhands takes your son out to play bouncy ball. In the ER cubicle, a flimsy curtain pulses in and out with the unseen breath of a heating vent. Your husband holds your face against his. You notice his tears. His hands smell faintly of Ivory soap and diesel. You imagine you're on the boat, cruising out to a difficult day's work in stormy seas. He whispers, "Whatever happens, everything will be okay." Your husband is no stranger to suffering, having endured two special forces tours of duty in combat zones.

You want better than *okay*. The physician comes in, speaks quickly; there's another, more pressing emergency.

"At this stage, we just let nature take its course," he says. "There is zero chance of your infant's survival if she's born now. We hear a normal heartbeat. Sometimes bleeding just happens. Go home and rest in bed."

Your mind turns over and over.

"Or wait here, and see what happens," the doctor invites. "You have insurance, right?"

You refuse to let your daughter die in a hospital a thousand miles from home. You've seen it in movies where women hide in the bathroom and miscarry and then return to the real world and get on with life. You think, *I can handle this*. You struggle to calm your breathing, to slow the churning of blood through the superhighway of your arteries.

Your husband turns out to be like a superman in an emergency. He's used to emergencies, stress, complicated emotions, contingency plans, pretending that things are okay when they're not. That afternoon, he transports you safely back to the motel room, stopping en route to buy a giant box of maxi pads. He helps your son turn the motel table into a new fort. Your husband is reluctant to leave you alone, but you insist. You're drifting in and out of sleep. He pulls extra covers over you, offers a glass of water. Your son brings your fun-meal toy and tucks his blue teddy bear in next to you. Then, the guys go out to do guy things: check on the boat and find ice cream. When you wake the next morning, you're not bleeding anymore.

weeks sixteen, seventeen

The next weeks are a blur of reading *The Little Engine That Could* hundreds of times to your son. This alternates between looking for Waldo and playing with puzzles that distract you moment-by-moment. Your husband hires a bookkeeper so all you have to do is rest. You are on medication to keep your muscles relaxed. But you feel tense, have migraines, don't know how to cope.

week eighteen

You decide that you should move back to your real home, that living in the motel isn't safe. You drive twenty hours and your mom comes to stay for a week. The apple trees blossom. You are still carrying your unborn daughter. You wonder if she will ever be able to climb an apple tree with her brother.

week nineteen

Your husband heads back up north to work, because there are payments to make and a crew to pay. It's all for the security of the family, but you wonder if any of it is worth it. Now, of course, there's the hospital bill, and another hospital bill because you started bleeding again. You are prescribed complete bed rest. Your sister comes to visit. She's your little sister, but now she takes care of you and plays with your son. She cheers you up with interesting conversations and she's a great cook, which is awesome because you've been forbidden to stand for longer than five minutes at a time. No more walks in the forest, chopping wood, building fires. No more exercise class. No more anything that made you happy. No more wine, beer, coffee, or sex.

week twenty

Your muscles atrophy from being on bed rest. A neighbor brings the mail. Your parents take your son to stay with them for a while. You are glad because he will have fun. You are lonesome, even though your husband now works from a harbor close to home. You rest and daydream. Friends send you cards and bring small gifts that help you get through the ever-longer days of springtime.

week twenty-one

One afternoon you feel strong, and decide to tackle one load of laundry. You have always found refuge in the simple repetitive task of washing and folding. A fancy, flowered envelope falls from one of your husband's jacket pockets. Graceful but unfamiliar handwriting, addressed to him at one of those instant post box places. You can't help yourself. You read it, while the dryer tumbles around and around and around, and you sink to the floor. Around and around, you are tumbling, hating him, hating yourself. Hating this woman whose name you recall him having mentioned as someone he'd known years before.

week twenty-two

You're freaking out on the inside. Your exterior has turned to stone, like a statue. A goddess statue, with certain body parts missing, strewn across a disaster zone. You bide your time, not sure what to do.

You want to confront your husband but wonder, really, what's the point? Part of you wants him to run away with her, leaving you and your son and your baby girl in peace. You feel betrayed in a way you can't put words to. You want to torch his clothes. You want to send a cryptic postcard to the return address on the envelope. You read the letter multiple times for clues. Then you hide it, this unwanted beast, this rabid rat of evidence. You hide it until you can figure out how to destroy it.

Your son returns home from his grandparent getaway and you fall into a rhythm of *Where's Waldo?* and *The Little Engine That Could*.

week twenty-three

You are too embarrassed to confide in anyone, not even your sister. You are no fun anymore. Of course he found someone else. Someone to take dancing, surfing, to dinner. Someone to share an entire conversation without interruption or crying. Someone who can enjoy sex without worrying about miscarriage. You assume that sex with her must be incredible, way better than anything you ever experienced with him.

week twenty-four

Your husband arrives home early one afternoon. It's obvious you've been crying, but he doesn't seem to notice. Or, maybe he actually doesn't look at you anymore. You are not the same person he married, the one who ran in races and swam in big waves in tropical waters way off the grid. The one who bicycle-commuted thirty miles a day. That girl is gone. Now you understand multiple layers of the word *invalid*.

But wait, he is carrying a big pizza box and your son is behind him, laughing and holding a bag of popsicles and special tea that Mommy is allowed to drink. You slip away into the bathroom and wash your face. You change into a thin summer dress that used to make you feel sexy and desirable. When you return to the main room, your boy says, "Mommy, you look pretty." You lie on your side on the couch and allow yourself to be taken care of. That night, after your son is tucked in and asleep, you pull the letter out of its hiding place and throw it in your husband's face.

week twenty-five

You realize you are living with a complicated guy who is running from his own fears. His anger is bigger than yours, and he has more experience than you in methods of marital deceit. He promises that *it doesn't mean anything*, and he rests his shaggy head with his little-boy-blue eyes next to your belly. You hold him like a soldier might hold a grenade. Breathing in, breathing out, wanting to believe that everything will be okay.

week twenty-six

Things aren't okay. You're in the hospital again and tired of trying to be strong. Part of you wants to be a cave woman, to wander near a river until she collapses, to let nature take its course. A very kind nurse mentions that if you make it to thirty weeks gestation, your baby has good chances for survival. She explains how moms in labor are transported to a special hospital in the city, where they're able to save infants smaller than three pounds. You owe it to your daughter to hold on to this idea.

week twenty-seven

You're not a fun mommy anymore. If there is one thing that your son is teaching you, it's the value of make-believe.

week thirty

Your daughter is born at the lifesaving urban hospital, and spends the next ten weeks in neonatal intensive care. You are surrounded with families whose children are in very delicate and complicated conditions. Your husband coaches you back to your feet, out the door, and inspires you to be stronger than you thought possible.

Your new normal is to live in a Ronald McDonald house with your son, a cheerful place full of families in crisis. You are in the dinosaur room and your husband becomes a road warrior, traveling back and forth from San Francisco to the far north, and he promises that things will be better once you are all at home again.

week forty

You bring your baby girl home from the intensive care nursery just when the apples are ripening. Your husband takes your son out on long hikes looking for birds or bears. Indian summer days slip into a routine. The sanctuary of home soothes you, while the erratic emotional terrain of the marriage frightens you. You figure out how to avoid discussing anything volatile.

week fifty-four

You want to return to work, and wonder if this is possible with your baby still fragile. You meet other moms going it alone. The doctor says she is growing just fine, and all her vital signs are normal, a healthy almost six-month-old. She is like a small angel and you love the hours in the middle of the night when you sit and nurse and rock and sing lullabies. Your husband is gone long hours and weeks at a time. A week home, a week away. You decide not to ask too many questions because he is a good provider and because you know you cannot handle any more anger or any more pain.

week sixty-five

Your sister comes to visit and she senses something is wrong, but you can't bring yourself to confide. Your son turns four. He and your husband build a new picnic table and you host a happy family party with everyone you know, lots of balloons, cake, potluck, laughter. You skate on top of a lake of gratitude. You know there is an abyss beneath, but you just have no idea how deep, how murky, or if you will survive.

week seventy-five

You're living day to day, until one afternoon, the phone rings. With tragic, surreal news. There's been an accident. You don't understand what happened. They transported him from the boat to the hospital, but he could not be saved. The crew, his friends, everyone is in shock. Of course, you don't believe it. A friend flies you up to the remote coastal town where you enter the hospital and expect to find your husband making a joke about his accident. They tell you he has been moved to the funeral home. These words bounce off you like there is a titanium hull around you. Words and emotions crisscross in many directions without making sense. You try to explain life and death to your son.

The Coast Guard tells you, "So often up here, people go missing. We can't even retrieve their bodies." You feel a touch of comfort in those words. You sign the first of many papers that will allow you to take what remains of your husband home. You climb into the boat and take his personal gear, his jacket, the ship's log. If there are other random love letters, you don't notice them. You give the crew authority to move the boat out of the harbor. You don't want to be doing all these things. You're catapulted to a planet called grief. Your children's new, favorite story becomes *Where's Daddy?*

week seventy-seven

People you love and people you have never met before come from near and far to pay their respects at the memorial. Your husband's closest friends have navigated the boat five hundred miles from there to home, with his ashes on board. You are in a daze. Your son plays with friends in the meadow. Apple trees and wild rhododendron bloom, daffodils everywhere. A massive bonfire. Slight breeze from the north. Jets fly in formation, dispatched from some unseen military base, swooping in low and then vanishing. His friends you'd never met, he'd never spoken of, from that secret band of brothers. Ravens noisy in the forest. Your infant daughter swaddled close, her deep blue eyes searching this sea of strangers for signs of her daddy.

week eighty-two

Your daughter crawls but doesn't walk, yet. The children are leading you, because they're hardwired to believe in the future. Every day brings new discovery. A sea lion, dead, in tide pools at the beach. Shells tumbling and turning and castles built in damp sand, then claimed by high tide.

"You blow the candle and you make a wish." Your son explains the ritual to his sister at her first birthday. The three of you are sitting outside. The cake is homemade, chocolate-from-a-box, a flavor your husband might have called *bittersweet*. With whipped cream frosting. You all blow, and the flame goes out. A thin plume of smoke swirls up to the sapphire sky. And that is how you move through the moments.

THE DAY I AM NOT OK

Jenny Kanevsky

*I*t is the day I am not OK. Driving on a road I drive daily. Each street corner, place of business, pothole etched in my consciousness. I feel the road rise and fall by the water tower, a gentle movement, the anticipation of the big hill, braking as I approach the YMCA, wave at friends in passing cars, take in the stunning Seattle city skyline.

That day, I almost lose my life. That day, I save my life, and my baby's. My older son is at preschool, an intimate in-home school. I, a seemingly competent adult, drive home with my baby. When I dropped off my three-year-old—my happy, spirited child—I went in with the baby and everyone cooed. I wore a mask—an ill-fitting mask that makes it hard to breathe. And then, somewhere between the drop-off and the corner store— the one with the giant cow on the roof—a switch flips.

Fatigue and helplessness wash over me, not in waves but in a tsunami of unexpected force. Tears spill down my cheeks. I grip the wheel with such urgency, my hands ache. They are white with rage. And I drive. I sit at the wheel in a massive weapon, a frightening place for a woman who suddenly thinks, *Maybe it would be better if I were just dead.*

I am at Morgan Street. The always-empty Pizza Hut to my left, the food bank to my right. And then I see it, to the exclusion of all else, a red and white semitruck. *A big truck for this road,* I think. *I've never seen such a truck on this road. Maybe it's for me. I'll just swerve. I'll let my car drive into it. It will be easy. It will be over.* Just over, the overwhelmed-ness, the sadness, the exhaustion. And then I'm seized by terror. *What if it's just an accident and we survive? Or I survive and the baby dies? I'm in charge of this person. My husband would hate me. How am I a mother? I am horrible. I am dangerous.*

And in an instant, the truck passes. I'm still driving. I glance in the rearview mirror and see my baby in his car seat. We are alive, there is no crash, no screeching of lights, no ambulance, no disappearing into the crunch of metal against metal. We pass the library, go through another light. People wait at the bus stop. Runners pound the sidewalk. We approach the downhill.

This is not good. These thoughts are not OK. I am not OK.

I cry all day, tears flowing freely but with no release. They just make me heavier. Prozac flows through my bloodstream, as it has for over a decade and throughout both pregnancies. I should be fine. I'm on antidepressants. I've done this before. I should be fine. I should be fine. I am not fine. I cry and cry and cry.

"I think something's wrong," I tell my husband. "I've been crying all day."

"You just had a baby, dear. You're tired."

"No, this is different."

"OK." Sometimes, he says OK when he's not sure what else to say.

"If I feel like this tomorrow, I'm calling the doctor."

"OK." And then he says, "Whatever you need." He *is* listening. He *does* hear me.

"I think something's wrong. I'm scared. I think I need help."

He hugs me. "It's going to be fine." He is at a loss, too.

I wake up the next morning and am heavier still. Fogged in. I could let another day pass. Every movement is endless. Days are lost with a new baby. Moments are eternal. But I call my doctor. I force myself. It takes every ounce of energy to navigate the receptionist.

"Yes, I'm a current patient. I just had a baby. I'm not doing well. I need to talk to someone—a nurse or my doctor."

I wait. I wonder for a strange second what they are doing. Does an alarm go off when they get a call like this? Do they hit a panic button? Likely, they are behind closed doors, speaking in hushed, urgent tones, talking about me. Finally, I hear a familiar voice. My doctor's PA. I can see her in my mind. I am ashamed. I am lost. How will I say these words, how will I tell her what I am thinking? And yet, somehow—in whispers—I do.

"Yesterday, I thought bad things. I was in the car with the baby. I cried all day. I'm so tired."

My voice is dead. I cannot admit that I thought about driving into a semitruck, thought about tons of metal crashing down on me and my baby. The baby I am supposed to protect.

"Where are you, Jenny? Are you home alone?"

"No. My husband is here. He's working downstairs."

"Where's the baby?"

"He's asleep. He's OK."

I realize why she is asking. She is afraid I will hurt him, or myself. I have already said as much. Oh my God. I could. I couldn't. I cannot be that person. I am not that person.

"Why don't you come to the office? You can be here with us, not be alone."

"I'm not alone. My husband's here."

I am hazy and out of focus but I feel relief. I am really not alone. I have told someone. They know. I can't un-tell now.

"I won't do anything," I say. "I mean, I know what you mean, and I won't." I can't say it out loud. I can't say, *"I won't kill my baby. I won't kill myself."*

This cannot be happening. I am the worst mother ever.

"OK. Hold on. Just sit, can you? I'm going to talk to the doctor."

Two minutes pass and my doctor, my sweet, tiny five-foot-tall doctor, gets on the line. Her voice is strong but calm. She missed both deliveries but was there for everything else: the preeclampsia and bed rest with my first child; the car accident with my second child, when I was hospitalized with placental abruption and put on bed rest; the month I gained over ten pounds and she gently, without judgment, talked about her own eating issues, planting a small, fragile seed that helped me pay attention to my body without hating it. She is gentle and caring.

When she'd first heard this baby's heartbeat, she was overwhelmed. "Listen," she whispered and her eyes sparked with amazement. I remember asking how she got so excited over every baby, every heartbeat. And she said, "So many things have to fall into place to make this happen. So many things have to work. It truly is a miracle." She loves her job. She cried with me when I miscarried after my first child. Actual tears. She looks me in the eye, always.

"Jenny. What's going on?"

I start crying again. Sobs rack my body. She waits. I tell her what I told the PA.

"OK, are you going to hurt yourself? Do you want to hurt the baby?"

I want to be sick.

"No. I won't. I won't do anything. I'm so tired."

"OK. I want you to call this psychiatrist. He's a postpartum specialist. He's very good. I'll call him as soon as we hang up so you won't have to wait for an appointment." The care in her voice is overwhelming. I cannot stop crying. I'm nodding at the phone. I manage an audible response.

"You can always come here. You can sit with someone in a room, bring the baby. You should not be alone."

"My husband is here. I'm not alone."

"OK. Call me in a few hours. Leave word at the front desk. I want you to check in every few hours. I mean it. I'm calling the psychiatrist now."

Twenty minutes later, her PA calls back. The psychiatrist is waiting. When I call, he answers the phone. No voice mail, just him. I have an appointment in two days. I am relieved and pan-icked at the same time. How will I make it another hour, another night, another two? How will I drive there? How will I go out in public? I'm both a shell of a person and a monster, taking up space, spilling out of sloppy clothing. Nothing fits me. I'm huge and awkward. I'm pale, un-showered, eyes red-rimmed, my breasts are swollen, my face is puffy, my body is thick and full. And empty.

His voice soothes. He tells me he can help, that I'm not alone, that he will see me soon. I cry the whole time talking to him, sobs of gut-wrenching relief.

This is not how I should be feeling two weeks after having a baby, my beautiful second son. I'm fortunate to have him. I already had one miscarriage. I'm forty. I'm in a daze of fatigue and shame. My mother is here now. She hovers over me, cooing, watching me breastfeed. Watching me *try* to breastfeed. *Try* to sleep. *Try* to be mother of both of my children with different and opposing needs. I cannot stand the watching. Please, stop watching.

I become obsessed with not having anything to wear to the appointment. Nothing fits me, only maternity clothes. I could easily wear them but instead, I'm frantic. Anxiety consumes me. I can't sleep. I can't think about anything but what I'm going to wear. It is the most important thing. It swallows me. I somehow go to a consignment shop and buy giant black linen pants and a red linen blouse. I don't look like myself, which seems right. I don't feel like myself. Everything is wrong. Nothing is me.

The psychiatrist is exactly who he needs to be. He is kind but brilliant. He knows. He explains what I'm feeling. This is not a therapy session like I have had in the past, where I talk and we go back and forth. He asks questions, I cry and nod. He talks. I'm a stain of un-ironed red and black linen on his Queen Anne sofa. He gently explains the fight or flight physiological changes in my body that are causing me to feel so overwhelmed, causing the anxiety. He explains how my history of depression predisposed me to this. He gives me a prescription for clona-zepam, an antianxiety medication. He says with my heightened protective maternal instincts, my adrenaline will continue to surge. I will be anxious. I won't sleep. And, as there is no real danger—there are no predators, no threats—there will be no release. But my body doesn't know that, it is just on alert. Awake. Panicked.

He also says, "You need to find a way to sleep six hours a night. Uninterrupted." I almost laugh. Almost. It would have been my first laugh since the delivery room banter.

Six hours. No matter what. He tells me my body needs to maintain even levels of melatonin. Don't turn on lights while changing diapers, use dark-colored lightbulbs, and other things. *How will I ever find dark-colored lightbulbs?* I feel another panic coming. *That's an errand. I can't do an errand.* It doesn't even occur to me that my husband will do it.

Most of all, I'm nursing. Nursing, nursing, nursing, and nursing. I think, *there's no way I can sleep six hours. And nurse.*

With my first son, colicky and never sleeping more than two or three hours at a time, I was wrecked. I couldn't put him down to sleep alone. He'd wake up, he'd cry. He had to be on me, touching me. I slept during the day. I nursed in the morning and we'd fall asleep together. Every day. I slept when he slept. We'd nurse in bed at night, and I'd fall asleep with him on my breast, my neck impossibly crooked. We'd sleep, nurse some more, sleep. I can't do this now. I have a three-year-old. I have responsibilities. I have too many responsibilities.

Somehow, despite my being a mess, crying, lost, unable to form complete sentences, the psychiatrist doesn't *tell* me how to get the six hours of sleep. He doesn't tell me what to do. Anyone can see I am unable to make decisions, to make a plan. But, he doesn't say it. He doesn't say, "You might want to consider not nursing, or not nursing at night." He doesn't say it, because even though he is the doctor and I am the patient, I am also the mother. It is not his decision to make. I am already thinking, *If I stop nursing, I'll be able to sleep. I'll take this medicine, I'll sleep. Tim will feed the baby. With formula. And it may actually be OK. Maybe, I'll want to live.* I don't tell him though. I feel ashamed. I should be nursing my baby. I should be.

He says the medication will work in three to five days. And slowly, it will work better, and more, as the weeks pass. This is glorious news because, as a person with depression, I am all too familiar with waiting for antidepressants. Three to five weeks is typical for any relief. If you're lucky. He says I will feel better soon; with the medication and sleep, I will start to feel better. And I believe him.

I come home from the appointment drained. My mother is there and the pressure to breastfeed—she breastfed me for over two years—is suffocating. I take the baby and nurse. I've been gone two hours, so my breasts are swollen and heavy and he is hungry. My mother has the grace to allow us privacy and I tell my husband what the doctor said. He is calm, listens, seems less worried. He doesn't process things like I do; he thinks, is quiet. He is, as always, an anchor for me when I flail and cannot come up for air.

And then I say it out loud.

"My mom is leaving soon. I want to stop breastfeeding. I don't care what she thinks. I need to sleep. Can you do nights?"

"Of course I can. It's not your mother's choice," he says. "If this is what you need, I'll support you. And you don't have to wait for her to leave. You can stop now." The words are barely out of his mouth and I'm sending him to the store for formula.

He loved feeding our older son. When I stopped nursing at ten months, or when I pumped, my husband gave him his bottle, gently rocked him to sleep. I could hear his soft whispers in the night, soothing our son. He is a wonderful, nurturing father. I am blessed. We are blessed.

My mother sees the formula and doesn't say anything, at least not with words. I know she disapproves, but she's leaving and it's not her baby and I am losing my mind. I am an adult, although I haven't felt like one in weeks. I am suddenly empowered; it's a tiny feeling under all the others, but it's there.

My baby boy takes the bottle with a passion. He is hungry and sucks away on Avent nipples. He is happy. He is eating. I feel nothing but relief. I love him and wanted to nurse him, but I'm empty. I'm more exhausted than I ever thought I could be and I want to sleep and live and smile again. My breasts hurt, but I sleep. I am engorged and miserable, but I sleep. I take the medication and in a few days, I feel less crazed, less scared, less like bugs are crawling under my skin. I start to feel more like a tired new mom with a beautiful baby boy. I have an older son who wants to help, to hold his brother, to coo at him, to play. I am a tired new mom with two healthy kids and a husband who is supportive and willing to share the nurturing, the caretaking, the everything.

Several weeks pass, maybe a month. Time is not the same with a new baby. I see the doctor weekly. He is pleased with my decision to bottle-feed. I tell him I'm sleeping. He smiles. He seems proud of me. Happy for me. I am proud of me. I am swimming in the black linen pants and red blouse. I never wear them again.

I feel better daily. And one day, maybe today, I am going to be OK.

MAKING TEA WITH PRESSED LEAVES

Melissa Uchiyama

I'm so relieved you were but a baby but O, your inno-cent skin scorched, made to know searing pain. I wanted to disappear in my disgust, melt down in one slick puddle of oil. I burned you quite badly, baby, my buddy.

In one moment I wanted to feel helpful, in control, success-ful, not needy, not recovering, not dealing with any postpartum malarkey. In a gust of new energy, I offered to make my visiting mother tea. She wasn't simply in for a long weekend, but to stay for over a month. She'd received the approval for her Family Medical Leave of Absence to sail through time zones, meeting me in the Far East. I needed to show her that not only was I fine with a second kid, in *Japan* (not too tired, certainly not feeling "blue"), but I could even help *her*.

"Oh, just sit down, Mom. What'll it be? Coffee? Tea? Can I whip you up some ginger snaps?" while still in 4:00 p.m. stale leggings and hair submitting to bare necessity. It didn't make the cut. Bursts of energy were all I had, time-released prenatals helping me nurse. Having my mom visit for two months right after giving birth to my second? It was going to be like Canyon Ranch, or, at worst, more bonding over, "What's all this fuss about colic and where shall we get our nails painted?" I knew, but must have forgotten, how painful exhaustion and keeping it together could be. I was frenetic because I had to be. I think I actually *was* okay, unless I felt attacked or criticized, less than perfect. In a country where I still couldn't fill out the most basic of paperwork, I often felt confused and left out of all the good information. I missed knowing that my *ku*, or ward, provides six sessions of babysitting. I could have gotten air, could have chased down a new nursing bra to replace my ratty-tatties from three years ago. I could have gone out for a quick lunch, alone. I could have maybe felt pretty and successful at least a few of those times. I don't remember much except what pictures are on Facebook. And the disaster.

But wasn't I strong to hold you, baby, and do nearly everything? I could breastfeed anywhere—whilst walking dogs, whizzing on rush hour trains through *Shinjuku*, up in the whipping air on a Ferris wheel. At the sink, while also brushing my teeth. Wherever. So I became accustomed to holding you. I could have held you through the whole of Japan while giving your sister pigtails. It was easier than you crying, so I made tea.

I held you as the metal French provincial blue teapot passed over your right calf, forged, and fired your feather-delicate skin. I branded you "new mother disaster," and when you didn't cry, I hoped all might be well. Maybe I imagined the graze. Maybe it was like the poof of powder. Just wipe it off. Just before the kettle cry, I pictured, thought about not saying anything. It was that humiliating, that sad.

But no. I saw it like smoke out of a barrel. First pink, then instantly, shockingly white. And you did not even cry at first— must have been shock over being branded for the sake of tea. On Mother's Day. I decided I better send back every card. I can be no mother. This lousy wretch was ashamed and altogether inconsolable. "Don't even call me a mom," I thought, moving ashen, room to room. I'll have to give it all back.

I called our English-speaking pediatrician. "What do I *do?*" in my smallest voice. I was under a chair, tail tucked. Talk me down from the bridge. I hid behind the idea that I was simply overtired, exhausted. Things were harder now that I had two. You can't just *nap.* Yes, burning my child must mean I need time for me, time to sleep properly. Something had to give. Something beautiful broke.

It was good my mom was there. It would have been hard not to lie.

I never told my sister-in-law. I would have omitted it from anyone, but the wrapped leg was telling. The principal and nurse of my daughter's school asked about it. I cheerfully brushed it off while my cheeks felt hot like sunburn, an internal scowl. I was more than vague when cornered. "He hurt himself," as if he were a cowboy, a bandit renegade barreling shotgun of a toddler at reckless speeds. Really, he was barely filling my arms, tush sitting in the smallest diapers. I celebrated our first Mother's Day together with him wrapped in liniment and sterile gauze. I gave him a second-degree burn. His worried sister looked on. I had let her down, too, in hurting her baby, as she called him. "How did it *happen?*" Her droopy, inquiring voice grieved. She wanted to know everything.

Deflated and raw, I took him to the dermatologist the next day. His leg was dressed in those peculiar hard plastic Band-Aids to protect the slow drip of skin healing, a hidden kneeling down in church when it's really time to sing. Moss mixed with mold growing up a wall. I damaged my boy. This "do not disturb" Band-Aid was not supposed to come off until a sign from God, until all oozy woozy sadness had passed.

That was more or less what the pediatric nurse told me on the phone. I had to buy this and put it on. Do not take it off in all capitals, "DO NOT." But the next day, here we were. I felt we needed to show someone more than my shame. *Take him.* I was with my mom, now seated across from the Japanese derma-tologist. Maki, our family's close friend and my daughter's godmother, played translator.

"Why is she asking so many questions? Why is she asking this again? Just help him!" Around and around we went, up over across that iron teapot. What was I doing before? On what side did I hold him? What kind of tea was I making? Have I done this before? She took notes. I used profanity. I had to. I needed help. And shade. I was nervous for my boy and deeply ashamed. I realized sometime later, while reporting to my husband, that she was checking my story, making sure there were no holes—that would be abuse.

The nurse peeled back my special sticker and everyone—doc, two nurses, mom, kids, receptionists, waiting room breaths—listened, and got a good look at what stupid, sad thing I did. Without warning or translated-anything, she popped the blister!

The *one* thing every site said not to do! There, next to my own mom, and kids I let down, I muttered, *"Bitch."* I may have said it a few times. She smiled and almost seemed to laugh with her nurses. They always seem to do this here—laugh when I am upset. I think they think it helps.

The doctor, white jacketed, clear-faced, smoothed on a generous dollop of medicine like it could have been custard. It was like taffy, pulled, or a smoothing of soft Alouette cheese on pepper crackers. He was dressed with Egyptian cotton gauze and secured with white medical tape we also took home. I cried teacups full of care. "Whatever they think of me, we are being helped," I thought. He would be okay.

We came back every day for two weeks. Every day like it was both the hospital and my detention center. Off with our shoes, and on with their peach, bland, shitty slippers. Every day having to remember socks because, "Oh my gosh, it's a dermatologist's office. What if some flaky scaly man has toe fungus and I have to slide my bare foot into his slipper?" Every day of taking out insurance cards and not straying too far from the neighborhood so I could make it to his medicinal lifeline, and to my reminder that I messed up. Weeks of every day on my best tired mother behavior, because the doctor must still be required to watch me and take notes.

Then, quite suddenly, just as summer roared with humidity, the doctor announced good news. I understood it first in Japanese, as she examined his shrinking site out from under the bandage. Her nurse repeated, then wrote it down. "Treatment will now be every other day, then every few days." I whooped and hugged his wide-eyed head to my chest, thanking the doc profusely.

Just three sessions after that, his leg healed, as baby skin heals quite remarkably. There is no mark, not a trace, not even in the right light. The cells are all new, with no scab, no scar or discoloration.

Now it's just me who must heal my damaged dermis, my mistake-making-mother skin. And whereas I thought I was solely responsible for treating my own wounds, the ones that burned each of my layers of skin and heart, I realize there is a team. If and when I muster the courage to get better, to ask for help, then I feel the love of community, past the raised-brow concern of the dermatologist. Past the suggestions and "ought-tos" from the put-together mamas, including my own. I hold my arms up, even with backed-up milk ducts deep in my armpits. There is freedom in saying, "Yeah, maybe I need help," even if you choke on laughter, choke back tears. Or, hey, let them fall.

There is the enveloping hug of family, the acoustic accompaniment of literary mothers, the ones who also aren't ashamed to drop the Band-Aids, even in front of Shame, in front of Perfection. The Band-Aids are only trash in the shadow of healing. I find the pots of black, jasmine, mint-whatever tea anyone is happy to make for me. Deep regret and then blisters, goopy ointment, and a falling away. O smooth over me with liniment, my dears. Bind me up with love. Who wants shame? I only call on healing, reconstructing love, and for my next Mother's Day, a double-dipper *vat* of Neosporin because sometimes stupid accidents happen. Sometimes a poor, tired mother looks away or misjudges distance or her own emotions. Sometimes, may I repeat, you just need to ask someone to make the fucking tea.

MY PERSONAL OCEAN
OF DEPRESSION

Laura Miller Arrowsmith

*I*t was easy. It was a lovely, romantic, beautiful idea. My husband agreed to it right away. We had adopted our first daughter from China, and the experience was glorious, divinely ordained, almost spiritual. And now. Now I spoke these words to my husband: "I have enough love in my heart for a second child." We imagined how the two would bond, two sisters from China, connecting in ways that no one would understand, loving us. Everyone smiling. The family photo was my favorite fantasy. Two doting parents. Two adorable little girls held in their laps, radiating love and warmth and peace.

All the long walks with our first daughter in the stroller. My husband and I walking together, speaking about the future. Making plans about the girls. We could do bunk beds eventually, they could learn Chinese, we would all cook dumplings together. Fun. That's what it was going to be. Fun. It was easy to be giddy, imagining all the family outings: the zoo, the park next to the library, oh and the family story time at the library. Yes, this was going to complete us. We would be a full-fledged family just as soon as we got those tickets to China.

The social worker warned us. Don't take your first daughter with you to China. Leave her with your parents. This is your only chance to be with your second daughter alone. You'll need this time to bond with her. But no. That just didn't feel right to us. No, we wanted to do this all together. We would all be there to meet her. It would be a group effort. A big welcome party for our newest member.

China was hot. It was June in Changsha, and it was simply the hottest time of the year in the hottest city. We fed our three-year-old ice-cream bars every two hours as we pushed her along in a stroller between stretches of shade, up and down the crowded, noisy street. It was almost time. Almost time to welcome a new little daughter, a new sister. The family portrait would be complete. We dodged cars and cyclists and wound our way through vegetable markets and teashops, killing time until the hour of our meeting.

And then there we all were. In a waiting room in a tall building on a random street. My husband and I staring at the clock. Our three-year-old daughter looking out the window. Waiting for one hour, then two hours, then two and a half.

And there she was. She was brought in by an adoption assistant, someone to help with the transition for our new little daughter between her foster family and us.

So beautiful and so small and fragile and vulnerable. Wearing a petite red and white flowered top with little red pants. She was placed in my arms, all teary-eyed and confused. And I had my first daughter sit next to me as we held her one-year-old sister together. Together, all of us now. Love, warmth, peace, unity. The family portrait completed. We made our way back to the hotel room, tired, curious, full of anticipation.

We joked and thought how cute it was that this new little daughter only wanted to be held by my husband. How sweet— Daddy's girl. In fact, she cried intensely every time I touched her or came near her. But she settled into my husband's arms just fine. A picture of contentment and ease. That was convenient, because something was going horribly wrong with my first daughter. Somehow, without me knowing when it started exactly, she began hitting me. She hit me in the elevator. She punched me during mealtime. She hit me and yelled hysterically during bath time. If I came within three inches of my second daughter, both daughters would cry and scream violently. Things were spiraling out of control and I was becoming hot and sweaty and nervous and confused.

The adoption agent came to our hotel room. It was evening. He needed paperwork. Signatures. He had a ream of forms to fill out and complete. It all had to be done immediately. But something was going wrong with our family. All four of us were crying, screaming, clawing at each other. We hadn't slept well, meals weren't working out, I was fantasizing about prying the window open on the fourteenth floor and jumping out. The agent looked confused. He kept insisting that we should relax, try to settle down, sign the papers, and he would be on his way.

We needed to get out of China. Things would be better at home. Our own beds. Our own food. Our own routine. That's what we needed. We held on to that hope, that promise. This would all settle down when we got home.

The trip home: disastrous. Everyone sick—bronchitis, coughing, aching, fevers, crying, screaming. Three missed flights. Hours and hours of waiting in vinyl chairs while both daughters cried and screamed, arms flailing, suitcases and bags being dragged behind us, banging into other passengers, into flight attendants. Standing in impossibly long lines trying to understand where to go when a flight had been missed. Guangzhou, Hong Kong, California, New Jersey, Virginia. Calling my father long-distance and sobbing and sobbing into the phone. We just wanted to get home.

And then finally—home. Suitcases unpacked. Everyone into warm baths and then sitting at the table eating scrambled eggs, Cheerios, juice, pancakes. We could finally breathe a sigh of calm and relief. Back to normal. Back home.

But something was still wrong. I would reach for my newest little daughter to hold her and my oldest would fly out of nowhere, smacking me in the arm and stomach. My three-year-old was vigilant and watchful, making sure I never got near my one-year-old.

And then my husband went back to work and I was home alone with my girls. Although I had jet lag and was still coughing and wheezing from bronchitis, I was ready to bond with my little one. But she wanted nothing to do with me. I would touch her arm and she would recoil. I would smile and wiggle my fingers at her and she would look away and cry. Once I made a little progress and held her on my lap for a minute, but my three-year-old was right there waiting for me, screaming crazily and smacking me in the face.

I sat on the floor for hours and hours every day between two crying, screaming children. One crying because she didn't want to be near me, the other crying because she wanted to punish me. I began crying too. I began talking to myself in front of the girls. Things like, "You don't like Mommy do you?" and "Why are you punishing Mommy like this?"

It was so painful to be simultaneously rejected by one child and punished violently by another child that I began scratching myself. I scratched my arm so hard that it would bleed. I imagined throwing my child against the closet door until she lost consciousness. I called my husband on the phone repeatedly while he was at work. I would cry and cry and tell him something was very wrong and that I wasn't sure I could hang on for much longer like this.

I made a list of friends to call but would have to hang up mid-dial because I was sobbing too hard to be intelligible. One friend called to say that some of them wanted to arrange a baby shower. When would be a good date? I could only answer in a low growl, "No . . . no . . . not yet . . . we're not ready."

I tried calling my mother, raising the red flag, letting her know I was falling apart, my family was disintegrating. But her words were shards of glass: "Why can't you just relax and enjoy your children? You've always been overly sensitive." I stopped using the phone. I stopped going grocery shopping because I would sob and sob as I walked up and down the aisles. When my husband came through the front door at night, I would have my purse ready and my car keys in hand and not even utter a word as I got in my car and sped away from the house, leaving him with our children. I would go to the movies and stuff popcorn in my mouth and sob uncontrollably for hours.

And then it got worse. After three months of realizing that I was failing at motherhood, something in me shut off. I zoned out and glazed over into a kind of coma. When my older daughter hit me in the face, I began laughing hysterically and waving my arms over my head. I mumbled in little chants, "I hate this, I hate being your mother, I hate this." I started avoiding my children and yelling at them when they came near me. Something deep inside me had been crushed and I was in utter despair. My friends wondered what happened to me, I stopped communicating with my mother and sisters, I never went outside, and when I passed by the mirror and glanced at my face, I was startled to see how joyless and distraught I looked.

I knew I had reached the lowest depths of my personal ocean of depression on one particular day when my daughters were both howling and crying and I calmly decided that I no longer wanted to be their mother. I called my husband on the phone and told him he had better come home early. I felt a sense of calm and peace as I looked through the newspaper for apartments for rent and visualized leaving home and never coming back. My sister dropped by unannounced and cheerily said hello. I pulled her into the other room and confided in her that I had made the decision to stop being a mother to my children. She looked puzzled and distressed and tried to reason with me. It was no use. I just wanted to run away and never come back, or go to sleep and never wake up.

My husband convinced me to hang on. Things would get better. We would get through this. He was worried. And he should have been. This hell continued. Four months. Five months. Six months. I would gaze out the window and think about putting my fist through the glass.

And then it happened. It was the beginning of January and it was really the smallest thing. It wasn't really even a thing; it was just a feeling. I was in the kitchen fixing breakfast for the girls and they were calm and I looked out the window and for a moment I didn't feel sad. For the first time in over six months, I actually did not feel sad. I looked out the window and noticed a bird. I saw rain on the street. There were some clouds floating by. And that was it. I suddenly did not feel distraught and hateful and angry. I looked from the window over to my daughters. And I saw them for the first time ever as little girls, small creatures that were alive and hungry and giggling and spilling juice on the table. There they were, just two normal sisters, eating breakfast like normal people, and I was just a normal mom cleaning up after them.

Afterward, the three of us sat on the couch and snuggled as I read *Goodnight Moon* in my best dramatic voice and held them both close in my arms. Once again, my tears flowed, but this time for love. For warmth. For normalcy. For the pure joy and gratefulness that finally, finally came into my heart.

BREATHE

Alexa Bigwarfe

I'm not sure how many times I passed the puddle of spilled milk before I finally told myself to clean it up. Had it been days? Certainly my husband would have noticed it if it had been there for days. It must have only been hours. Lord, it felt like days.

My inner voice chastised me for leaving it there. After all, no "normal" person would leave spilled milk on the floor. No "normal" person would allow her house to get to this state.

What the hell was normal anyway? I did not remember how to feel "normal." I felt tired. I felt numb. I felt a sense of overwhelm at all of the duties that needed to be done each day. I just wanted to crawl back in bed and sleep. For days. Maybe even for weeks.

But three little people depended on me to get up each day. And no one was coming to my rescue.

Maybe I would just leave. I fantasized about getting in the car and driving somewhere far away. I would find a hotel (or better yet, a beach house—it was a fantasy after all) and just sit in the quiet, alone, until I couldn't stand it anymore. I thought it might take several weeks to get to that point. Maybe then I would be healed. Maybe then I could be a loving mother.

On my way back to the kitchen, I passed by the milk puddle once more. And again, I ignored it. Why should I clean it up anyway? It would only be a matter of minutes before one of the children spilled something else. There was always something to clean up. It never ended. My eyes pricked with tears and I felt like screaming at that stupid puddle of milk.

I hated this. I hated all of it. The panic started to swell in my chest.

Closing my eyes, I reminded myself to breathe. Just breathe. This too shall pass.

The soft mewling of my tiny baby in her swing distracted me from the milk on the ground and the impending panic attack. She was cozy and comfortable, just beginning to stir, soon to awaken. My heart ached as I watched her. My miracle baby. How I wanted to be rocking in the chair, holding her, covering her with kisses and relishing her sweetness. Cherishing her. Being grateful that she had lived, even though her twin passed away in the NICU. But I could not do those things, at least not on a regular basis. She spent much of the day in the swing, where she was safe. So that I could breathe. I just needed to breathe. It felt like I could never get enough air anymore.

I knew that I loved her. I loved all of my children. But I was suffocating. How could I be what they needed? They needed so much. All day. And I wanted to be free of it. Of them. I did not want to do the mothering.

No. It was not that I didn't want to be a mother. I did not feel *capable* of being a mother.

These sweet children deserved so much more. This must be why God let Kathryn die. I couldn't handle three children. How could I have ever handled four?

Somewhere in between the fight to survive and the desire to love them, I felt like a monster. I once admitted to a friend (a friend without children) that I could now understand how a woman could be driven to the point of drowning her children in the bathtub. I saw it in her eyes as soon as the words left my lips: "Monster!" I did not want to harm my children. I was not thinking about drowning them. But I could finally somewhat comprehend how a mother could get to that point. I didn't share that thought with anyone again.

The isolation of my days made my emotional state even more fragile, but I could not physically manage the effort involved in taking the three children out. It was so stressful to get them ready, pack everything up, and go someplace. One day when I tried to attempt it, I probably made seventeen trips back into the house because I kept forgetting something, or someone needed the potty, or a diaper needed changing, or my four-year-old left his shoes somewhere in the house, and so forth.

As it was, I had a narrow window for being out of the house. My routine was regulated by an evil breast pump and my daughter's feeding tube. My pumping schedule remained at every two to three hours because my micro-preemie could not nurse and it was important to me to give her breast milk. If I did not pump regularly, my supply dwindled. We had to feed her through a tube that had been surgically emplaced in her stomach. She was getting better with the bottle and I hoped that the tube would be removed soon, but in the meantime, it was not something I wanted to do in public. It was just easier to stay home.

If I did make it out from under house arrest, I usually felt worse, not better. Getting together with other moms was not a pleasure. I had no energy to keep up with my older two children, and they would often run amok, further wearing me down. I did not perceive the other moms as compassionate or understanding. I felt judgment. After all, the baby was over five months old, and I'd had three whole months while she was in the NICU to get myself together. Yeah, right.

No one understood. I was alone. It was not worth it to leave my house.

Those were some of the darkest days of my life. I was up early to pump, hoping I could finish before the children woke. I felt like a zombie in a B-list movie. My body was so heavy. I would schlep to the kitchen—wild hair, morning breath, mismatched fuzzy socks, which I might have worn for two days in a row—and move through the motions of making scrambled eggs or cereal for the kids. It took every ounce of brainpower I could muster to carry out the duties that had to be done each morning. Step-by-step I had to walk myself through the simple process of surviving: feed the children, dress the children, attempt to brush their teeth and brush their hair. Who am I kidding? I don't think I brushed my daughter's hair for weeks. "Pick your battles," became my mantra.

So, no, I didn't care about that spilled milk on the floor. Or the overflowing trash cans, or the stench coming from wherever it was coming from. I did not care that my two-year-old had just colored all over the wall. Add that to the beautiful streak of blue paint on our white kitchen cupboards and the greasy lip balm circles all over the living room wall.

I no longer put any effort into makeup or styling my hair.

My daily uniform consisted of my maternity jeans (yes, five months after giving birth), an oversized shirt, bright socks, and my Birkenstocks. I brushed my teeth most mornings. We ate hot dogs and takeout pizza and chicken nuggets because I couldn't bring myself to cook.

The children overwhelmed me. Noise—loud music, toys, social settings—completely unnerved me. I was what you might call a "hot mess."

But somehow I faked my way through it.

Could this emotional distress have been caused by the grief of losing one of my girls? Maybe. But I didn't think so. I had compartmentalized those feelings, and I knew the difference of the extreme heartache and pain when I felt a wave of grief wash over me.

This was unlike that pain, and it was something I had experienced before. When my first child was born and for about six months afterward, I felt a similar level of disconnect. It was more manageable because I did not have other children, and I did not feel the same level of overwhelm. I remember being alone in my home with the baby, and letting him sit in his swing (where he was content and safe) for as long as he would stay there. The lyrics "One is the loneliest number" would play in my head over and over and over, until I wanted to scream. I did not know it was not normal for a new mother to want to hand off her baby to someone else as soon as she got the opportunity. It wasn't for a lack of love, but rather, a lack of connection because of a battle I didn't even realize I was fighting.

This time I was more aware, even while trudging through such a deep fog. Sort of from afar, like an out-of-body experience, I recognized that I was depressed. Not from grief, although I'm sure that compounded it. I needed help. Help came in the form of a bottle. Or several bottles. I had my antidepressant dosage doubled. I drank wine. Every night. Late at night while everyone else was sleeping, I would curl up on the couch with my glass (bottle) of wine and watch some brain-numbing television shows. Those were the only moments of "normal" I seemed to find.

I had nowhere to go and no one to talk to. So I started talking to strangers. I found communities on Facebook with other people who were going through their own challenges. I made friends online. I poured my heart into writing and connecting with others who validated my feelings. I turned to blogging, where I found other mothers who were experiencing similar situations and admitted they didn't always feel capable of being a mother. Through the comfort of strangers, I realized I was not alone, and I was not a bad person. Slowly, I began to heal. I quieted the dark voices in my mind. I remembered how to breathe.

Some days those bothersome voices return, encouraging me to just grab my jacket and run for the hills. To leave it all behind. To find myself again. I hear those voices telling me I'm not a good mother, and I should stop trying to be one at all. Those instances are fewer and farther between, and I am mostly enjoying my time with my children, despite the daily challenges of motherhood. I found a wonderful therapist who is helping me learn how to replace those lies in my head with these truths: "I *am* a good mother. I love my children. It is normal to struggle. I am *not* alone."

You, my friend, are not alone either.

DEPRESSION IS A NUMBERS GAME

Kim Simon

4 blocks.

To get from the parking lot of the shopping mall to the front door of the New Parent Support Group, I had to walk 4 blocks. 4 blocks of steering a stroller through herds of teenagers on their way home from school. 4 blocks of an overflowing diaper bag tapping at my knees. 4 blocks of praying that my sweet, pouty-lipped baby would stay sweet and stay asleep until I was safely cocooned in the air-conditioned classroom that would allow me to breathe again. In the span of 4 blocks, I had to outrun the fear and loneliness that had followed me around every corner of motherhood.

I never imagined that falling in love with a tiny human being could strip me so completely of my confidence.

4 blocks was the distance from my old office to my favorite French cafe. I could walk 4 blocks in high heels and a pencil skirt, just to reward myself with a chocolate croissant. 4 blocks was a quick break after a morning of back-to-back meetings, or

a particularly trying session with anxious clients. 4 blocks was nothing. On Sunday mornings, my husband and I walked the 4 blocks from our doorstep to our favorite downtown coffee shop. 4 blocks was a vacation from chores and deadlines and responsibilities. 4 blocks was freedom.

And then, on an inky black night in May, we drove 4 miles (in about 4 minutes) when my water broke at 39 weeks. As I leaked meconium-tinged fluid all over the floor of the emergency room, I wondered out loud if perhaps we were 4 minutes too late.

We timed the minutes between contractions, and subtracted the hours that were left until my scheduled C-section the next morning. We added the growing headcount of nurses who rushed around at 3:00 a.m. to prepare me for surgery, to the number of times that my mom asked them if we were really going to be OK. When Max arrived, underneath the lights of an ice-cold operating room, I took 3 deep breaths as his first hearty cries replaced my fear with the hope of new beginnings. We counted tiny wrinkled fingers and matchstick-thin toes. I ran a shaking thumb over his impossibly soft cheek. I kissed him 1 time for every minute of my life that I had spent waiting for him. As our family of 2 became 3 in the space of a heartbeat, I was overwhelmed by how my ability to love instantly multiplied.

In our first weeks at home, I was sure that the answer to my parenting success would lie in the numbers. In my 30 years, I had come to rely on controlling the uncontrollable with outlines, and equations, and schedules and lists. Most of what new moms encounter can be explained away by numbers. We count wet and dirty diapers. We report back to kind-faced nurses who scrawl tally marks on a dry-erase board. Lactation consultants take charge of breasts that once belonged to us, rattling off equations of how many nursing sessions in how many hours equal how many ounces gained. The clock mocks us as we tiptoe out of the nursery and settle down to sleep, waking exactly 17 minutes later when the baby screams again. I scratched notes in a journal and entered every move that Max made in an app on my phone. And then, sometime after I learned that I could keep a child alive and before I learned that this parenting gig wouldn't kill me, the world started spinning. My breasts produced 2 drops of milk, instead of 2 ounces. My son vomited 3 times in an hour, and my husband knelt beside us to clean the carpet, for the 10th time that week. If babies were a numbers game, then something didn't add up.

I was sure that my tears were the only part of the equation that made sense. Of course I was upset! My baby couldn't eat without getting sick, I couldn't nurse him without getting help, and no one under our roof was sleeping for longer than 45 minutes at a time. When I saw the look of panic in my husband's eyes, I assured him that this was normal.

"There's a learning curve." I smiled. "We're clearly at one end of it. For now. It will get better." That's what the kind grandmas in the grocery store tell you when you are flushed and fumbling for your wallet in the checkout line while your baby screams and screams. That's what the books tell you when you are mindlessly flipping through crisp new pages, desperate for answers and solutions and a plan that actually makes sense.

But things didn't get better.

I fell in love with Max from the very second I heard his tiny heartbeat on a monitor in my doctor's office. When he was finally safe in my arms, I poured every ounce of energy that I had into being the perfect mom. I sang to him. I snuggled with him. I laughed, and rocked, and tickled, and dressed, and bathed him. On the surface, I was the perfect mother. I was earning a 4.0 in motherhood, but I was failing miserably at everything else. I was surviving. My baby was thriving. I had the luxury of staying home to take care of him, and the honor of being the one to teach him and wear him and sing to him and nap with him every single day. Max filled me with joy, and gave me a purpose, and made my life complete.

I was furious when that wasn't enough to keep depression from finding me.

I thought I could outrun it. I thought I had left it behind. Depression is what robbed me of the year that I was supposed to spend studying abroad, traveling with a performing arts group. Depression made me sleep away how homesick I was, and finally forced me to fly home alone to a life that made sense. Depression made me miss my college classes, and forced me to stay in school for an extra 2 years. Depression pushed me to go on too many dates, with too many of the wrong guys, because the adrenaline of being desired felt better than any medication ever could.

Depression and I had a long history. We were like on-again, off-again lovers, but I was sure that we had broken up for good this time. Of course I wouldn't need to solve the equation of depression when I was finally "grown up." It would be easier when I finally had everything I ever wanted. *Until I finally had everything I ever wanted.*

My 20-something self would have told you that depression is a numbers game. Depression adds up the fears and irrational doubts and rounds out the equation with panic attacks. Depression solves for "x," with "x" being everything that you haven't yet mastered about taking care of yourself. Depression doesn't care that you are madly in love with your baby. Depression doesn't care that you haven't had a hot shower in 4 days, or that your baby just pooped through his 3rd outfit of the morning, or that you desperately wanted to breastfeed. Depression doesn't care that you have a college degree, or a strong marriage, or an uncanny knack for knowing exactly what makes your baby laugh. Depression follows you home from the well-baby checkup and whispers in your ear that perhaps you misunderstood the doctor, and what she really meant was that there was indeed something terribly wrong with him. Depression wakes you up before your baby does, and sends you careening down the hall in a panic, convinced that he has stopped breathing. Depression mocks you as you drive to a friend's house as the sun sets, nudging you to pull over to make sure that he's really buckled in safely. Depression masks your successes and highlights your mistakes. Depression gnaws at your confidence, and turns 4 blocks into the longest walk of your life.

I knew that equations would save me. I went through the familiar process of writing down what my next steps would be, as if seeing them on paper could force my body to move in that direction. 1 class. 1 "Mommy and Me" group. 1 time each week. A reason to get dressed, to put on makeup, to feel like a human being again. 1 opportunity to reach through the darkness and push my swanky stroller and bottles of formula toward the light. Or at least toward a bathroom that had a changing table in it.

But first, I had to get in the car.

Depression is exhausting, and babies are too.

First, I had to wake up. First, I had to flip the rusted coin of new motherhood. Heads, attempt to shower before the baby wakes up (gambling the extra minutes of sleep I could have indulged in). Tails, rake my fingers through my hair and scrape the messy ends into a bun. Shower tomorrow. Or the next day. And so the identity shift began. I'd throw on jeans, then take them off when the button rubbed against my swollen C-section scar. The new me wore yoga pants. I'd put on a nursing tank and cry, because the new me wasn't able to breastfeed. I would make sure that Max looked trendy and precious and darling in his tiny baby jeans and sneakers, then cry some more because he was impossibly perfect and I was impossibly broken. And then he'd poop. Up the back of the tiny baby jeans, and down into his sneakers. And somewhere between cutting his onesie off and throwing it in the trash, I would realize that there was no other way to escape this. If I was going to be Max's mom, I had to keep walking.

I only had to walk 4 blocks.

I only had to drive 7 miles, and walk 4 blocks, with a 2-month-old, on the first Monday morning that I felt brave enough to venture out into the world on my own.

I had waited 30 years to be a mother. I had survived 39 weeks of carrying a squirmy, squishy, perfectly formed little human being in my belly. I had a college degree in Psychology, for Christ's sake, which only took me 4 (ok, 6) years to earn. I was used to standing in stilettos in front of a room full of people, lecturing them on domestic violence, and adoption, and crisis counseling. I was great at taking the broken parts of people, and helping them find ways to piece themselves back together.

Until my own motherhood broke me apart.

Depression is a numbers game. If you leave it alone for too many months, it will sneak in through the side door and make itself at home.

I forced myself to walk.

Those 4 blocks turned into 3 more, when the mom with the skinny jeans and wide smile asked if I'd like to get coffee. *My confidence grew.* 7 blocks turned into 7 miles, as we drove to the park to sit with our babies on brand-new blankets in the grass. *I had somewhere to be.* 12 years with my best friend from college turned into a lifeline, when I finally allowed myself to tell her the truth about how lonely I was. 1 friend turned into 5 friends, with 5 babies who cried and fussed and smiled like mine. *I saw my motherhood mirrored in their eyes.* 7 miles turned into 27 e-mails, as we planned each Mom's Night Out and shared tips on baby food and temper tantrums and nap schedules. 1 support group turned into 2 music classes. 2 music classes turned into 3 preschool days. 3 preschool days turned into a community of families who made us laugh and invited us in and caught us when we fell. And my tiny 6 lb. 2 oz. baby boy blossomed and smiled and danced and grew. And then he turned into a big brother, exactly 4 years later.

Depression was a numbers game. Max's first 4 years were nestled among zoo adventures and picnic lunches and playdates and blanket forts. But depression counted the hours until he was asleep, so that I could safely dissolve into tears when I was alone. Depression assured me that my husband must be cheating on me, because I was too miserable to be loved. Depression calculated the weeks between when my mom would visit, because I was sure that I couldn't manage the load of mothering on my own. Depression taunted me when my best friend reached out, because I was sure that she had all of the answers and I was the only one who was struggling.

So at 6 months pregnant with my second son, I stacked the deck.

I was done gambling against the house. Depression can count cards.

I found a group of doulas who would hold my hand through my labor and surround me with strength in the weeks that followed. I found a therapist who asked me to be honest about what terrified me the most. I talked to my OB about taking an antidepressant, and wrote out a detailed birth plan so that the hospital knew the trauma that I carried from my first birth.

This time, when I multiplied the minutes of sleep lost by the days that my husband had to work late, I got the number of hours that a kind, wise doula sat beside me and showed me how to breastfeed. When I tallied up the evenings that I spent crying, I presented them to a calm and compassionate OB, who divided them by the number of milligrams that I would need to keep my depression at bay.

And as the hours became days, and the days faded into the blissful months that infants fly through, I realized that I no longer had the responsibility of deciphering the equations. I started keeping track of the things that mattered again. First words and first steps, first dinner dates with my husband without dozens of texts to the babysitter. First hugs between brothers, first whispers at bedtime, and the first time my husband looked at me as if to say, "We're going to be just fine." I've always hated math, and releasing the desire to control things allowed me to embrace my ability to enjoy them.

Motherhood doesn't suddenly get better. *You get better at it.* You allow yourself to let go of the pain, and you force yourself to find your strengths. You have to. That's what moms do. We pick up the broken pieces and put them back together. Even when we are the ones who are broken. Our children see us emerge from the darkness. They see us summoning our courage, building on our strengths, and choosing every hour to fully live. They fall in love with us as we fall in love with them, and it is the only thing that teaches us to love ourselves. They learn that our love for them is exponential, and we *become* the foundation that we have spent a lifetime searching for.

Motherhood always has an answer. *You* have always had the answer. Depression is a numbers game, but it's nothing you can't solve.

RECOGNIZING THE DARKNESS

Lea Grover

The open library door cast a thin rectangle of light from the street beyond the front yard. Tangled shadows fell from the bathroom window, where the moon shone beyond the trees in the backyard. At the end of the hallway, the two lights merged, pouring in from the living room and kitchen.

My feet were silent as they padded forward. I was practiced at wandering the house at night. At eight years old I rarely slept, and when I did my sleep was punctuated by fits of restless sleepwalking. On this night, still early in a school year that promised as much abuse from my peers as the last, I was, without knowing the word, depressed. On previous nights I'd moved from my bedroom to the television and back again, watching dozens of episodes of *F Troop* and *Bewitched*.

On this night, I decided the only way I would sleep was if I were dead.

When I reached the kitchen, I dragged a stool from the table to my mother's under-the-cabinet knife rack, and climbed up to it. I pulled out her largest knife, smaller than the animated butcher knives in Looney Tunes, but sufficient. I stared at the knife, imagining how it would feel to have a piece of metal slide into my heart.

I put the knife back, climbed down, and went to bed to wait for dawn.

Over the next fifteen years, I fought depression. I slowly built up a toolkit to keep me from returning to that dark place, that part of my brain always planning not for the future, but for the end. I thought I was cured. I may have been, in a manner of speaking.

I grew up, and I fell in love.

When Mike popped the question, I didn't hesitate. I told him yes, absolutely yes, and the next day we went downtown and picked out a ring.

That evening, he had a seizure. A CT scan showed us pictures of masses, deep in his brain. Inoperable tumors.

Four days after that, his surgeon told me in private: he had stage four cancer, and eighteen months to live.

I looked at the dark place I'd once known and I shut it out. I pushed him into experimental trials. I made sure he ate healthy foods, steered him away from antioxidants, promised him he would beat the cancer. Our friends rallied around him, our families came together. Mike was sick, one of the 13,000 people in the United States to be diagnosed with astrocytoma that year.

When he started getting depressed, everyone understood. He had terminal cancer. That's *supposed* to make you depressed. It took one e-mail to his doctor to get Mike on mood stabilizers, and his battle against the tumors continued.

"Ignore the tumors," I told him. "Focus on life."

As the tumors shrank, we did what married people do. We had children.

Our twins came in a flurry of excitement and terror—we'd both lost our jobs in the recession. I looked in that dark place, and I shut it out again.

"Ignore the doubt," I said. "Let's both go back to school and focus on life."

We did. We both got new degrees, and Mike got a good job downtown.

And then our third child was born.

For the first time, I was a stay-at-home mom, alone, out-numbered by my children. For the first time, I wasn't leading the charge, my eyes shut tight against that darkness as we forged ahead into our Happily Ever After.

For the first time, we were there. We'd made it.

And then the darkness swallowed me.

Twenty years after my first childish fling with death, I found myself battling depression again, imagining painless suicides that separated me from the reality of life surrounded by children.

I thought I knew depression. I thought I understood its flavors, its lies, its broken promises. I thought that a lifetime of depression had prepared me for anything. That if I had been able to recognize the depths of it before I fell in, I could stop myself from sinking.

Ignore the darkness, I told myself. *If you pretend it's not there, you can walk out of it.*

I had panic attacks every few hours. I learned they were from a condition called D-MER, Dysphoric Milk Ejection Reflex. Instead of oxytocin, my brain was producing panic-inducing endorphins when my milk came in. And even when I realized my brain was sabotaging me, I still told myself I wasn't depressed.

It's just the D-MER, I said, sobbing hopelessly every time my baby needed to eat. As though D-MER and depression were unrelated.

I told everybody I was fine, at first. I told them I was tired, or didn't feel well, and they understood. Of *course* they understood—I had three kids under three. I had every right to be tired and unwell. They didn't question me.

But the thing about depression is that it distorts how you see the world. They weren't understanding; they were grateful to have an excuse to be rid of me. They weren't compassionate; they secretly hated me and wanted me to be lonely.

Depression isn't something you can compartmentalize. It infects every aspect of your life, every relationship. I resented my husband for not being depressed, and pushed him away. I found myself unable to enjoy being around people, and stopped leaving the house. I loathed myself, my post-baby body, and silently sneered at anyone who dared call me beautiful.

I stared at myself in the mirror, hating every inch of my body and soul.

You could just take all the pills in the cabinet. There's enough Codeine in there. There's plenty of booze in the dining room. You wouldn't have to worry ever again. You wouldn't have to be a disappointment. You could just be gone.

Friends who gathered to congratulate Mike on his survival dismissed my struggle when I began to complain of feeling isolated or hopeless. What reason did I have to be depressed? Mike was alive, and now that we had our Happily Ever After, all I needed to do was sit at home and care for my three beautiful children.

Only I couldn't care for them. Numbness had taken over my ability to empathize, emotions were painful, and I struggled to shut out the few that worked their way into my heart:

Guilt, that the children deserved a mother who wouldn't break down and cry for no apparent reason.

Shame, that my two-year-old twins spent their time begging me not to cry, to play with them, to not be angry or sad.

Love, which I couldn't stop myself from feeling, but which wrapped around my heart and squeezed until I couldn't breathe, until I thought my chest would collapse around it and I would die simply from having to *feel*.

The depression lied to me, telling me my family would be better off without me. That I didn't deserve the expense of a sitter and therapy. That I could wish it away if I wanted to, so I must somehow want to be depressed. The depression told me I would never be happy again, and I believed it.

If I pretend it's not real, it's not real, I told myself.

Depression masked itself in my internal monologues, and told me with my own voice I didn't have to fight it.

And why would I lie to myself? I wondered.

Twenty years after I stood on a kitchen stool in the darkness, contemplating the force it might take to push a knife into my heart, I stood on the balcony of my third-floor walk-up, imagining how easy it would be to accidentally fall to the sidewalk beneath.

Twenty years after I learned the many colors and textures of depression, a new variety consumed me. Postpartum depression was unlike any other, more isolating, more self-hating, more violent. I would imagine myself driving into the lake, all the children strapped into their seats, and the thoughts nauseated me. I imagined my two-year-old twins, prodding my corpse where it hung in a doorway, and collapsing in tears on the hallway floor. PPD consumed me, and I hated myself for it.

Because *I* didn't deserve the luxury of depression. I had a healthy husband, beautiful children, a home, and an education. I had *everything*.

My husband had spent the previous years fighting a *real* disease. Brain cancer, in his own head, was as invisible to anyone as my depression, but we didn't question it. He was sick, *really* sick, and he might die.

It wasn't until I began crafting a plan to leave my children and husband in each other's care and take my own life that I understood how truly sick I had become.

That was when I started looking for help.

The thing is, help is easy to find. There are therapists everywhere, and there are pharmacies in every town where you can fill a prescription for an antidepressant. I would never have waited months to start treating Mike's cancer. But I waited most of a year before treating my own postpartum depression.

We're learning more about postpartum depression all the time. We're learning how a flood of ante- and postpartum hormones can trigger latent bipolar disorders, anxiety, all manner of mental illnesses that we already had susceptibilities for. Like an infection in an old, not-quite-healed scar.

We say people who commit suicide "kill themselves," but that's not always true. What's true is that a disease kills them— a disease that uses their own bodies and thoughts as the weapon.

We like to think that our brains are above the petty

illnesses that plague the rest of our bodies, but it's not true. Our brains are as susceptible to fatigue and disease as our bladders, our lungs, our livers.

The truth is that every year, 39,000 people in the United States commit suicide. Three times more people die from suicide than astrocytoma.

The truth is that every time I compared the two in my mind, cancer and depression, I felt sick to my stomach. I felt like I didn't *deserve* to call myself sick, not in comparison to Mike. That some diseases were legitimate, and depression was not.

While brain cancer is terrifyingly fatal, postpartum depression is terrifyingly common.

My husband's brain went a little bit wrong. Cells that were supposed to carry information to his nerves decided instead to reproduce like mad. To build structures out of cells that should have been brain and squeeze until his life was gone.

My brain is very much the same. Cells that were supposed to trigger serotonin and oxytocin instead let loose an array of chemicals that sapped my energy, exhausted my muscles, and depleted my ability to experience happiness until my brain convinced itself it no longer wanted life at all.

My husband and I had the same amount of control over those processes. None.

Brain cancer and depression are both diseases. Neither one has a cure, but they can both be treated successfully. There can be recovery and remission. But there is no "Happily Ever After."

There is only healing, and vigilance. Remembering that when the depression surfaces, it is not a judgment of your ability to live, or to enjoy living. It is a symptom of a disease affecting your brain, and there's no shame in treating it.

There is a time when the sun rises, and the silence of midnight hallways and hopelessness is replaced with little arms that wrap around your legs and lighten your soul. There is the familiar comfort of casual smiles. The day comes when you can say, "I'm fine," without feeling like an impostor.

My Longest Winter

Allie Smith

*W*e drove twenty miles per hour on the interstate. It was raining hard that day. Sitting in the back, between two car seats, I kept turning my head to look at each baby. Rich would periodically peer over his shoulder and ask if they were okay. They were sleeping, so I assumed they were. I was still dumfounded that the doctors thought we were capable of taking care of them. Sure, we'd been taught how to bathe and feed them, administer their medications, and perform CPR, but always under the watchful eye of a nurse. I'd been so consumed by all the setbacks during the seven weeks in the NICU—acid reflux, sleep apnea, aspiration issues—that I'd thought little about bringing them home. Sometimes it seemed as if they would never come home.

But here they were. Each boy was tethered to a sleep apnea machine that would alert us if they stopped breathing. It was as if we were medical interns with very little training, instead of new parents. I was overwhelmed by the fear I felt and by what I didn't feel.

I have a secret that I've never shared with anyone. On that slow journey home, and for months afterward, I didn't feel love. I genuinely cared about them, and was certainly concerned with their well-being. But that overwhelming joy that usually manifests in the form of pheromone-inducing euphoria? Nope, I didn't feel that. I wanted to, and sometimes conjured up a happiness that I thought was love, but mostly I was going through the motions because those boys did not feel real to me.

The first couple of months were a blur, so I naturally assumed twin exhaustion was the reason for my apathy. The boys were on a four-hour feeding schedule. It often took an hour to feed each baby, and if I was alone that meant two hours. Then I would pump, sterilize their bottles, do laundry, and repeat it all again. Barrett was colicky and would usually erupt just when Rich got home from work. We'd eat takeout and stare blankly at the television, as we administered the evening feedings. Then I went to bed, because I usually had the middle-of-the-night shift, while Rich handled the early mornings before he went to work. It was winter, and we weren't allowed to take the boys anywhere except the pediatrician's office. Since they were born ten weeks premature, there was a high risk of contracting RSV.

It was a long winter.

∽

Despite overwhelming exhaustion during the first trimester, Rich and I rode an intoxicating wave of excitement and anticipation about becoming parents to twins. We believed we'd hit the parenting lottery. After all, we'd only half-tried to get pregnant—and ended up with twins. How lucky were we?

The white picket fence life that I once dreamed about was turning out better than I'd ever imagined.

∾

At my sixteen-week appointment, my ultrasound took longer than usual. I was a little bored, because the doctor wasn't chatty. He kept studying the monitor. When he stood, I started to get ready to go, but he patted my shoulder, smiled, and told me he'd be right back. I lay back down. When he returned, there was another doctor with him. As the two men gathered at the screen, the new doctor asked the original if he'd checked to see if there was a third baby.

Gulp. Okay, they had my attention now. I was up on my elbows. Twins? Sure. Triplets? No, thank you.

Half an hour later, I was grasping the arms of the chair in front of the doctor's desk, as he explained that I had a condition called Twin-to-Twin Transfusion Syndrome (TTTS). Although my babies were in separate sacs, they shared a placenta, which meant they were identical. When my egg split, creating two sacs, it didn't completely separate. The babies shared some blood vessels, and Twin A was sucking all of the amniotic fluid from Twin B. Twin B was "stuck," and would die without the nutrients he needed. Twin A would most likely suffer cardiac arrest because of the excess fluid.

I started crying. Before I knew it, Rich was by my side, but I didn't remember calling him. I became hysterical. I was put on bed rest, where I assumed a fetal position for days. There were phone calls to be made and there was research to be done, but I didn't do any of it. I refused to speak to anyone except Rich.

∾

We had to fly to Tampa to have intravenous laparoscopic surgery performed inside the womb, to cauterize the conjoined blood vessels. The procedure itself went well, but the first twenty-four hours were risky, because the trauma of the surgery was sometimes too much for one or both of the babies. At the first postoperative ultrasound, I held my breath until I saw the first heartbeat. I didn't smile until I saw the second.

We weren't out of the woods, but we'd won a major battle.

∾

After the surgery, which was performed mid-September, I returned home, and to my bed. The goal was to get me to thirty-six weeks, which was just after the New Year. I was supposed to lie on my right side as much as I could endure; for reasons I didn't quite understand, it was deemed beneficial. I was supposed to consume an unusual amount of Ensure. I was supposed to hope and pray and be cautiously optimistic. On the advice of the doctors, my baby showers were canceled. It was gently suggested that we not buy anything "personal" for the babies. I understood. The fate of the boys was still uncertain.

I was exhausted by fear and welcomed the respite of bed rest. I wanted to be alone. I wanted peace. I wanted quiet. And that's exactly what I got. Oh, the days were very long, stretching out one after the other. With so many hours of solitude, scared and bored, a wall formed around my heart.

At four o'clock each afternoon, I would turn off the TV and listen to classical music. As I lay on my right side, staring out the window at the changing leaves, my hip prickled with pain. Rubbing my belly, I wondered if I'd ever meet my boys. I made deals with God as the sun descended into the horizon and the sky turned black, like a shadow passing over my heart.

As my belly grew, my appetite diminished. I had to eat, I knew that, but I couldn't taste anything. When I did consume food, my heart burned. When I would feel the discomfort of my stomach expanding, or a baby would push too much, I'd panic that there was excess fluid and we were in trouble.

But week after week, I got good reports. The doctors' smiles appeared to be more genuine, rather than pitying. Milestones came and went. I made it to twenty-four weeks, and then twenty-eight. The boys reached two pounds. Halloween and Thanksgiving passed. Everyone in my life started to get excited. Optimism blossomed all around me, although it never once touched my heart.

At my thirty-week appointment, I was shocked to see a Christmas tree in the lobby of the hospital. Dumfounded, actually. Rich gently explained it was December 1.

After the ultrasound, we were told Twin A had stopped growing and that he was in distress. I was being admitted to the hospital immediately, so they could administer steroids to speed up the growth of the lungs. A C-section would be performed the next day. We went from zero to sixty, just like that. Long, boring, lonely days to being rushed up to labor and delivery for a steroid shot, an epidural, and the ten-week premature delivery of our sons.

The hospital priest came to see me late that night. He held my hand and said a prayer. I cried, needing and missing my mother. The overwhelming loneliness I felt that night prevented me from getting any sleep.

❦

"Allie, look, our son." I turned to my side, where Rich was holding the tiniest little creature I'd ever seen. Barrett. Two pounds five ounces, bright red, and mad as hell. Rich was crying. I'd never seen him cry before.

Where was the other one?

My other son, Hunter, wasn't breathing when he was born. They resuscitated him and then he was rushed out of the delivery room, before I got to see him.

❦

When I woke up in my hospital room, Rich was by my bedside. He quickly told me both boys were alive and in the NICU, but I wouldn't be able to see them until the next day. I accepted that injustice without a fight, threw up from the anesthesia, and drifted off to sleep.

The following morning I was wheeled up to the NICU where we found Barrett in an incubator, under the blinding glare of a bright light. He'd had a blood transfusion overnight. I stood to get a better look and all I saw were flailing arms and legs. He reminded me of a scared and trapped little bird. I wiped my tears and fell back into my wheelchair.

Hunter was across the aisle in another incubator, baking under a bilirubin lamp. He was yellow, and his face was swathed in bandages, which secured the tube that connected him to a respirator. We wouldn't see his face for two weeks. He was bigger than his brother, at two pounds and eleven ounces, but much sicker. His lungs were not as developed as Barrett's.

I went back to my room. As I was wheeled down the hall, we passed rooms full of flowers, balloons, babies, joy, and laughter. Entering my own room, the silence painfully echoed. I was released four days later, but I didn't bring any babies home with me.

∽

Once the boys were home, I struggled. Aside from the work and resulting exhaustion, I felt an odd disappointment. *Is this all there is?* It was boring and mundane and they slept all the time. The irony was that I'd resented the NICU nurses for doing my job. I was jealous whenever I'd see them embrace my babies. Yet in my own house, I was afraid to hug them too tight. I was afraid they'd break. I was disconnected, as if I were taking care of someone else's children. I felt shame and guilt, because what I should have felt was happiness and relief. My boys had beaten the odds—they were home.

I lived with an unrelenting terror that I'd do something wrong, and the stress often caused me to do just that. Once, I accidentally messed up their medications and had to call poison control. Thankfully the double dose of Zantac wasn't serious. I recorded every ounce they consumed and obsessively checked their apnea monitors to see if they were working. On the rare occasion that the alarm went off, I'd experience a flood of panic that surged through my body and sent my heart into spasms.

I cried a lot, but assumed it was from exhaustion. I was a very task-oriented mother. I wouldn't go to bed until everything had been checked off the list. I had a schedule and I stuck to it. I rarely let anyone help. I had it all under control.

Not once did it occur to me that I was depressed, not until four years later, when I gave birth to my third child. My daughter's arrival was blissfully surreal in contrast—it was the happiest time of my life. That's when I knew my boys had been robbed. They didn't get the bonding, breastfeeding, or cuddles that their sister did. They got a different mom, one who was terrified to love them. They deserved more. My pregnancy had been so traumatic, and my memories of that time were (and still are) etched in my soul. My memories infringed upon my heart's ability to open up and let them in. My memories, and the fear they instilled, polluted those first few months with my sons. There's a reason I can't remember much of that first year, and it's not exhaustion. It was shock and anxiety. I couldn't function normally, because I was haunted by what we'd been through.

Eventually, and mercifully, I felt a shift, a tiny flutter in my heart as my boys plumped up and the machines and medication went away. When their eyes were open more than they were closed, my smiles returned. As spring dawned, the constant tension in my shoulders eased ever-so-slightly as I slowly let go of my anxiety. Without even realizing when it happened, I discovered the love that had been hiding in my heart. Fourteen years later, it's stronger than I would have ever imagined, often painfully so. My boys seem unaffected by my behavior during that long winter. Perhaps someday, I will be, too.

MY MANY MOTHERS

Becky Castle Miller

I ignored my two small children until my guilt over-
came my apathy. My socks caught on the splintering
hardwood floor as I shuffled into the dining room, clutching
my stained bathrobe closed with my fist because the belt was
gone. I poured Cheerios from the box straight onto the cherry-
wood table. I switched on cartoons for my kids—at ages three
and one, their favorite show was *Blue's Clues*—then I disappeared back to my cave. The heavy bedroom curtains blocked
out most of the sunlight, and I pulled my blanket over my head
to shut out the rest. I escaped into sleep.

I did this more than once, but fewer times than twenty.

Dear God, I hope it was under twenty.

The process of bringing my second child into the world
had left me unable to enjoy him or his older sister. Or anything
else in life. My husband, Matthew, worked long days with a
grim commute on either end, and my days were lonely expe-
ditions over foothills of laundry and mountains of dishes. I was

not mothering. I was barely even caretaking. I somehow started my kids on the day, and somehow got them back into bed at night, but the hours between were a blur.

The best thing I did for my children during that year and a half was stay alive for them. I had no hope for the future, and no light in the present, so death seemed reasonable. I thought about how I would do it, and by a miracle, my imagination stretched out far enough ahead to picture the aftermath when I was gone. I saw my children dealing with grief every day for the rest of their lives—much as I was dealing with grief every day of my life—and I knew that I couldn't shove those rocks into their pockets.

I could stay alive, but that wasn't good enough. They deserved better. I was failing, barely functioning between crying spells and stretches of sleep. I was still trying to keep up with freelance clients and volunteer work, but I could only cope in public for brief periods of time before I retreated to my car to cry. In the short, tense hours he was home, Matthew suggested that my struggle was a character defect, laziness. Neither of us knew that I had the clear symptoms of a serious illness, until a friend gave me the word "depression" to explore.

Which I did, via the Internet. On one test, I had seven of ten symptoms. On another, eleven of thirteen. On the Goldberg scale, zero means no depression and fifty-four or higher means severe depression. I scored sixty-one, off the chart. My WebMD-fueled self-diagnosis was clinical depression. My armchair therapist self-analysis unpacked a fuzzy understanding that I was crumbling under the burden of long-ignored emotions: a broken heart and the loss of every home I'd ever had, through twenty-five moves.

Giving my disaster a name didn't fix it. But it did give me the hope that I could be fixed. If I were sick, maybe I could get healthy again.

The problem was, I couldn't self-heal from depression. The nature of the disease stripped away my ability to fight it. Like drowning in a cold lake, the hypothermia numbed before the water even closed in overhead. Depression had made me a child again—unable to care for myself—so I needed a mother to nurse me back to health.

The military culture in which I grew up saddled me with both emotional repression and the fierce independence that resisted the help needed to overcome it. I had unconsciously pulled away from my family to make my own way, and I had leapt out of the nest with my emotional wings undeveloped. I needed to be mothered myself, and I needed to relearn how to mother my children, but I was far away from my family.

So I braved the distance, loaded the kids and my baggage into the car, and drove all day to my parents' house. It wasn't the same home I'd left when I had struck out on my own, as they had moved three times since then, but it held the same furniture and the same pictures of me and my brothers on the walls.

My mother, Donna, and I sat in rocking chairs, and I tried to dig from my soul years of buried emotions and sum them up. But I didn't understand my feelings enough to communicate them to my mother. I finally just asked her to pray for me. She did, slipping into the guest room after I had tucked myself in, like she used to come into my bedroom every night when I was little. She perched on the edge of my bed and gripped my hands and prayed for me. Not easing into the familiar bedtime prayers for a child, but stumbling over the complex, confusing prayers required for adults. We had left too long a gap in praying together, and I had grown up in the meantime.

When I drove away, I know she continued to pray, closing the distance the best way she knew. Then she was far away again, and I needed more hands-on mothering.

I tentatively started reaching out closer to home, afraid of rejection if I made my struggles known beyond my closed front door. "You haven't been yourself since your son was born," my friend Nikki offered, softly, so as not to offend. I wasn't offended; I was greedy to hear more. She told me about painful relationships and psychiatric treatment. She normalized my need for help with her "Me, too." *Me, too; you're not alone; you're not the only one.*

Convinced by Nikki to seek help, I started seeing a counselor, Christine. With her own grown children my age, she served as a professional mother for me. I cradled a throw pillow on my lap and shredded Kleenex with my fingers while I told disjointed stories that didn't add up to my current misery. Christine extricated the memories like a mother plucking gravel out of a skinned knee. She gave me a name for the night I fell apart: an emotional breakdown. She washed me with advice instead of antiseptic and covered me with book recommendations rather than Band-Aids. At the end of our sessions, she sent me back outside to play, stronger and braver.

She also taught me how to mother myself. "Some of the emotional difficulties you're finally dealing with happened ten years ago," she said. "You hit pause on it. So when you deal with these emotions now, it's not twenty-nine-year-old you dealing with them. You're nineteen again. Think about the girls you volunteer with. If one of them came to you like this, how would you deal with her?"

My fingers relaxed with a surge of compassion. I was so much kinder to them than I was to myself.

"You need to be gentle with yourself," she said. "Treat yourself now like you would treat that nineteen-year-old girl."

My midwife Nicole also mothered me. She was younger than I was, and had no children yet, but she listened with a mother's sympathy as I sat on her exam table, gripped my knees, and detailed my personal checklist for recovery. I had been in therapy for months. I was trying my best at self-care—healthy diet, exercise, vitamins, sunshine, spiritual growth—but I couldn't stop the crying and the suicidal thoughts. She provided affirmation: "You are doing everything right. You're still not getting better. It might be time to consider medication." Nicole took personal responsibility, calling the maternity hospital to find me help. They wouldn't admit me to their postpartum treatment center because it had been over a year since my youngest child was born, so she pressed on and found me a private care provider.

Providentially, this psychiatric nurse, Laura, had been one of my midwives during my first pregnancy, so she was familiar with healthy-me. She had gone back to school for certification in psychiatry, and now she had room in her new practice to take me in. Like a mother with the key to the bathroom medicine cabinet, Laura diagnosed and prescribed. Major Depressive Disorder. SSRIs. We teamworked our way through types and dosages till we found what worked for me, Celexa and then Zoloft. We slogged together through the setback of an early miscarriage and the hormonal and emotional fallout. Gulping grape-flavored syrup is a treat to a preschooler, but swallowing the pills that helped me stop wallowing was not so enjoyable. The medications made me feel hyped-up, like I'd overdosed on espresso. They suppressed my appetites for both food and sex.

But they also forced the misery to retreat, allowing my natural vivacity to resurge. One day, months later, I stepped into Laura's office with a smile, and she said, "You're wearing yellow. I don't think I need to ask how you're feeling."

When Matthew understood my diagnosis, his perspective changed. He educated himself about mental health. We learned that partners of those with mood disorders need support too. He saw a therapist himself, so that he could become healthier. We went to marriage counseling together. The accusing words faded as we figured out how to navigate an altered relationship. Matthew created time and space for me to go running and continue in counseling. He saw the limits of his own ability to comfort me, so he encouraged me to be mothered by a support network of friends.

A few of those friends in particular gave me hands to hold when I was falling fast. Gwyn abandoned a party she was hosting to take my phone call from halfway across the country. She deciphered my incoherent words and murmured soothing affirmations. She taught me mantras I repeated to myself and then later to other hurting friends. *Your feelings are legitimate. I'm sorry it hurts for you. You can say the same things over and over as many times as you need to.* And I did. She made herself available on-call at all hours to respond by e-mail and text.

Jenn fixed me with food. When I didn't have the energy to cook, she took me out for cheeseburgers, and we slurped strawberry milkshakes through striped straws. She served me cookie dough like it was chicken soup. We ate it straight from the mixing bowl, talking with our mouths full.

With their care, and with the medication and therapy, I recovered. Now I am healthy, and I have two more children. My third, I carried, birthed, and breastfed while taking antidepressants, because I was terrified of plummeting into darkness again. My fourth was born at home in a new country, the Netherlands, with no medications and no recurrence of depression.

I learned how to mother my children by the way all these women mothered me. In the mornings, I'm up with coffee, scrambling eggs with one hand and packing lunch boxes with the other. We bike together to their school, even in the rain. When their little bodies get hurt, we go through boxes of bandages and bottles of Benadryl. When their hearts ache, I try to give them child-sized words for their gigantic feelings. I talk through my own emotional processing and coach them in theirs. They are free to say, "I am so angry, Mommy!" and, "That makes me sad."

I tell them, "I'm sorry it hurts. I've felt that way too."

At night, I tuck them in and sing off-key, and I pray for them. Then it's my turn to fall into bed, the good kind of tired.

My many mothers gave me time and presence. The best mothers give those things. They form secure attachments with their kids, so their children know they can adventure out from a home base of safety. I've helped my toddlers learn to walk while giving them both my hands to hold, then one, then only a pinkie. Then they're off on their own without realizing it. Eventually I could walk through my emotions on my own in healthy ways without falling. The many mothering hands hovered as long as I needed them, and they still remain close when I wobble.

HANGING ON BY A THREAD

Susan Goldberg

I keep coming back to dental floss.

This is a problem. The writer in me knows that I need to open with a strong image, and, ideally, that I should close with that image, making—no pun intended—a neat loop of a narrative, tidying up all the (forgive me) loose ends.

But what I keep returning to is the nightly ritual of flossing. I've been a model flosser for decades, a dentist's dream, scraping away at the grit between my teeth even on nights when I'd had a few drinks, even when I was exhausted, even when the tedium of oral hygiene was the only thing between me and my bed and my bed was so, so attractive. I flossed out of a sense of obligation, because it felt good, but most of all because I had long taken flossing as a bellwether of my own mental health: no matter how bad things were, I'd always figured, they couldn't be dire if I was still managing to floss. There was still hope. I mean, no one on the brink of madness, of utter collapse, says to the guys in the white suits, "I'll be with you in a second—I just need to floss my teeth."

Or do they?

You probably knew I was going to say this, but for the record: in retrospect, I'm not sure that flossing was such a good bellwether.

I'm pretty sure I didn't floss for the first few nights after my first son, Rowan, was born, a little over ten years ago. I'd had a planned C-section (he was breech) and that first week in the hospital—with its midnight shift changes and baby weigh-ins and 2:00 a.m. lactation consultations—was a blur of day and night, pain medication, and sweet exhaustion. We had decided to co-sleep, so I tucked my baby next to me in my hospital bed at night, much to the night nurse's disapproval.

"He'll get used to that," she said.

"I *want* him to get used to that," I retorted, so confident. (Spoiler alert: no one got "used to" anything involving sleep.) But by the time we got home, I was ready for routine, a clear demarcation between day and night, rest and wakefulness.

The problem was, there was very little routine, very little demarcation between day and night. There was very little rest. There *was* lots of wakefulness, though: hours and hours of it, those hours punctuated by increasingly fitful moments of sleep and, eventually, no sleep at all, even when the baby slept. Months passed with my partner, Rachel, and I juggling the nights in which our son woke as often as every forty-five minutes, soothed back to sleep only by breastfeeding or, if we were lucky, a pacifier. In the same manner in which we had chosen co-sleeping, we had also eschewed the use of a pacifier in Rowan's first few weeks. I'd read Katie Allison Granju's book on attachment parenting, which pooh-poohed the idea that a truly loved baby would gain comfort from an artificial piece of chemical-laden plastic rather than his mother's breast or, in a pinch, a parental finger. But ten days in, with my nipples cracked and sore and our arms cramped from holding them up at odd angles while the baby sucked on our fingers, we caved. We needed some relief, even though it, like the C-section instead of the natural birth I had envisioned, felt like a loss to me.

We slept in shifts—Rachel going to bed by nine to take over at 2:00 a.m. with bottles of pumped milk, me shuffling about the house with the baby sleeping against my chest in the sling, hoping to ease him into bed and catch a couple of hours of sleep (after flossing) before I could surrender responsibility.

It wasn't just sleep. My mother had died six months earlier. We'd just moved to a new city and I knew practically no one. Rowan had been born at the end of November and the weather had turned bitterly cold—getting out of the house involved shoveling, warming up the plugged-in car, and scraping the frost off the inside windows with my credit card. Leaving was a daunting prospect, and I had nowhere to go, anyway, so I didn't leave the house. Instead, I read books about infant sleep and paced the floors, day and night, with my baby.

Those books: Marc Weissbluth and Dr. Richard Ferber and Baby Whisperer Tracy Hogg and the Sears family and the anti-pacifier Granju with her tome on attachment parenting. They nearly killed me. There's a picture of me, in the early days, sitting on the sofa with my laptop on my lap, the baby sleeping next to me on the couch. It's a simple enough shot of modern life with baby while Mom catches up on e-mail. But if you could read the thought bubble above my head, it would have been filled with warring impulses: *What kind of mother are you, letting your baby sleep on the couch—on his stomach, no less? He could die.*

In my head, Hogg hissed at me to *Start as I meant to continue*: if I wanted my baby to sleep regularly, in his crib, through the night, then what kind of asshole was I being by letting him sleep on the couch? And then Granju would chime in: *What kind of monster are you for staring at your computer instead of staring lovingly at your child? Why is he sleeping on the cold, unloving couch cushion when he could be nestled against your chest, the rhythm of your beating heart in sync with his? You'll break him, you know. You already have.*

They never stopped, those voices. They kept me company in the day, kept me awake in the middle of the night. Somewhat ironically, I was ghostwriting a parenting book of my own during my son's first few months, pretending on paper to know exactly what I was doing. And I'm ashamed to admit it here, but this is just how far gone I was: when Hogg later died of cancer, and when Granju's son died of a drug overdose, my bitterness toward these two utter strangers overshadowed any empathy I felt for them. *Serves you right,* I thought initially. My apologies to them both.

There was the bonus, added complication of doing it all as a queer parent. Rachel and I had thought so much, planned so hard, bucked the system, created this baby with barely anything in the way of role models or support other than a couple of books on female fertility and the advice of a few friends. Our friend Rob agreed to donate sperm, and we did the inseminations at home, handing off the "receptacle" and its milky contents like a baton and then watching episodes of *Survivor* while I lay with my hips elevated on a pillow. It took only three cycles for our little science experiment to work and me to get pregnant—clearly, I thought, we were good at this parenting thing. Clearly, with our smarts and resourcefulness and eagerness, our sheer force of will, our penchant for negotiation and creative problem-solving, we could get through anything. Admitting that we couldn't—that our longed-for, meticulously planned baby hadn't brought the joy we imagined he would, hadn't turned us into the perfect version of the complete queer family—felt like an added failure.

These were the pre-Facebook days, and I longed for something like Facebook, some kind of beacon in the night where I could commune with other parents as I rocked and paced with my baby. Who's awake at two, three, four in the morning? Who's scared? Who's lost in grieving? Who else can no longer recognize herself? Who else is desperately looking for someone to help her feel less alone, to make sense of these feelings, to tell her that it's going to be okay—or, more to the point, to say, *You're not okay. What you're going through is real, and even common, but you're not okay. You need help.*

No one did. Friends nodded and clucked sympathetically, offered to come over for an hour or two so that I could nap, but of course I couldn't nap, so what was the point? My doctor never asked.

"I'm having a hard time," I finally said one day on the phone to my father. "I know," he said. "I know." But the conversation never went further. No one mentioned postpartum depression, suggested that maybe I should see someone. At one point, I phoned the District Health Unit to ask if they had any services that would help us sleep train the baby, because I was so tired. They phoned back and berated me for even considering letting him cry it out. *What kind of asshole are you?*

Eventually, the baby slept. First in five-hour chunks and then, after marathons of sleep training that nearly killed me and Rachel (and during which we nearly killed each other), through the night. Eventually, I took a Mindfulness-Based Stress Reduction course, got some perspective. Eventually, spring came, and then summer. Eventually, things got a bit better, then a lot better. We had a second baby.

"What sleep philosophy will we use?" I asked Rachel, justifiably terrified.

"Whatever gets everyone the most sleep," she answered, and we threw out all the books and went with what worked for us.

Through it all, I flossed. And I survived.

But I'm scarred. Recently, I talked about those times with a good friend, one of those no-holds-barred conversations that goes immediately—no small talk—to the painful core of things. "No one said anything," I said, and was suddenly racked with tears I didn't know were still there, ten years after the fact. We talked about the seemingly respectful, entirely uncomfortable silences each of us had maintained at different points in our friendship, when both of us knew something was wrong, but didn't want to overstep, didn't want to intrude, even though the hurt and the pain and the damage were obvious. And we made a vow to each other to speak up, to be the friend who says, "I think something's wrong."

On so many levels, we need to learn how to have these conversations with each other, to find ways to speak up about our own pain and acknowledge each other's. New parents need education about postpartum mood disorders well before their babies are born—and not just light references to the "baby blues." Our midwives and obstetricians and family doctors need to check in regularly. We need to establish circles of safe friends and family members who can intervene, gently, to say, "I think something's wrong. Can I help you get some help?" We need conversations—not just with the warring voices in our heads, but with each other and with the people who can help.

I still floss regularly, but every so often, even just a few times a year, I skip a night. I skip it for all the usual reasons: too tired, up until 2:00 a.m. dancing, just don't feel like it. But I also skip it to remind myself that sometimes, it's okay to take a break. I skip flossing to remind myself that my sanity, my well-being, are much too complex and complicated to be reduced to a single, arbitrary ritual of self-care. In other words, sometimes, flossing is just flossing—not the single, tenuous thread holding me together, keeping me from falling into the brink.

CRANES

Laura Haugen

One day I will tell you the story of the blizzard in April that stranded thousands of cranes in frozen fields, halting their migration north. I'll describe to you how beautiful and surreal the falling snow appeared, how helpless and lost the cranes looked as they stumbled around in the fog, how my witnessing this freak event changed me forever.

But right now I am watching you zoom around the room, arms outstretched, mimicking the graceful arc of the demoiselle cranes you saw on the Planet Earth video we watched. You delight in replaying the triumphant flight of these cranes over the snowy peaks of the Himalayas, and nothing is about to stop you.

If there's one sure thing I've gleaned from you in your four years, though, it is your unquenchable thirst for knowledge, a wild curiosity about everything on this earth, and I know it's just a matter of time before I need to tell you more, much more. You will want to know all I know about cranes, and your insistent questions will tug at me as if steadily unraveling the thread of a hem until I spin you stories that light your imagination aglow.

I love your questions, Little One. And there is so much to tell you.

Lately I've been thinking a lot about the story of us, your birth story. It's one that I haven't recounted in full to anyone, and yet when the time comes, I hope I can share it with you. I believe that the stories we tell help shape our identities and our understanding of the world. The narratives of our heritage, our family's beginnings, and our entry into this world serve as lenses through which we view the very essence of who we are. How we are each unique and all connected.

I've often wished that your birth story resembled others I've heard from new moms in our playgroups and social circles. There are the stories propelled by suspense and drama (the frantic car ride, the flat tire, the stranger who rushes in to help deliver the baby in time), those interspersed with slapstick comedy (the fainting husband, the obscenities shouted during labor), the ones claiming extraordinary ease or a magical syncing of natural rhythms (the baby who pops out unexpectedly while the doctors suit up, the candlelit home birth surrounded by midwives and soothing chants), and countless other heroic tales of plucking babes from loins and plopping them at the breast.

This is not that kind of story, and I'm not sure I know where to begin.

I struggle to find the correct starting point, the appropriate frame, and the right trajectory of your birth story, even after all this time. We could speak about the barely five-pound baby who was determined to enter this world five weeks ahead of schedule despite her parents' utter lack of preparedness. We could remark upon that fierce first cry, the head of blonde curls that made the doctors smile and call you "très jolie" in your first moments of life. We could recall your feistiness in the NICU, how you expressed in no uncertain terms that you were not to be poked and prodded with excessive wires and tubing, that you were fed up with the round-the-clock disturbances. We could tell it as a story of flair and grit and perseverance and strength, which you've shown us in abundance.

But that is not all.

We can't talk about your story without mentioning how in love we were with you from even before your first stirring inside me. I could describe the overwhelming joy I felt holding you on my chest for that first moment and peering into your curious and worldly eyes before the doctors whisked you away, the ache of being apart from you after an inseparable eight months. We could speak of the many ways your father and I struggled to be there for each other throughout the labor and all that followed—we were still new at this—but also how we were reaching and mostly succeeding in becoming a family. We could remember rejoicing with pride at each of our firsts: feeding you, bathing you, singing to you as you searched our faces. A humble story of love and good intentions and finding our footing and comfort in each other after a shaky beginning —this too is the arc of us.

Still, these are only pieces of the whole story. For all the strength it contains, the story is also about weakness. For every achievement, there were setbacks. For all the joy, an unspeakable sadness. A significant chapter of our story, Little One, was about darkness and how we stumbled through it. I wanted to spare you and the world this darkness, so I kept it hidden deep within me for a long time. I didn't realize until I saw the stranded cranes in the snowstorm that it was no longer mine to keep.

The day we saw the cranes, we were driving on the highway to spend a long Easter weekend away from the city. You were two, and you sat behind me in your car seat, chattering away cheerfully as I pointed out the cows and windmills and your dad drove. It had been snowing on and off since morning, mostly in light, scattered flurries, but suddenly it came down thick and we were caught in a heavy snow squall as we drove through a stretch of farmland. Traffic slowed to a near standstill, and with hours more driving ahead of us, we decided to turn around and head home rather than risk getting stuck in the storm. It was then that I caught a glimpse of the horrific scene in the fields all around us.

For as far as I could see, the fields were covered with dazed and faltering cranes, barely moving. Some would shuffle a few steps and fall, others struggled to spread their wings or shake the ice from their frozen limbs. Their slender frames hunched against the whirling snow, creating eerie specters, and a thick fog began to envelop them. I kept gasping and pointing out at the fields for several moments before I could make sense of what was happening. There were thousands of these birds spread out over miles of frozen fields, and long after we passed the last of them, I couldn't shake their look of sheer anguish and helplessness.

It was a feeling I knew too well.

Women often say that the pain and suffering of labor disappears the instant they hold their new babies in their arms.

That's the line I hear in the childbirth-as-a-competitive-sport league I run with sometimes. But I know plenty of women for whom this was not the case, especially those who encountered difficult labors and complications beyond the birth. Many of us carry around a complex mix of guilt, shame, anger, and fear because we were not so fortunate and we feel like failures. We stumble through the first phase of motherhood feeling lost, trying to will the fog away but not comprehending how we came to be enshrouded in it.

In the anguished looks of those cranes, I'm certain I recognized a feeling of being forsaken. An instinctive call had beckoned them north with the promise of warmth and safety and the natural rhythm of life, only to lead them to a cold and dark tundra. What was supposed to be magnificent turned ghastly. The cranes—just like the wounded and dazed mothers I saw every day in the NICU—seemed to be beseeching the skies above them, asking, "Why me?"

For a long time as a new mom, I stood frozen on that tundra, feeling forsaken. I questioned what I could have done differently; I beat myself up for having been too active and doing too much so late in the pregnancy, I wondered why I hadn't rested more or eaten differently, I asked myself how I could have failed at carrying you for the full nine months. I was angry that my body had let me down in the final stage of the pregnancy, then failed me again in refusing to open up in labor, and I felt so ashamed that I hadn't protected you. I had expected childbirth to be an empowering and beautiful experience, but when the doctors told me that my labor wasn't progressing, that my baby was in distress, and that I'd have to be cut open, I felt complete helplessness. I raged at the indignities of daily life in the NICU for you and all of us battered creatures.

The flight out of the darkness was a long and arduous journey for all of us. While we celebrated our homecoming from the NICU, we were haunted by the memory of the other little babies we had seen around us daily, some of whom we knew would face gargantuan challenges for life, and others who never made it home. It was difficult to shake the feeling that tragedy lurked at every corner, that in any moment things could go terribly wrong. We struggled in your first year through your continued health issues—sleep apnea and acid reflux and difficulty nursing. The second year too was punctuated by more tests and worry and sleepless nights. Missed milestones and a series of therapy sessions. How we fretted over you, Little One, not knowing how or when we'd make it through to easier times.

Even as I listened to two-year-old you chattering in the backseat as we drove past the snowy farmlands that April, I hadn't stopped fearing that we'd face more setbacks, that our course would never completely right itself, that I'd keep failing you.

I fretted over those cranes all the way back home that day too. I cried for them, I searched for them, I prayed that they made it out of the storm and all the way to a more hospitable place. Then a few weeks later I came across a photo online of a flock of migrating birds spotted north of us. I told myself these were at least some of the cranes we had seen, that surely some would have made it out alive. I let myself breathe a little more freely after that. I thought about how the future offspring of those cranes might bear the mark of those dark days, as if somehow the memory of snowy fields and icy wings and a compass gone haywire were imprinted in their DNA as a safeguard for their future survival. It was a thought that comforted me, gave me strength, as I tried to put my days of worrying behind me.

It was around that time that I began to realize that we, too, had rounded the arc from our dark days in the NICU and the trials that followed, to a place of relative safety, warmth, and light. I realized it was time to tell the story, the dark chapters and all. You've grown into a spirited and bright four-year-old, Little One, and we've come so far from the fog. Despite all the hardships that set us back, made us more fragile, they also made us stronger, smarter, better able to weather the storms that come our way. I think because of our ordeal, we celebrate our joys more readily, express our affection freely. We know when to turn around and head home to avert unnecessary danger. Because of our stumbling through the cold and bleak darkness, our compasses are recalibrated now, set dependably toward the light.

One day soon I'm sure I'll be able to point out to you a flock of birds in formation above us. Or maybe we'll see a single slender crane teetering in a treetop, ready to launch into the sky. We'll talk about the magic of their seasonal migrations, their triumph over cold and inhospitable climates, the beauty and mystery of nature. But I'll also tell you about the cranes stranded in frozen fields as they tried to make their way northward through an April blizzard. I know it will sound familiar to you, because it's part of our shared story, the story of our very beginnings and how we found our way. Soon it will be your story to carry on and carry with you as you take flight along a trajectory all your own. I'm watching you now, Little One, with your arms stretched wide and your chin jutting up as you race around the room. The afternoon sun lights up your face and I can already see you soar.

SHATTERED AND WHOLE:
EMBRACING AMBIVALENCE

Sarah Rudell Beach

I always thought Corelle was supposed to be unbreakable. Their website says it's "smart, strong, [and] stylish." Yet there I was, staring at the remains of a white Corelle plate shattered into hundreds of pieces on my cracked vinyl countertop, my chipped linoleum floor, my messy kitchen sink, and my stylish stainless steel toaster.

But I did not feel stylish. Or smart. And certainly not strong. I felt like a maxed-out and disheveled mother, as shattered as her cheap dinnerware.

The kitchen, filled moments before with yelling and whining and screaming as I emptied the dishwasher at the end of a long day, fell oppressively silent. My children, then ages four and one, stared at me.

My husband was out of town. He'd been out of town for the last five days. I was tired, exhausted, and overwhelmed.

And I had just smashed a plate on the kitchen counter.

My anger and aggression shocked me. I thought moms who got so mad that they shattered a plate to get the attention of their whining children only existed on the Lifetime Movie Network.

I quickly tried to recover.

"Oh, no! I dropped the plate!" I said. "Silly Mommy!" I faked a weak smile.

My four-year-old looked at me suspiciously. Was this the first time she realized her mother could lie?

"You slammed it because you were mad at Liam," she said, matter-of-factly.

"Oh, no," I lied. "It slipped."

But I *had* slammed it. *Hard.* Because the whining and yelling and complaining had been too much.

What precisely led me to take a plate and crash it full force into the counter? My memory of this incident is like the dramatic opening of that Lifetime movie—cut to the crazed mother, stunned children, fragmented dishware, and disheveled kitchen. Cue the dark and heavy music. What could those cherubic-looking children have possibly done to produce such a clichéd mommy meltdown? I still don't know.

All I know is that something I had once thought unbreakable was now broken, lying in thousands of pieces in my dirty kitchen.

❧

Before having children, I rarely cried. In fact, for years of my adult life, I would tell the story of how the only time I could recall crying in recent years was when I had overdrawn my bank account. I felt so ashamed, and then angry that in my humiliation the bank would charge me an extra $30.

But crying became a big part of my experience of early motherhood, especially after the birth of my second child. I remember too many nights of putting the kids to bed, and then sitting on the couch and crying. For hours, the tears wouldn't stop.

That wasn't me.

Motherhood had transformed me. And I didn't know into what. I simply knew I didn't want to be broken, crying on my couch each night.

Perhaps a shattered plate is the perfect metaphor for modern motherhood—many of us today are becoming mothers later in life. We experience years of independence: career success, clean homes, adequate sleep, and a schedule that is entirely our own. And then a tiny seven-pound creature upends the whole foundation. Our sleep is fragmented, our lives are tethered to the needs of a small stranger, our careers are put on hold, our homes are strewn with toys and all sorts of infant containment and swinging devices, and the whole notion of a *schedule* becomes laughable. We may encounter the profound ambivalence of motherhood—a simultaneous desire for our old life combined with a powerful love for our new life with our child. Our whole identity feels fractured by competing desires.

I think many of our postpartum struggles derive from this ambivalence, from wrestling with this absolutely normal part of motherhood that is demonized in our culture. *What mom would admit that sometimes she doesn't like being a mother?* Though I couldn't put it into words in my plate-smashing days, I can see now that ambivalence was at the heart of my postpartum depression.

For the first seventy-two hours after my daughter was born, it felt so easy. My entire world had shrunk to the size of that small hospital room. I had a bed, my husband had his chair to sleep in, we had a private bathroom, and I had someone bringing me three meals a day. If my daughter was fussy at night, I could simply page the nurse and she would whisk her away to the nursery, where, I assume, because I never actually saw it, a combination of swings, warm blankets, and kind night-shift nurses would rock and soothe my fussy child so I could sleep.

Approximately every half hour I was warned that, by virtue of having a C-section, I was at greater risk for postpartum depression; I should call them if the baby blues lasted longer than a few weeks. They were there to help me. *I'll be fine*, I told them. *How hard could it be?*

I felt the first stirrings of ambivalence when I arrived home after my three-day stay in the hospital. I longed to be at home, in my own bed without all those needles in my arms. And at the same time, I was panicked. How can these doctors allow me to leave with this little seven-pound human? How can the only test for readiness to leave the hospital be the fact that we have both pooped in the last twenty-four hours? That doesn't seem to be a challenging standard for parenthood approval.

I returned home and everything looked different. *I* was different. I was a mother, but I had no idea *how* to be a mother. Sure, I had read a lot of books in preparation for having a baby. I devoured those books, and took notes. *Labor won't be what I expect*, okay. *My identity will change*, no big deal. *Babies sleep sixteen to eighteen hours a day.* Fantastic! I went to the classes at the hospital, and had baby showers where I received things like wipe-warmers and other first-world necessities for raising children.

None of it—not the books or the showers or the childbirth classes—prepared me in a way that helped me understand my new role or revealed my new self to the larger society. All I had in my toolkit were completely useless platitudes: *You'll be fine! Rely on your mother's intuition! You'll just know!*

But I didn't *just know.* I had read that I would be able to identify my baby's different cries—different vocalizations meant she was hungry, cold, wet, scared, or in pain. I even watched YouTube videos of an adult woman imitating the cries of infants, pointing out the variations in tone, pitch, and tongue position that I should listen for. But when my daughter cried, which she did *a lot,* it was just loud and sent me into a panic. I couldn't distinguish any differences between her cries and concluded I had no mother's intuition.

When she was a week old, I could finally drive again (the doctors had told me to wait a week after the C-section). I was nervous to drive my car, because the last time I had done so was a week before her birth, when my vision began to blur and my blood pressure spiked, and I drove to work in a crazed panic, unable to see the road in front of me, guided only by my peripheral vision. Which was pretty much how motherhood felt at that moment.

I decided I would venture to the mall to buy my daughter some clothes. Every pregnancy book I read advised that I skip purchasing 0–3 month sizes, as they would be too small for most babies. But my daughter was a peanut, and all her clothes were too big. Not for the last time, I cursed the advice of parenting books and told my mom that I needed to go out and get some clothes. I nursed my daughter, and handed her to her grand-mother.

It was my first time leaving her, and I didn't feel sad. I didn't feel anxious. I didn't really feel anything, except a power-ful desire to escape. *That* was what panicked me—shouldn't I be freaking out about leaving my child? Isn't having a kid like having your heart walking around outside your body or some shit like that? *I am leaving my heart! And I'm not sad! I need to run an errand, and I am totally okay with leaving my child. WHAT THE HELL IS WRONG WITH ME??*

Still I bent down, kissed her fuzzy head, and said, "I'll miss you," even though I knew I wouldn't. I felt I had to say it. What would my mom think if I just left breezily, as if I were leaving her to watch the dog? Aren't mothers supposed to cry in agony when they leave their children for the first time? Shouldn't I be powerfully *attached* to her by now? The lack of immediate love for my baby weighed surprisingly heavy in my anxious heart.

One night at dinner, a few weeks later, I confessed to my husband that I didn't yet feel this amazing and powerful love for my daughter. I felt overwhelmed and tired and angry. And, somehow, I also felt numb.

"It all just feels so *intellectual* right now," I told him. "I'm doing what I read in my books, and taking care of her, but I don't feel like I've bonded with her." Motherhood felt like a job, and I was carefully completing all the duties listed in the job description. It didn't feel like something I did with passion and intensity. In fact, I was starting to think I didn't really like this new career path, and I resented my overly demanding employer, which just added to my feelings of failure. Aren't I supposed to be head-over-heels in love with her? Aren't I supposed to be *loving every minute* of this?

In the early months with my daughter, there was a lot of crying and pacing around my small house trying to get her to nap. I remember days when I didn't even shower, let alone brush my teeth, because my Velcro-baby wanted nothing more than to be held all freaking day long. When she was about four months old, I signed us up for a mommy-and-me class because we *had to* get out of the house. On the first day, the instructor welcomed us to the class and asked us to introduce ourselves. "And tell us the one thing that has most surprised you about motherhood so far," she added.

Where would I begin? I had so much I wanted to share with my fellow tribe of mothers: how *unprepared* I felt, how *boring* it was at home with an infant, how tired I was, how little she slept during the day. Could I tell them that some days my growing love for my daughter was equally matched with a powerful yearning for my life before she was born, and I was terrified that one day the scale would tip to the dark and scary side?

But then I listened to the other mothers share how unexpectedly powerful their love for their child was. Or how amazing it was to see older siblings bond with the new baby. Story after story of unexpected but wonderful and positive aspects of motherhood. One mother told us, "I guess I'm just surprised by how much I still feel like me! I still do the things I did before having her. I can sit and read a magazine when she naps, so I still have time for myself." *Are you fucking kidding me?*

What kind of mother was I that the first things I thought of, out of all of my unexpecteds, were *negative*: the things I dreaded, the darkness I was now convinced only I experienced? My verdict was in: I was a terrible mother.

Once my maternity leave ended, and I went back to work, I figured things would get better. *I'll be myself again!* And for a time, it felt like I was. But when I went back to work after my son was born, and tried to balance full-time work and caring for two children, the darkness and depression returned.

∽

We often see two extreme versions of the new mother—smiling and serene, or murderously crazy. The media give us airbrushed images of celebrity mamas, with gorgeous postpartum bodies, pushing their bundles of joy in designer strollers. Or they give us Susan Smith archetypes, like Carrie in *Homeland*, who abandons her baby (after nearly drowning her) to escape to the safety and stability of fighting terrorists in Islamabad. These polarized archetypes make no room for the vast middle ground in which we mother. They make no room for serenity and rage to exist in the same person. They make no room for ambivalence. They make it really hard to recognize when we need help.

I resisted getting professional help for the longest time. At first, I didn't think I was actually depressed. Depression medication commercials showed people who couldn't even get out of bed, despite that adorable dog looking at them with the sad face wanting to play ball. *I get out of bed every day and go to work and make dinner—if I were depressed, I wouldn't be able to function!*

I was also scared to get help. The most terrifying parts of my postpartum depression were the intrusive thoughts. As I made dinner in the kitchen, I had disturbing images of dropping a knife on my daughter. When she was six months old, we stayed in a vacation home with a gorgeous spiral staircase in a tiled entryway. All I could see when I went up the stairs were images of my daughter falling to the ground below and smashing her head open. I held her tight to my chest and raced up the steps in horror. After my son was born, I walked to my car in the parking lot at work in a panic each afternoon, convinced I would open the doors to the horrifying discovery that I had forgotten to drop my children off at daycare. I knew I would never deliberately hurt them, but those frightening images wouldn't leave me alone.

When my mother and my husband encouraged me to see a psychiatrist, I thought, *No one can give me a pill that will make me a normal mom!* I figured I would just have to make peace with the fact that I would be a mom who didn't really like motherhood, who played the part even though it didn't feel quite right. *I can't reveal these terrible thoughts to anyone,* I told myself. *I can make this work.*

And then one day I smashed a plate on the kitchen counter out of frustration with my children. It wasn't working. I hadn't found peace. I picked up the phone and told my doctor, "My baby is already sixteen months old, but I think I have postpartum depression."

∽

Motherhood is often described as a journey. I think it's the hero's journey, the universal myth described by Joseph Campbell. The heroine is called to an adventure, an arduous undertaking. She crosses the threshold as she begins her transformation, often with the aid of helping friends and mentors (like Yoda, or her mother). Before her metamorphosis is complete, she plunges alone into the abyss, the proverbial "dark night of the soul." The mother-heroine faces difficult tasks and trials, and she suffers loss and agony as she journeys through the darkness. But she ultimately resurfaces and rejoins the world, bringing with her an elixir—the holy grail—that brings healing and wholeness.

When the heroine-mother is lost in the abyss of post-partum depression, the magical elixir can seem elusive, but it exists. For me, it was the combination of medication and meditation that saved me from the fire-breathing dragon. I broke my silence, and discovered that many brave women have battled the same dark demons.

The next step is for the heroine to bring the insights and blessings from her profound journey into her everyday life. She finds atonement—at-one-ment—by integrating her two worlds. For me, integration means acknowledging and accepting that sometimes motherhood is amazing, and sometimes it sucks. I know now that ambivalence about motherhood is absolutely normal. I know that my depression was not my fault and did not happen because I was a bad mother. I know those dark and scary thoughts were my depression, and not me. I know that becoming whole doesn't mean loving motherhood all of the time. I know that being a good mom doesn't mean I must deny my ambivalence. I know that I can be a mom, and still be *me*.

Perhaps the ultimate boon from my journey is my story. I desperately wanted to become a mother. I had a beautiful baby. I didn't fall in love with her right away. But today I love her, and my son, intensely and fiercely. I cried a lot right along with my babies, and sometimes wondered why I'd ever had them. And now I cannot imagine my life without them. I love being a mother, and I also love when my house is quiet and my children are not around. I love being with my children and I love being at work. Motherhood contains multitudes.

We can be shattered, and we can become whole again. That smashed plate ended up in my trash years ago. But it's still part of the mosaic of my motherhood journey: beautiful and grotesque, dark and shining, and gorgeously, amazingly complicated.

Q & A *with* JESSICA ZUCKER, PHD

∽

Dr. Jessica Zucker is a Los Angeles-based clinical psychologist
and writer specializing in women's reproductive and maternal
mental health. She primarily works with women struggling
with fertility issues, pregnancy ambivalence, pregnancy loss,
during transitions in motherhood, prenatal and postpartum
adjustments, perinatal and postpartum mood and anxiety disorders, pregnancy and postpartum body image concerns, and in
the midst of relationship challenges after the birth of a child.
Jessica contributes to myriad publications, including the *New
York Times*, the *Washington Post*, *BuzzFeed*, *Glamour*, *Medium*,
Modern Loss, *Every Mother Counts*, and *Goop*, among others. In
addition, Jessica has contributed to various books pertaining to
the maternal mental health landscape.

We were honored to have the opportunity to ask Dr.
Zucker about her perspective on this collection as well as her
clinical work with women who have perinatal mood disorders.

JESSICA & STEPHANIE: What were your first impressions as a
clinician after reading the essays?

DR. JESSICA ZUCKER: I am in awe of the candidness and the
beauty interwoven through the revelations discovered in pain.
These essays illustrate such stunning range and poignant depth
—from a lyrical perspective and also the treacherous emotional
landscape of perinatal and postpartum mood and anxiety disorders. There is something incredibly powerful about com-

mitting your story to the page, to expose your struggle to yourself even when you are the one who lived it, and to share it with others.

Even if the traumatic experience was many years ago, reflecting on such a challenging journey can evoke difficult memories, potentially stirring up feelings such as guilt, sadness, anger, regret, grief, hope, gratitude, and many other emotions. Writing about these periods of anguish in our lives can also help us make sense, over and over again, of our heartache and fortitude. Writing provides a perspective that yields or even sheds light on the process of catharsis. It is one thing to read clinical papers and scientific studies about postpartum depression, but it's another when the actual person who lived it shares their personal narrative in such vivid and riveting detail.

In my clinical practice, I sit with women navigating perinatal and postpartum challenges every day. Hearing about the glaring statistics that one in seven women are affected by postpartum mood and anxiety disorders doesn't necessarily help women feel less alone. It is reading essays like these that have the potential to promote resonance and healing for those suffering. The accessibility of the writing and the cogency of these horrendous experiences bring to life this incredibly complicated disorder that ravages too many new mothers.

J & S: How does a new mother know when her feelings and thoughts can no longer be considered "normal" and she should seek help?

JZ: It can be quite tricky to know when her feelings and thoughts are no longer within the "normal" range, particularly due to the logistical and emotional stamina new motherhood requires. For example, things like sleep deprivation, hormonal changes, birth trauma, a hard-to-soothe baby, and emerging into this newfound role as a mother inevitably make for quaky ground. The ingredients are tough.

Most people struggle to some degree as they get to know what motherhood is all about. The enormous responsibilities that come along with raising a human being can be confounding. When nagging feelings become more prominent or if negative feelings persist, then it is likely time to seek help. Approximately 80 percent of women experience what is termed the baby blues after giving birth. Symptoms might include weepiness, irritability, fatigue, mood changes, and insomnia and might last up to about two weeks.

It is important to note that the baby blues are not postpartum depression. Baby blues are considered "normal" and even expectable. If the baby blues persist or worsen past the initial couple of weeks in motherhood, then attention should be paid and additional support galvanized. It is tempting to hope that these postpartum difficulties will go away on their own, but research reveals that when postpartum depression is left untreated, the symptoms can worsen and become intractable.

J & S: What does recovery often look like for a woman experiencing PPD?

JZ: Recovery comes in all shapes and sizes, and can be quite circuitous in some cases. There isn't a one-size-fits-all approach to treatment or to the emergence from postpartum depression.

What I hear most from women turning the corner from postpartum depression into a place where they actually enjoy being mothers is, "I can't believe I didn't get help sooner. I was ashamed to share my feelings and hoped they would go away on their own. It didn't feel possible to thoroughly appreciate motherhood and experience joy. Now I do."

Understandably, people typically have a variety of feelings pertaining to seeking help, being in therapy, needing treatment, and/or taking medication. These feelings sometimes create significant roadblocks to getting professional help in a timely manner. Ideally, a woman experiencing postpartum depression is in treatment with a therapist who specializes in women's reproductive and maternal mental health issues. In addition, it is optimal if she consults with a reproductive psychiatrist, providing her with additional clinical insight and support. If she wants to involve her partner in the treatment, couples therapy can be another important tool to revitalizing the family structure.

J&S: What should women considering pregnancy know about postpartum depression?

JZ: Women considering pregnancy should be informed about potential risk factors, signs and symptoms, and treatment options for postpartum depression. Given the fact that postpartum depression is a public health crisis, affecting over one million women in the United States each year, it is vitally important that women have a solid understanding of what has been named the most common complication associated with childbirth.

Being armed with this knowledge will serve to better help

women who do in fact experience a postpartum mood or anxiety disorder identify symptoms early. The sooner women get the help they need, the better off the family can function. The passage of time does not make postpartum depression dissipate. Therefore, prompt treatment is the ideal course of action when new mothers meet the criteria for a perinatal or postpartum mood or anxiety disorder.

Pregnant women in my clinical practice often share that they are scared to know the facts for fear that it will heighten anxiety or even make them more prone to experiencing postpartum depression somehow. I reassure the mothers-to-be that being up to speed on what to pay attention to after birth can actually create less anxiety because it means they can spot potential problems without confusion. Rather than waiting weeks or even months to reach out for help if postpartum depression should arise, women who understand what to look for are in a position to feel better faster.

We will be donating a portion of our book profits to Postpartum Progress, an incredible organization for women dealing with postpartum depression and other perinatal mood disorders. If you are struggling, we encourage you to utilize their vast resources for seeking help. Learn more at http://postpartumprogress.org.

AUTHOR BIOS

Alana Joblin Ain

Mother, writer, and teacher, Alana Joblin Ain earned her MFA in poetry from Hunter College in New York City, where she has taught creative writing and literature. Her writing has appeared in the *New York Times*, *Dossier Journal*, *Crab Orchard Review*, *Quarterly West*, and *RealPoetik*, among other publications. Alana lives in Brooklyn with her husband, Dan, and their two children, Autumn and Samson.

Laura Miller Arrowsmith

Laura Miller Arrowsmith is a teacher, writer, and mother. Her writing reflects her ongoing desire to capture and describe the often lonely, deeply vexing times of motherhood so that others might laugh, cry, and share in that universal longing to be a good parent. She has published numerous essays and articles on parenting, faith, and community building in *Brain, Child Magazine*; the *Loudoun Times-Mirror*; and the *Washington Post Magazine*. She lives in Leesburg, Virginia, with her husband and three children. She can be reached at larrow9@verizon.net.

Suzanne Barston

Suzanne Barston is the author of *Bottled Up: How the Way We Feed Babies Has Come to Define Motherhood, and Why It Shouldn't*, the creator of the international "Fearless Formula Feeder" community, and the cocreator of the #ISupportYou Movement. She is currently working on her first novel, which has absolutely nothing to do with infant feeding (thank god). She lives in the Los Angeles, California, area with her two kids, husband, and a very peculiar mutt.

Elizabeth Bastos

Elizabeth Bastos is a Baltimore freelance writer and mother of two. Her work has appeared in the *Rumpus*, the *Baltimore Sun*, *McSweeney's*, WYPR, the *Boston Globe*, the *Motherlode* blog of the *New York Times*, and *Book Riot*, and she writes an urban nature column for *Baltimore Fishbowl*. She is currently working on a book of essays about the Venn diagram of parenting and anxiety disorders. Her personal blog is *Goody Bastos*.

Sarah Rudell Beach

Sarah Rudell Beach is a teacher, writer, and mother to two little ones. She is the creator of *Left Brain Buddha*, where she explores ideas and practices for mindfulness, and shares the challenges and riches in her journey to live and parent mindfully in a left-brain, analytical life. She is also the Executive Director of Brilliant Mindfulness, LLC.

Alexa Bigwarfe

Alexa Bigwarfe is a freelance writer and author. She is the coauthor of *Lose the Cape: Realities from Busy Modern Moms and Strategies to Survive* and editor and contributor to the book *Sunshine After the Storm: A Survival Guide for the Grieving Mother*. She launched her writing with the blog *No Holding Back*, as an outlet for her grief after the loss of one of her twin daughters to Twin-to-Twin Transfusion Syndrome (TTTS). Alexa is a wife, mother of three, dog owner, and advocate.

Jennifer Bullis

Jennifer Bullis holds a PhD in English from the University of California, Davis, and taught community-college writing and literature in Bellingham, Washington, for fourteen years. Her poems appear in *Iron Horse Literary Review*, *Natural Bridge*, *Heron Tree*, *Wherewithal*, *Tahoma Literary Review*, *Bellingham Review*, and *Journal of Feminist Studies in Religion*. Her poetry collection, *Impossible Lessons*, was published in 2013 by MoonPath Press. She blogs about poetry at www.jenniferbullis.com.

Kristi Rieger Campbell

Kristi Rieger Campbell's passion is writing and drawing stupid-looking pictures for her blog, *Finding Ninee*. It began with a memoir about her special-needs son, Tucker—a memoir she abandoned when she read that a publisher would rather shave a cat than read another memoir. Kristi writes for a variety of parenting websites, including *Huffington Post Parents*; has been published in several popular anthologies; received 2014 BlogHer's Voice of the Year People's Choice Award; and was a proud cast member of the DC Listen To Your Mother show. She almost always leaves home in either Uggs or flip-flops.

Denise Emanuel Clemen

Denise Emanuel Clemen's fiction and essays have appeared or are forthcoming in the *Georgetown Review* (including an honorable mention for their prize), *Two Hawks Quarterly*, *Literary Mama*, *The Rattling Wall*, *Fiction Fix*, *Knee-Jerk*, *Chagrin River Review*, *Delmarva Review*, *New Plains Review*, and *Serving House Journal*. She's received fellowships to the Virginia Center for the Creative Arts, Vermont Studio Center, and Ragdale Foundation, and was an Auvillar fellow in France in 2009. Her memoir, *Birth Mother*, was published by Shebooks in 2014. Denise blogs at leavingdivorceville.blogspot.com and deniseemanuelclemen.com.

Dawn S. Davies

Dawn S. Davies is the recipient of the Florida International University UGS Provost Award for Best Creative Project and the Kentucky Women Writers Gabehart Prize. She has been awarded residencies with the Vermont Studio Center and Can Serrat. Her work has appeared or is forthcoming in *Real South Magazine*; *River Styx*; *Brain, Child*; *Hippocampus*; *Cease, Cows*; *Saw Palm*; *Border Crossing*; *New Plains Review*; *Literary Orphans*; *Green Mountains Review*; *Ninth Letter*; *Fourth Genre*; *Chautauqua*; and elsewhere. You can find out more about her at dawnsdavies.com.

Estelle Erasmus

Estelle Erasmus is an award-winning journalist and former magazine editor-in-chief. She has contributed to several anthologies, including *My Other Ex: Women's True Stories of Leaving and Losing Friends*. This year, Estelle will also have essays in *Love*

Her, Love Her Not: The Hillary Paradox, edited by Joanne Bamburger and published by She Writes Press, and in *Recipes with a Story* by Blue Lobster Book Co. Estelle's writing is found on *Brain, Child*; the *Washington Post*'s *On Parenting*; *Purple Clover*; *Marie Claire*; *xoJane*; the *Huffington Post*; *Working Mother*; *Role Reboot*; *The Mid*; *Erma Bombeck Writers' Workshop*; Felicity Huffman's *What the Flicka?*; and other publications. She was named a BlogHer Voice of the Year 2015 for her story "Giving Up the Ghost Baby," published on *Purple Clover*. Estelle is a SheKnows Parenting Expert, and a member of the American Society of Journalists and Authors (ASJA) and the American Society of Magazine Editors (ASME). Estelle blogs about raising a young daughter in midlife at *Musings on Motherhood & Midlife* and is on Twitter at @EstelleSErasmus.

Maureen Fura

Maureen Fura is a storyteller and activist. She recently coproduced, wrote, and directed *The Dark Side of the Full Moon*, the first documentary exposing the barriers of care when women face a mental health crisis during pregnancy and the postpartum period in the United States. She is the mother of two beautiful sons and birth mother to a fearless young woman who hates brushing her hair as much as she does. Maureen has a story in the *Badass: Lip Service Anthology*. She lives in Miami.

Nina Gaby

Nina Gaby is a writer, visual artist, and psychiatric nurse practitioner living in New England. Her anthology, *Dumped: Stories of Women Unfriending Women*, was just released this spring by She Writes Press. Gaby has contributed to numerous anthologies and periodicals, including *The Maternal Is Political* and *I Wanna Be Sedated* by Seal Press, *I Wasn't Strong Like This When I Started Out: True Stories of Becoming a Nurse* by In Fact Press/Creative Non-Fiction, and fiction in *Lilith* magazine and Paper Journey Press anthologies, and she has guest-blogged on numerous sites, including Brevity.com. She is currently working on a series of mixed-media three-dimensional memoir vessels, and her sculptural porcelain is in the permanent collection of the Renwick Gallery of the Smithsonian. Gaby is thrilled to be included in this anthology and feels it will serve as an important addition to the literature on trauma and postpartum depression; most importantly, as personal narrative rather than academic, it will be accessible to the women who will most benefit from it. Gaby can be found infrequently blogging at www.ninagaby.com.

Susan Goldberg

Susan Goldberg is a writer, editor, essayist, and blogger, and coeditor of the award-winning anthology *And Baby Makes More: Known Donors, Queer Parents and Our Unexpected Families* (Insomniac Press, 2009). Her personal essays have been featured in *Ms.*, *Lilith*, *Today's Parent*, and *Stealing Time* magazines, as well as in several anthologies and collections. She is a contributing blogger for VillageQ.com and *Today's Parent*, where she blogs regularly as *The Other Mother*. In 2012, Susan was chosen as one of BlogHer's Voices of the Year community keynote speakers, and has twice been a VOTY honoree. She is one of approximately thirty Jews in Thunder Bay, Ontario, where she lives with her family.

Lea Grover

Lea Grover is a writer and speaker living on Chicago's South Side. Her writing has been featured in numerous anthologies, including *Listen To Your Mother: What She Said Then, What We're Saying Now,* and on websites ranging from the *Huffington Post* to *AlterNet* to the *Daily Mail Online,* and she speaks about sex positivity in parenting, and on behalf of the RAINN Speakers Bureau.

Laura Haugen

Laura Haugen is a graduate of Northwestern's Medill School of Journalism and Georgetown's School of Foreign Service. She has worked as a journalist at various publications and served as a diplomat in Washington, DC, Oman, Bosnia and Herzegovina, Serbia, Tunisia, and Jordan. She is currently a freelance writer and lives in Berlin, Germany, with her husband and nearly five-year-old daughter.

Eve Kagan

Eve Kagan is a writer, actress, international theatre teaching artist, and yoga instructor. She is a Harvard graduate with an EdM specializing in Arts in Education. Her essays have appeared in the *Huffington Post* and *Teaching Artist Journal,* and her short story "Spit the Truth" can be found in the anthology *Dark City Lights: New York Stories* (Three Rooms Press, April 2015). Eve travels the world with her husband, almost two-year-old daughter, and seven-year-old English Setter.

Jenny Kanevsky

Jenny Kanevsky's debut mystery novel, *Chosen Quarry*, is available on Kindle, and she blogs at *In Other Words* (http://jennykanevsky.com). She is a regular contributor at *Huffington Post*, *The Good Men Project*, and *BLUNTMoms*. Her work is also featured in the recently published anthologies *I Am Here: The Untold Stories of Everyday People* and *Motherhood May Cause Drowsiness, 2nd Edition*. She lives in Austin, Texas, with her two sons, now ages thirteen and ten.

Kate Kearns

Kate Kearns is a poet, mother, manuscript editor, wife, and business owner, jumping on all the equipment in the writing playground. This is her first personal essay. Kate earned her MFA in Creative Writing at Lesley University. Her poetry collection, *How to Love an Introvert*, was released in 2015 through Finishing Line Press, and her short fiction has appeared at *Mash Stories*. You can read her blog and follow her publications at www.blacksquirrelworkshop.com.

Karen Lewis

Karen Lewis lives in rural northern California where she leads workshops with California Poets in the Schools and directs the Mendocino Coast Writers Conference. Her essays, poems, and fiction have appeared in *Hip Mama*, *Iron Horse Literary Review*, *Instant City*, *Literary Mama*, and in magazines for youth. Her daughter now lives and works as a mountaineer, and her son is a business strategist and chef.

Celeste Noelani McLean

Celeste Noelani McLean is the woman behind *RunningNekkid*, where she explores the intersection of grief, mental health, and her Pacific Islander ancestry. Her writing has been featured on *BlogHer* and has appeared in *SisterWives Speak* and *Stigma Fighters*. She left her island paradise home over twenty years ago and has been trying to figure out how to get back ever since. She currently lives in Seattle with her husband, Ian, where they raise two children, grieve one, and make each other very, very happy. You can find her at her blog, www.RunningNekkid.com.

Becky Castle Miller

Becky Castle Miller is the Managing Editor of *Wyn Magazine*, providing resources and hope for mental and emotional healing. In 2009, she had an emotional breakdown that uncovered heartache, loss, and undiagnosed postpartum depression. Now she's figuring out a healthy life with her husband and four children as American expats in the Netherlands.

Randon Billings Noble

Randon Billings Noble is an essayist. Her work has appeared in the Modern Love column of the *New York Times*; the *Millions*; *Brain, Child*; *Literary Mama*; *Los Angeles Review of Books*; the *Georgia Review*; *Shenandoah*; the *Rumpus*; *Brevity*; *Fourth Genre*; and elsewhere. A fellow at the Virginia Center for the Creative Arts and a resident at the Vermont Studio Center, she was named a 2013 Mid Atlantic Arts Foundation Creative Fellow to attend a residency at The Millay Colony for the Arts. Currently she is a nonfiction editor at *r.kv.r.y quarterly* and Reviews Editor at *PANK*.

Kara Overton

Kara Overton is a wife, mother, teacher, and proud survivor of postpartum anxiety. She lives in southeast Iowa with her husband and two daughters and works as a high school English teacher. She enjoys untangling her thoughts on her blog, *An Adventure Story*, where she writes about the triumphs and trials of motherhood. You can find her on Twitter at @overtonkara or at her blog at www.anadventurestory.com.

Jill Robbins

Jill Robbins is a wannabe wine snob and sometime runner from San Antonio, Texas. She has a degree in social psychology, which has so far been unhelpful in understanding the behavior of her husband and three children. She writes about adoption, motherhood, and midlife on her blog, *Ripped Jeans and Bifocals*. Jill is a regular contributor to the *Huffington Post*, *BLUNTMoms*, *Babble*, and *Mamalode*, and she is also a BlogHer 2015 honoree. She's also been published in the *Washington Post*'s *On Parenting* and is a proud member of the 2015 cast of Listen To Your Mother, Austin. Her work has also been featured on *Scary Mommy*, *Mamapedia Voices*, *In the Powder Room*, *SheKnows Parenting*, *Midlife Boulevard*, *Beyond Your Blog*, and other places around the Internet. Her print publications include the December 2014 issue of *Mamalode* and three upcoming anthologies about motherhood. She someday hopes to write the books that are living in her head.

Alexandra Rosas

Alexandra is an award-winning blogger and BlogHer Voice of the Year four years running. She is a published author, live storyteller with the nationally acclaimed *The Moth*, and coproducer of Listen To Your Mother Milwaukee. You can follow her adventures of life in a small town where she tries hard to go unnoticed on her personal blog *Good Day Regular People*. She is a contributor to *Huffington Post*, *Purple Clover*, *MetroParent*, and several other online sites. Offline, she lives in Wisconsin with her husband and three sons. But she's mostly online on Twitter and Facebook.

Dana Schwartz

Dana Schwartz is a lifelong fiction writer who recently discovered a passion for personal essays. She received her MFA from Fairleigh Dickinson University in 2008. Since then two of her short stories were finalists in contests and published in the following journals: "The Moment of Departure" in *New South Journal* (2014), and "On the Ground Looking Up" in *Crab Orchard Review* (2008). She contributed to The HerStories Project on female friendship and was a cast member of the Lehigh Valley 2015 Listen To Your Mother show. She writes about the creative process and motherhood on her blog, *Writing at the Table*, contributes monthly to *The Gift of Writing*, and is currently working on a novel. She lives in New Hope, Pennsylvania, with her husband, Steven, and their two children, Emma and Leo.

Jen Simon

Jen Simon is a *Huffington Post* blogger and a *Babble* contributor. A freelance writer, her work has appeared on *Scary Mommy*, *Elephant Journal*, *Your Tango*, *The Frisky*, *Kveller*, *Nerve*, *Women's Health Online*, and more. *Mothering Through the Darkness* is her fourth anthology, her second with the HerStories Project. Jen stays home with her sons—a toddler and a sleep-challenged five-year-old.

Kim Simon

Kim Simon is a freelance writer and mother, who divides her time between directing The Simon Family Circus, and chronicling it. Her essays on parenting, social justice issues, and current events have been featured on the *Huffington Post*, *MSN Living*, *Mamalode*, *Scary Mommy*, *xoJane*, and other online magazines. She is the cofounder of the I Support You project, and the facilitator of the parent support group "The Truth About Motherhood." Kim is a frequent guest speaker, presenting on the motherhood identity shift, the "fourth trimester," and infant feeding choice. Kim lives in the San Francisco Bay Area with her husband and two little boys. She can be found telling the truth about motherhood on her personal blog *Mama By the Bay* (http://mamabythebay.com), on Twitter @mamabythebay, and on Facebook.

Katie Sluiter

Katie Sluiter lives in Zeeland, Michigan, with her husband and three young children. She holds a master's degree in English and teaches Language Arts to eighth and ninth graders. She blogs about being a teacher and mother at *Sluiter Nation*. You can also find her documenting her life on Facebook, Twitter, and Instagram.

Allie Smith

Allie Smith is a wife, mother of four, and freelance writer living in the suburbs of Atlanta. She's a columnist for *My Forsyth Magazine*, a book reviewer for *Chick Lit Plus*, and a contributor to The Family Legacy Center. Her work has been published on the *Huffington Post*, *Scary Mommy*, *Full Grown People*, and several other publications. Allie has a bad case of wanderlust and can often be found surfing travel websites and planning her family's next epic road trip. She blogs about parenting, autism, travel, and books at *The Latchkey Mom*.

Maggie Smith

Maggie is an accomplished poet, but, amazingly, this is her first personal essay. Maggie Smith's second book of poems, *The Well Speaks of Its Own Poison* (Tupelo Press, April 2015), was selected by Kimiko Hahn as the winner of the Dorset Prize. She is also the author of *Lamp of the Body* (Red Hen Press, 2005), winner of the Benjamin Saltman Poetry Award, and three prizewinning chapbooks, the latest of which is *Disasterology* (Dream Horse Press, forthcoming 2015). A 2011 National Endowment for the Arts Fellow in poetry, Maggie has also received four Individual Excellence Awards from the Ohio Arts Council and fellowships from the Sustainable Arts Foundation and the Virginia Center for the Creative Arts. She lives with her husband and two children in Bexley, Ohio, where she works as a freelance writer and editor. You can find her at her website, www.maggiesmithpoet.com.

Michelle Stephens

Michelle Stephens writes from the home she shares with her husband and their two daughters. In addition to being the in-house cookie baker, nose wiper, milk maker, diaper changer, and potty helper, she writes a bimonthly column for the *Brattleboro Reformer*, a southern Vermont daily newspaper. Her work can be found on *Mamalode, BonBon Break, BLUNTmoms*, and on her personal blog, *Juicebox Confession*.

Melissa Uchiyama

Melissa lives in Tokyo with her delicious family—two kiddos and husband. As a mother, teacher, and writer, she buzzes around Tokyo, stopping to smell every flower. You can find Melissa's work at *Literary Mama, Kveller, Tokyo Cheapo*, and her own blog, http://melibelleintokyo.com.

ACKNOWLEDGMENTS

∽

We could not have put together this book without the help of so many.

First of all, we'd like to thank the hundreds of women who shared their postpartum stories with us. Your stories are brave, beautifully told, and so important for others to hear. It's a difficult choice to write about this private, difficult experience, and we are appreciative of every woman who sent her story to us.

We are grateful to all the supportive women who make up the generous She Writes Community for their patience, advice, and expertise.

Our talented editor Lauren Apfel again provided daily support, feedback, friendship, and an ear for language. We are in awe of her skills and her generous spirit.

As part of this project, we sponsored our first writing contest. We'd like to thank the judges of that contest—each accomplished and brave women in their own right—for volunteering their time: Julia Fierro, Lindsey Mead, Kate Hopper, Lisa Belkin, Dr. Jessica Zucker, and Katrina Alcorn.

We are also thankful for the continued support of our HerStories Project community: our current and former contributors, students, and readers. It's been an amazing two years since we put up the first guest posts on our blogs about female friendship, and we couldn't have done it without all of you.

And then there are our families, who put up with hundreds of hours of phone calls, computer time, and preoccupied parenting to make this project possible. We are grateful for your love and your support, every day.

ABOUT THE EDITORS

Kate Borgelt Photography

STEPHANIE SPRENGER is a freelance writer, editor, music thera-pist, and mother of two young girls. Her work has been featured in *Brain, Child* magazine, *Mamalode*, *The Mid*, and *In the Powder Room*, and she is a regular contributor to the *Huffington Post* and *Scary Mommy*. She was a member of the 2013 cast of Listen to Your Mother Denver and the 2015 cast of Listen to Your Mother Boulder. Stephanie was named one of BlogHer's 2014 Voices of the Year. She lives in Colorado with her family and can be found online at stephaniesprenger.com.

Adrian Quackenbush

JESSICA SMOCK is a freelance writer, educator, and editor. A Phi Beta Kappa graduate of Wesleyan, she was a teacher for more than a decade before returning to graduate school to finish her doctorate in educational policy from Boston University in 2013. She was a finalist for a Bammy Award for her writing in the field of education research and policy. She lives in Buffalo, New York with her husband, son, and daughter. Jessica's writing can found at her own website, School of Smock, at Brain, Child Magazine, and at the Huffington Post.

THE HERSTORIES PROJECT is a writing and publishing community for women. We offer a variety of online writing courses, feature a bi-monthly personal essay column, HerStories Voices, to which writers can submit guest posts, and our HerTake advice column explores modern friendship through reader questions. We have previously published two books—*The HerStories Project: Women Explore the Joy, Pain, and Power of Female Friendship*, and *My Other Ex: Women's True Stories of Leaving and Losing Friends*. *My Other Ex* was selected as a Finalist in Foreword Reviews' IndieFab 2015 Book of the Year Contest. Find out more about our books, our courses, and other opportunities for writers and readers at herstoriesproject.com.

SELECTED TITLES FROM SHE WRITES PRESS

She Writes Press is an independent publishing company founded to serve women writers everywhere. Visit us at www.shewritespress.com.

Three Minus One: Parents' Stories of Love & Loss edited by Sean Hanish and Brooke Warner. $17.95, 978-1-938314-80-3. A collection of stories and artwork by parents who have suffered child loss that offers insight into this unique and devastating experience.

A Leg to Stand On: An Amputee's Walk into Motherhood by Colleen Haggerty. $16.95, 978-1-63152-923-8. Haggerty's candid story of how she overcame the pain of losing a leg at seventeen—and of terminating two pregnancies as a young woman—and went on to become a mother, despite her fears.

Make a Wish for Me: A Mother's Memoir by LeeAndra Chergey. $16.95, 978-1-63152-828-6. A life-changing diagnosis teaches a family that where's there is love there is hope—and that being "normal" is not nearly as important as providing your child with a life full of joy, love, and acceptance.

Breathe: A Memoir of Motherhood, Grief, and Family Conflict by Kelly Kittel. $16.95, 978-1-938314-78-0. A mother's heartbreaking account of losing two sons in the span of nine months—and learning, despite all the obstacles in her way, to find joy in life again.

The Doctor and The Stork: A Memoir of Modern Medical Babymaking by K.K. Goldberg. $16.95, 978-1-63152-830-9. A mother's compelling story of her post-IVF, high-risk pregnancy with twins—the very definition of a modern medical babymaking experience.

Fire Season: A Memoir by Hollye Dexter. $16.95, 978-1-63152-974-0. After she loses everything in a fire, Hollye Dexter's life spirals downward and she begins to unravel—but when she finds herself at the brink of losing her husband, she is forced to dig within herself for the strength to keep her family together.